MY RACING
HEART

MY RACING HEART

THE PASSIONATE WORLD
OF THOROUGHBREDS AND THE TRACK

Nan Mooney

HarperCollins*Publishers*

HarperCollins books may be purchased for educational, business, or sales promotional use. For information please write: Special Markets Department, HarperCollins Publishers, Inc., 10 East 53rd Street, New York, NY 10022.

FIRST EDITION

Designed by Mary Austin Speaker

LIBRARY OF CONGRESS CATALOGING-IN-PUBLICATION DATA

Mooney, Nan, 1970–
     My racing heart : the passionate world of thoroughbreds and the track / Nan Mooney.—1st ed.
          p.   cm.
     ISBN 0-06-019853-2
     1. Mooney, Nan, 1970–   2. Horsemen and horsewomen—Washington (State)—Seattle—Biography.   3. Horse racing—United States—Anecdotes.   I. Title.

SF284.52.M62A3 2001
798.4'0092—dc21
[B]   2001042196

02   03   04   05   06   QF   10   9   8   7   6   5   4   3   2   1

To My Grandmother

Contents

Acknowledgments and Explanations

As is unavoidable when you're dipping into the past, much of this book is based on my recollection, other people's recollections, and my recollection of other people's recollections. Among so many other things I've learned from the racetrack, I will include the shaky nature of truth. I have not invented too much, except to change some names and blur a few details where it was kinder that way or couldn't be helped. But horse people—my grandmother included—are reluctant to be confined by factual boundaries. I hope any small inaccuracies will be forgiven in light of the larger spirit of the truth.

A number of books and magazines have been particularly useful in clarifying and elaborating upon what was stowed in my memory. Most notable are *Wild Ride* by Ann Hagendorn Auerbach, *Laughing in the Hills* by Bill Barich, *Across the Board* by Toney Betts, *Damon Runyon: A Life* by Jimmy Breslin, *The Nature of Horses* by Stephen Budiansky, *Horse Racing: A Book of Words* by Gerald Hammond, *The Kentucky Thoroughbred* by Kent Hollingsworth, *They're Off: Horse Racing in Saratoga* and *The Great Black Jockeys* by Edward Hotaling, *The History of Horse Racing* by Roger Longrigg, *The History of Thoroughbred Racing in America* by William H. P. Robertson, and those loyal standbys *Blood-Horse,* the *Daily Racing Form, Sports Illustrated,* and the *Thoroughbred Times.*

Aside from those already mentioned in the text, for whose passion, enthusiasm, and cooperation I am exceedingly grateful, there were a number of others on or around the racetrack who were kind enough to volunteer information and support. My special thanks to Steve Anderson, Tony Cobitz, Suzanne Depp, Bob Duncan, Tom Durkin, John Fort, Arthur Hancock III, Dr. Ted Hill, Jay Hovdey,

Fran LaBelle, Drew Mollica, Gasper Moschera, Steve Nagler, Ray Paulick, Jay Privman, Phyllis Rogers from the Keeneland Library, Andy Serling, Rick Violette, and Stuart Zanville. And thanks also to the photographers and photo experts who graced me with their talents: Brandon Benson, Carol Crandall from the National Museum of Racing, John Fort, and Joy Gilbert.

When it comes to those who have nothing whatsoever to do with racing, I have been even more fortunate in the way of ideas, humor, and healthy doses of compassion. Thank you to my parents, Robert and Jacquelinn Mooney, for their remarkable patience and generosity over the past thirty-plus years. And thank you to those people with no blood ties at all who provided opinions, sounding boards, beds, meals, and aid of every possible description: Alan, Jenny, Liz and Andrew Berliant, Crispin Fievet, Eve Karlin, Pamella Pearl (and Pierre), Kirsten Prather, John Radanovich, Michael Simon, Richard Simon, and Bryce Williams.

Special, special thanks to Martha Brockenbrough and Adam and Lucy Berliant for brainstorming, food, drink, vision, and interior decorating advice. (Not to mention a title.) I can't wait until it's my turn to return the favor.

I am especially grateful to my editor, Diane Reverand, for her guidance and propensity for taking risks. I am lucky beyond belief to have found her. Also to Janet Dery for letting me drag her out riding and for fielding a steady stream of questions and concerns.

This book could truly never have happened if it were not for two people. The first is my grandmother, who I think, I hope, is looking down just about now with a big old grin.

The second is my agent, Tanya McKinnon, who traveled miles beyond anything I even knew to ask, put up with the at times considerable insanity, and never ceased to believe that there was something—and someone—there.

Introduction

An Unconventional Romance

T he course of my seduction has been long and slow. Long and slow and surprisingly intimate when I consider the full list of my seducers: the jockeys, the trainers, the hot-walkers, the gamblers, the tipsters—and, of course, the horses. I can trace that seduction back years or decades, or just a few weeks to an ordinary race on an ordinary October day at Belmont Park racetrack: the seventh race of nine on a Thursday afternoon card, three-year-old colts running a mile and an eighth.

I'm standing on a mottled patch of grass near the far turn, coat clutched around me, head low to duck the blade of wind swirling leaves across the nearby parking lot. There are no other spectators braving the cold, just me, damp and shivering, leaning against the rusty chain-link fence bordering the rail.

The starting bell sounds. Hidden at the far end of the mile-and-a-half oval track, the horses burst from the gate. I feel them before I can see them, a steady bass-note rumbling of hooves against dirt that travels up through my legs and shakes my heart. Then they appear just below the opposite rail, a kite string of jockey caps sailing together like a single unit. Seconds later, the horses explode around the far curve. For an instant they are coming straight at me, a wall of rippling muscle with riders perched above bent taut like bows. And for an instant a childhood memory splashes across this adult canvas.

I am nine years old again, wild, dust-streaked, and reckless, hurtling down the barn road aboard my cousin's pony, crouched jockey-high in the saddle with my back curved tight over the horse's neck. The wind whips my eyes, forcing tears that fly away behind us, mingling with the dust. We—horse and I together, because it would be impossible to separate us now—rattle the ground like something's shaking loose, like the whole earth twists in our wake as we rocket across.

In front of me, a copper-penny chestnut breaks from the rear of the pack and begins streaking up the outside. He's so close I can see the map of veins risen up under his skin and hear the thwack of the jockey's whip slicing through the air, the same sharp swish I used to make with the broken end of a dogwood stick.

I feel that pony unfolding beneath me, the flicker of muscles against my nine-year-old thighs as her stride turns long and graceful, fluid as music. The two of us, laced together, have finally broken free. We tear past the mulberry tree and I let loose a victory call—part rebel yell, part Indian war whoop—as my cousin crosses the invented finish line a neck behind. I throw my fist into the air so hard it rips a hole through whatever fabric is holding everyone else down to earth. I almost touch the sky.

Far down the Belmont track, the thunder-run of Thoroughbreds has eased to a barely collected prance. As the chestnut breaks off for the winner's circle, I drift back into the semiheated clubhouse to wait out the twenty minutes until the next race. Walking through the linoleum-tiled hallways, I glance up at the photos lining the walls, yellowing evidence of racing's rich past. Nestled among portraits of Franklin Roosevelt, a cluster of Vanderbilts, a child Jacqueline Bouvier posed on a picket fence, hangs an action shot: three horses rushing at the camera with jockeys crouched tight to their necks. It takes me several minutes to figure out what's wrong, but when I do I experience that same thrum of excitement that comes from watching a race. The horse at the forefront, the one just seconds from crossing the finish line, has all four feet lifted off the ground. He and the jockey on top of him have literally taken flight.

The course of my seduction has been long and slow. In more than two decades, this horse racing has become my heartbeat, my high altar, my childhood dream. Our relationship has roots twisting back almost a century and leaves still unfurling, pushing today open into tomorrow. This is my love story, an unconventional romance between a woman and a sport.

IF YOU travel to the core of any true romance, you'll eventually find something unbreakable, something you could throw yourself against again and again and know it would never crumble. When I go back to my earliest encounter with horse racing, I find my grandmother, Mary Stuart Mooney. I called her May-May, a name she inherited from a cousin who couldn't get his mouth around the word Mary. She had long white hair that she coiled up every morning with gold bobby pins and a light-blue silk ribbon. She could tell a mean story, but she couldn't tell a lie. And she knew everything there was to know about the racetrack.

If I thread together the various pieces of May-May's life, arrange the stories she used to tell to form the woman I came to adore, every one of them might be sealed with the image of a horse. She was born in 1889 into a South churning in the wake of the Civil War. It would be seven years before Henry Ford completed his first automobile, and horses were still the engineers of daily life. May-May knew them as she knew her brothers and sisters, better than she knew her parents, who both died of fever when she was eight. She was raised on Spesushi Island, a family-owned compound with covered porches and wide dormer windows that looked out across the Eastern Shore of Maryland. The household was ruled by her eccentric and patriarchal grandfather, an archconservative backer of the Bourbon government who demanded women sedate and long-skirted. May-May tucked up those skirts whenever possible, and she was anything but sedate.

On her seventh birthday, her grandfather surprised her with a coal black pony and a white cart with cherry red wheels. May-May sneaked out to the barn early the next morning, shuffling through the field grass with her nightgown pulled up to her knees, wrenched the wheels off the cart, and hid them in the hayloft. Then, bareback and barefoot, tearing across fallow cotton fields, May-May taught herself to ride. In the years that followed, she would learn to sit a horse properly, to turn her mount with a nudge of her knee and stop him with the tiniest cock of her wrist. She would take prizes in jump racing and dressage and spend afternoons mucking out stables until harness grease permanently stained the fingers her grandfather had intended for nothing rougher than white china cups.

In 1906, when she was seventeen, fresh from the Hannah Moore finishing school—where sports of all kinds had been forbidden lest they overly excite the girls or permanently displace their "pelvic organs"—May-May's bent for horses immediately drew her across the bay to Baltimore's Pimlico Race Course. These were Pimlico's glory days, local racing newly broken free from antigambling legislation that had shut down tracks around the country. May-May reveled in the celebration. All that spring she ducked out early from a whirl of debutante teas to hitch a ride to the track with her brother, Robert, hiding under a travel rug for the first few miles in case they met her grandfather on the road.

While the young society ladies flirted in the grandstands of the Old Members Clubhouse, May-May followed Robert and the other men outside the whitewashed building and down to the wooden rail circling the track. There she began studying the horses. She learned to spot the straight knees and perfect angle of head to chest that indicate a well-balanced runner, and soon applied her findings to the very unladylike art of betting the ponies, stepping up to the bookmakers in person instead of paying a boy to run for her as most of the other women did. She and Robert started up a competition, betting on the third race every day. They would meet up outside the bookmakers' circle just after the race and compare empty pockets or handfuls of coins, until eventually Robert lost patience with a little sister who usually won twice what he did. Some of the money she reinvested in chancy long shots on the next racing day, but most went toward replacing the pairs of pearl-buttoned pumps she ruined picking her way through the mud around the horse paddock.

May-May spent years draped over that Pimlico paddock fence, fantasizing about riding races herself. In the cocksure male domain of the track, such a possibility remained as remote as duking it out with a bare-knuckle boxer. Eventually May-May decided to seek adventure elsewhere, territories where such rules had scarcely found time to form. She boarded a cross-continental railcar and spent ten years exploring the far edges of the country, first New Mexico and then Alaska. It wasn't until the 1930s, soon after settling in Seattle with my grandfather, that May-May returned to the racetrack.

A decade earlier, Washington State had jumped aboard a national antigambling bandwagon, which crippled the sport for much of the twenties. In 1933, after laws permitting racing finally flew through the state legislature, May-May borrowed my grandfather Bob's Model T and bumped across miles of poorly paved roads toward the Longacres Racetrack just south of the city. Though women everywhere had been lifting their hems and dancing the Charleston to the tune of the twenties, racing had refused to keep apace. May-May still found welcome only as a spectator in the two-fisted, backslapping male domain of the track. Again she had to turn elsewhere to curb that hunger for full-scale participation.

As the nation shuddered under the Great Depression, May-May homed in on her lifelong yearning to run a racehorse. She bought a couple of broken-down American Saddlebreds—a showy but slower and less temperamental breed than racing's Thoroughbreds—and hired a lean-lipped Kentucky trainer named Hugo Dunn. Together she and Hugo polished their pair of ugly ducklings, Dr. Rhythm and Countess Highland, until fit and gleaming. They entered them in trotting races, run around smaller tracks, with each horse hooked to a spindle-wheeled cart that streaked across the dirt like a dogsled over snow. While other owners retreated to the stands, toasting the end of Prohibition with flasks of legal gin, May-May shocked the local equestrian community by pulling on the leather riding boots Robert shipped from Baltimore and driving Dr. Rhythm and Countess Highland herself. Since there was no women's dressing area, my grandfather rigged a curtain across Countess Highland's stall and posted a hand-lettered sign:

LADIES
KEEP OUT

According to May-May, the ladies always did.

ALMOST FORTY years passed from the day May-May first sauntered out of Countess Highland's stall with straw poking from her hair to the day I was born one Sunday in January. Forty years in which she kept driving out to Longacres and following broadcasts of the Triple Crown races first on radio, then on fuzzy black-and-white TV. Forty years in which she held onto that maverick passion for Thoroughbreds until she found someone to pass it onto, a girl in dirt-stained blue jeans who, like her grandmother, always had trouble confining herself to the stands.

I was born into a happy well-adjusted family, living in a happy well-adjusted Seattle neighborhood. When I came along, a drop of something foreign somehow got into the water. I was not a happy, well-adjusted child. As far back as I can remember, I was moody and potentially explosive, an emotional time bomb capable of regularly reducing my even-tempered mother to tears. When my parents couldn't find me, it usually meant I'd run away from home with my jacket pockets full of tangerines and Oreo cookies, or was curled up on the floor of the den closet with a flashlight and a pile of library books. I spun elaborate fantasies featuring me as a changeling infant left by fairies and hobgoblins in place of my parents' child. My intensity scared me. I felt as if I'd been born in a body too small for what it contained, an outer casing meant for going to bed on time and playing quietly when all I wanted to do was throw things and run wild. I did my best to squeeze down whatever kept welling up inside. It refused to go away.

I loved visiting May-May. She was the one person who understood my rebel leanings, who wasn't constantly telling me to shape up or settle down. We were both different, and May-May didn't seem to care. She never baked me a birthday cake, bought me a baby doll, or sang me to sleep. Instead, one May afternoon when I was seven, she sat me down on her rosewood sofa, splashed Ficklin port into two beveled juice glasses—three-quarters full for her, just a splash for me—and opened a box of Aplets & Cotlets candies. She flipped her orange-tinted color TV to something called the Kentucky Derby. Then she declared it time we begin my racetrack education.

As the horses filed onto the track, May-May used the swivel end of the corkscrew to point out long shots and favorites. She announced their names—Seattle Slew, Mr. Redwing, Iron Constitution—and I recorded them on cream-colored stationery to take home and learn later, my large, careful letters filling the sheet until I had to flip it over and write across the embossed seal on the back. She floated terms like *hand-ride, speed-pop,* and *throwing crosses*—tantalizing fragments of a language I'd eventually speak in full. And she began stitching together pieces of racing history, stories sluiced in grit and glamour snaking back centuries. Those stories transformed her from a grandmother with soft cheeks and sharp opinions into a fairy-tale figure—Cinderella's godmother, Aladdin's genie—bearing untold riches. No prolonged courtship was necessary. In that single afternoon, a triangle formed among me, my grandmother, and the racetrack. May-May gave me a place to run wild.

At seven, I thought May-May was the only role model I'd ever need. Our racetrack afternoons spurred an immediate and all-consuming infatuation with horses, and with that first Kentucky Derby, I started to nurse my own dreams of becoming a champion jockey. All through grade school, I lived for summers spent on the Maryland farm belonging to May-May's sister Kate. Flying bareback down her dirt roads aboard a renegade pony named Little Sugar, I taught myself to ride. Sugar would buck and wheel, testing the limits of my horsemanship and usually finding them in thirty seconds or less as I slipped off her fat back onto the ground. Sometimes I'd still be hanging on to the reins as she dragged me home, bumping through the long grass until we reached the pinewood gate, where Sugar would stop and I'd climb aboard yet again. I used to toss an ancient English saddle across her back, jack up the stirrups as high as they would go, and tear across the fields in a high jockey crouch.

Each year May-May and I studied the top contenders for the Kentucky Derby. Come spring, I'd lie awake at night picturing myself on the favorite, orchestrating another record-breaking come-from-behind stretch run to victory. By the fifth grade it was clear I'd wind up closer to five-foot-eleven than the optimal jockey height of five-foot-two. I measured myself daily on the Sesame Street height chart tacked to our basement door. By the time I outgrew Big Bird, I'd suffered my first-ever broken heart.

"You can feel sorry for yourself or you can get on with things," May-May told me as I sat slumped in one of her parlor chairs. I got on with things, as she always had.

That year, our family started spending part of each summer at a ranch in Montana. There I fell for a high-strung dappled mare called Grey Lady who'd thrown her last rider and broken his back.

She was part Thoroughbred; a grandparent on one side had been a racehorse who never made it at the track, and her ancestry showed. The wranglers had to close her in a stall to saddle her without getting kicked. I'd linger outside the door, watching the whites roll into her cloudy blue eyes and recognizing that need to break free. I began offering up my hand, cupping the end of a carrot or an apple core, and held stick-still as her nose explored my fingers. When a flood of new guests took up all the available horses, I volunteered to ride Grey Lady. Somehow, the slow-drawling ranch owner convinced my mother to agree.

Grey Lady and I melded in those first weeks together, darting breakneck through the pine trees to round up stray cattle. By the following summer, we were winning barrel races out from under a handful of grown men. I drew confidence from the danger, certain Grey Lady would never toss me off her back but still pitch-tuned to the fact that she could. I even toyed with the idea of becoming a rodeo rider until an ex-bronco buster at the local Blue Nugget Tavern showed me the scars of twenty-three broken bones.

"You ride like the devil," one of the wranglers told me. "You're gonna get yourself killed."

"I ride like my grandmother," I corrected him. "And she's ninety-two years old."

I COASTED into adolescence with all the confidence of someone who, armed with nothing but a hat and red cowboy boots, had gone neck and neck with the devil. Throughout grade school, I'd played leader to a pack of horse-crazy girls. My racetrack patter was an exotic talent, my huge collection of plastic model horses the envy of the neighborhood. After sixth grade, I moved on to a private prep school with a cutthroat social crowd, one far more intent on impressing two-legged creatures than four—a pursuit I didn't quite understand. All I knew was that in the course of one summer vacation I seemed to have turned impossibly tall and gawky, incapable of dressing or talking or dreaming the way you were supposed to do. At a time when all I wanted was to fit in, the racetrack suddenly set me apart. So the horses went into hiding.

If friends came over, I'd take down my race posters and bury my riding boots at the back of the closet. When the clutch of popular girls made whinnying sounds at soccer practice, I blushed scarlet but pretended not to hear. I didn't tell May-May any of this, framing vague answers when she questioned me about school. Instead, I neatly split my life in two. Sitting on her rosewood sofa, I was still an adventurer, sleek and brilliant as a racehorse, not someone who, hard as she pretended to belong, couldn't seem to fool anyone— even herself—into believing that she did.

After three lonely years, I decided to leave Seattle for St. Timothy's, a horsey East Coast boarding school set on acres of rolling green countryside, where I fantasized I'd be surrounded by my own kind. I packed a trunk with my *Horse Encyclopedia,* jodhpurs, and *Sports Illustrated* photos of my favorite jockey, Angel Cordero, and ventured cross-country. In my dorm room that first afternoon, I lingered in the window seat overlooking the stables. It even smelled right, like cut grass and fresh-turned dirt. Here I could start over again. Here I would belong.

My roommate, Augusta from the Hamptons, blew in later that day with three hand-tooled English saddles and her own Arabian in tow. She immediately began plastering our walls with royal blue best-of-show ribbons and photos of the horses she'd left back home. When I pulled out Angel's picture, she arched both plucked eyebrows. She looked like she'd smelled something bad.

"I thought you rode."

"I do. Western, English, bareback. Everything."

"But that's the racetrack."

"You couldn't ride those horses."

"I wouldn't want to."

"I would," I snapped back at her. "I'd kill for it." Instead, I quietly folded up Angel and stuffed him under my kneesocks. It seemed the only possible way to preserve my racetrack romance was to bury it deep inside.

That initial month at St. Timothy's brought on a parade of girls like Augusta whose lives didn't extend beyond the show-horse ring, who equated Seattle with cowboys and Indians, and the track with just the opposite of class. In every corner of the campus, I found someplace I didn't fit. I was too rough for the horsey girls, too soft for the rebels, never quite arty or athletic or just plain cool enough to belong. I missed May-May, and Seattle. And, though they were all around me, I even missed horses. Then one night, curled on my side waiting for the 11:00 P.M. lights-out, I replayed an old fantasy, the kind of daydream I was supposed to have long out-grown. I was racing Angel down the homestretch of the Kentucky Derby, pulling away in the final furlong to leave him trailing in the dust. I lingered over each detail—clods of dirt cracking against my face, strands of horsehair beneath my fingers, the rat-a-tat of the announcer calling my record-breaking stretch run—and that old excitement began to stir. For the first time in weeks, I felt like myself again. The next morning, while Augusta brushed her teeth, I took Angel out of the bureau drawer and tacked him up on my bare side of the wall. When Augusta saw him, her button nose crin-kled, but she didn't say a word. In some unspoken contest, I'd come first across the wire.

Standing up to Augusta, and feeling her back down, gave me the courage to stop worrying so much about not fitting in. And so I came out of the closet as a racetrack lover. I hiked my school tunic above my knees to flash the scars I'd won learning to devil-ride and racked up detention points reading Dick Francis books in study hall, stories like *Nerve* and *Risk* and *Bonecrack,* the very titles of which encapsulated my adventure dreams. I threw a bowl of fruit salad at Mary Swan Lamarr when she kept switching the TV from the sports report to *Miami Vice.* I even disowned my first-ever boyfriend, a junior named Bernie from the Lawrenceville School for Boys, after he claimed jockeys weren't real athletes since all they had to do was sit down.

When I returned to Seattle that spring, I went straight for Long-acres racetrack. As I crossed the half-empty parking lot, I felt as if I'd emerged from underwater. I'd never bet before, but that day I found a 12–1 shot named May's Regal Girl. I called May-May from a pay phone and read her the filly's racing history line by line. We both agreed she didn't have a chance, but May-May told me to put

$10 on her to win. I did, and May's Regal Girl came through by a nose, edging out the competition the same way I'd edged out Augusta, and finally convincing me of something May-May had been saying since that first Kentucky Derby.

Racing's not about what you expect. It's about letting go of expectations, taking a gamble. How else could you possibly fall in love?

UNTIL MY junior year of high school my life had been all about me—which horse I would ride, where I fit in or didn't, whether to visit May-May, or go swimming at someone's house by the lake. I'd faced nothing more crushing than Augusta's crinkled nose and my aborted jockey career, both of which I'd managed with reasonable aplomb. I was convinced the world couldn't dish out anything I couldn't handle. Then, when I was seventeen, May-May died, just a month shy of her ninety-eighth birthday. Her death wasn't a surprise—she'd been bedridden for several years—and at the funeral some whisperers even called it a gift. Maybe so, but it wasn't one I felt ready to receive. With her went my one source of full-scale acceptance, my constant reminder not to be scared of who I was.

My family espoused the doctrine of stiff upper lips and by default so did I, standing dry-eyed next to my father at the funeral. Two weeks later I bought a box of Aplets & Cotlets, uncorked a dusty bottle of port from the corner of my father's wine cellar, and sat down to my first solo Kentucky Derby. I meant it to be a sort of homage, a pledge to May-May that my allegiance to the racetrack wouldn't waver. As I stared at that confluence of Thoroughbreds, all I could see was that our relationship had taken a permanent detour. I wasn't the devil-rider anymore, or the fantasy jockey. I wasn't even a granddaughter. Without May-May, the space for such childhood things seemed to disappear.

That afternoon, I painstakingly removed every one of the seventy-plus plastic horses still lining my bookcases. Some had names written on their bellies in indelible black marker, Babe and Duchess and Baryshnikov—the latter spelled horribly wrong. Some had forelegs I'd snapped by playing too hard and crookedly stuck back on, leaving behind surgical scars oozing gouts of Elmer's glue. One by one I wrapped them in tissue paper and stacked them in cardboard boxes. I untacked Angel's photos from my bulletin board, folded each perfectly in half, and lay them flat across the top. I taped the boxes shut, tied string around their middles, and carried them to the basement, stacking them in a corner under the furnace. In their place I began constructing a new kind of survival zone.

May-May's death precipitated a tumble which began my final year of high school and gathered speed for almost a decade. On the outside, I was finessing the world, moving first to Los Angeles then New York, graduating college with honors and landing jobs in the film and publishing industries. People constantly praised my independence and sense of adventure, and I became an expert at illusion—nearly convincing even myself that the right restaurants and travel plans and expensive leather sandals could somehow line up to create something meaningful. The adult framework I'd chosen at seventeen was skewed, a lampshade tilted to light up only a comfortable portion of my emotional landscape. I had acquaintances, not friends, glamorous jobs with little substance, a series of relationships that seemed to crumble after the fourth or fifth date. I'd created a tidy unit, a veil of self-protective lace, through which I could watch life without having to touch it. From the outside, I was polished and impenetrable, as neatly packaged as those plastic horses still hidden in the basement. But inside I felt the echoes of that changeling child, trapped in an impossible tug-of-war between the search to fill myself up and the fear I would overflow. I felt lonely and knee-deep in depression, and eventually began seeing a therapist. I didn't reveal much to her, afraid whatever I'd lost when May-May died couldn't be recovered. If I let down this slick outer structure, I'd be left with nothing at all.

I never stopped following racing during these years, still buying the *Daily Racing Form* and *Blood-Horse* magazine, but I started to look at horses in what I convinced myself was an "adult" way—focusing on the science of the sport instead of the soul. I kept my emotional distance, calculated odds, and examined running patterns and past performances to predict the winners, dissecting

Thoroughbred flesh as if it were a geometry theorem. In a brilliant self-protective coup, I mastered the art of going to the races without really going at all. Then I had convinced myself such an analytical approach was a sign of maturity. Now I can recognize the rawer stuff going on underneath. Racing, my bedrock of passion, had been spliced with loss, and I didn't know how to separate the two. So I just let the whole thing slide out of my heart and climb to the safer high ground of my head.

Somehow, I'd gone and chosen Augusta over the track.

IT REQUIRES remarkable effort to keep running from yourself. Just a few months after my twenty-eighth birthday, I finally got caught. By the Kentucky Derby. It was the spring after I'd moved to New York. I had a new job and a new city to master—a new illusion to sustain—and I'd erased racing from my life entirely. It seemed easier that way. Then one Saturday in May, I was buying a telephone at Radio Shack when strains of "My Old Kentucky Home" drifted over from the electronics section. I followed, half-hoping for a Louisville basketball game, but knowing with that internal racing compass May-May had so firmly implanted that it was Derby Day. My decade's worth of defenses rose up and ordered me to turn immediately and push my way out the double doors. I couldn't. I stood rooted before a line of six-inch-square televisions. I didn't know the horses and the jockeys were just colored dots on the screen. I came at it raw, as I'd come at it only once before, as a seven-year-old girl on May-May's rosewood sofa. The starting bell sounded, the horses burst from the starting gate, and I started to cry.

It began as just a trail of tears down either cheek, but seconds later they grew into full sobs, so I had to press my palms against my mouth to hold anything inside. The store employees stood around me in a mortified semicircle until one collected the courage to scuttle up and ask if I was alright. I nodded, and he backed away, as if afraid to catch whatever'd struck me. I managed to pull it together for the three blocks back to my apartment, but as soon as I got inside, keys still dangling from the top lock, I crumbled. For two hours, I lay on my bed and wept. I unwrapped all that grief for me and May-May and the little girl rocketing down the barn road and finally let it breathe.

The next day I took the Belmont Special train to Long Island.

I went back to the racetrack.

THE TRAIN to Belmont stops at street level. Only after you've taken an escalator ride up and traversed the hundred yards of cement thruway separating the station from the track does the course finally unfold before you. It's massive, a mile and a half around, with dirt harrowed soft and pillowy until the first set of hooves begins spitting it up towards the sky. That Sunday, I leaned against the corrugated metal siding of the thruway and stared across the track, waiting for the wonder that used to fill me instantly when I was seven and twelve and sixteen. A decade of ice was too much to melt through in a single moment. I looked out at the racetrack and felt nothing at all.

I was tempted to go home, and might have done so except that the next train wasn't until three hours later. Instead, I paid my $2, flipped through the turnstile, and made for the far turn of the track. If you've come purely for the horses, the far turn is the place to be. The race is yours for just a moment—when the horses barrel around the bend, torque their speed its final notch, and unfold for home—but in that moment comes the strongest possible Thoroughbred hit. You see the jockeys' faces as they coax their mounts still faster, threading them through holes in the pack to give them space to run. You see the horses dig their hooves in deep or begin to wobble, sense who's tiring and who's preserved enough to rocket right on down the stretch. You see dirt and sweat and popping veins. In placing myself there, I'd opted for full racehorse immersion.

Only a few true Thoroughbred fans gather at the far turn—those who don't mind missing the finish, which happens nearly a quarter of a mile up the track; those for whom sharing in sheer momentum weighs more heavily than cashing in a bet. So it was easy to find a spot along the rail. All afternoon fellow aficionados came and went around me—leafing through programs, downing hotdogs, resting their elbows next to mine on the chain-link fence. On the surface we had nothing in common. The average race fan is maybe fifty-plus and male, dressed in some plaid or polyester ensemble that couldn't have been fashionable even when he bought it thirty years before. He smokes cigars, hacks ands spits, carries a bunch of wadded-up betting tickets in one hand and a beer in the other. But underneath he and I line up perfectly. We're part oddball, part loner, and permanently sweet on Thoroughbreds.

A racing fan knows. That afternoon men old enough to be my grandfather walked up to me and started gently talking horses as if we'd been meeting up every afternoon for the past twenty years. They provided an instant and unspoken camaraderie, a current of acceptance whatever my cracks and flaws. I stood there among them and stopped worrying about holding my splintered self together. Instead, I watched ten races in a row, Thoroughbred after Thoroughbred rippling across a track. Gradually I felt something start to surface, a flicker of Sugar's back muscles against my thighs, a note of the devil-rider's rebel yell. I felt the ground shaking beneath my feet.

I kept going, every Saturday and Sunday I could spare. Always alone, letting the gap widen between the old life I'd constructed and the new one I meant to live. That deadening depression began to pack up and disappear one fragment at a time. It would be too simple to say I lost my passion when I lost May-May and found it again when I returned to the track, but those tears did wash clean many of the barriers I'd constructed. They left behind a diamond clarity that lit up just me and the horses. They brought me back to my most essential parts—to daring and purpose, Grey Lady and Angel Cordero, to how it felt to have something in which to believe.

I discovered that the space where I'd once housed racing was still very much open, and eager to be filled. I began to read up on the history of the sport, quilting together May-May's stories and those from a dusty library of old racing books, until I could chart lines wending back generations. I rediscovered my romance in these chronicles: royal Arabian coursers and delicate Kentucky breds; racehorses swapped in frontier poker games and young slaves tossed up as America's earliest jockeys; tracks run by international playboys, and trainers nursing stockyard horses all the way to the Triple Crown.

Since the earliest days of the New World, horse racing had been a mainstay of North American culture. In 1493, when Columbus landed in Hispaniola on his second voyage, his ships carried twenty-four stallions and ten mares. Wherever horses went, running them was sure to follow. A century and a half later, a shipment of mares from London to Jamestown, all of them "beautiful and full of courage," according to the boat's records, set the colonial sport upon its way. By 1790, a race conducted by the Virginia Jockey Club pitted a horse owned by George Washington against one from the stable of Thomas Jefferson. Three years later, Lexington, Kentucky, legislators advised public action to curb the impromptu races continually clogging city streets. The traditional European track consisted of one long straightaway with the finish line stationed directly under the royal box, but it was in America, land of democracies, that the first oval racetracks were developed to ensure that *all* the viewers saw *all* the action *all* the time. In the ensuing centuries, the sport would encounter attacks from politicians, reformers, evangelists, and zealots. It refused to die away.

I started to befriend New York's racetrack community, both fellow fans and those behind the scenes. I visited Belmont in the early mornings when the horses do their training, and hung out with the mostly Hispanic and South American grooms who worked the stables, watching them run currycombs over colts worth seven-figure fortunes. Talking with trainers and jockeys as they monitored morning gallops, I came to understand why they'd chosen to rest their futures upon four fragile legs. And I crafted a treasure hunt of sorts, searching out those featured players, Angel and others, who'd at one time helped my relationship to the races along its way.

Best of all, I met racehorses, loads of them. I rubbed their ears, untangled their manes, and fed them peppermints. (Horses have a sweet tooth, evolved long ago to search out the richest sap-filled grasses.) Then I stepped back, still and forever awed, to watch them wheel and dance and pour on their ungodly speed.

A FULL year and a month after that Radio Shack Kentucky Derby, for the first time since I was seven years old, I didn't turn on my television to watch the third leg of the Triple Crown. Instead, I rode the train to Belmont Park to root firsthand for Charismatic. Though he'd been written off by most as the foggiest sort of pipe dream, this chestnut colt had won the Kentucky Derby at odds of 33–1, followed it up with a victory in the Preakness Stakes, and now sat poised for the first three-race sweep in more than twenty years. A crowd of eighty thousand people had assembled, dense and humming, like those crowds I imagine from the forties when racing still meant society rolling up in Silver Phantoms. These weren't just the misfits with their cigars and clashing plaids. They were blue bloods flown in from Kentucky, blond, perfumed southern women with flowered hats on the arms of suntanned men in blue blazers and college ties. They were twenty-something urbanites, wearing sandals and dragging beer-stocked coolers, embarked on a once-a-year foray to the track. And they were grooms, morning exercise riders, and assistant trainers, some still in muck-caked work boots, who'd decided walk the few yards over from the barns to witness a bit of history. We all stood pressed hip to hip along the back of the clubhouse boxes and I dug my hands into a stranger's shoulders, balanced high on my toes to see.

Charismatic shot strong from the gate and settled in against the flank of the front-runner, a filly called Silverbulletday. The two glided in tandem down the backstretch, taking the far turn easily, tucked in tight to the rail. Then, just a furlong—an eighth of a mile—from the finish, Silverbulletday started to fade. Charismatic's jockey, Chris Antley, pumped his fists along the horse's neck, demanding anything that was still left. Charismatic answered. He cocked into full sweet gear and, as he ripped toward the finish line, I almost couldn't watch for wanting. I closed my eyes for the briefest of seconds and felt Sugar's mane laced through my fingers. The breath caught in my chest. I opened my eyes.

Then Charismatic's left front ankle snapped mid-stride.

At first, I thought he'd just given up, run dry except for a few awkward steps propelling him third across the wire. As he pulled up past the finish, his sides sweat-slick and heaving, the wreckage sifted its way to the surface. I watched Antley tumble off Charismatic's still moving back and sink to his knees, cradling the injured foreleg in both arms, watched Charismatic fling his head up and down, a rhythmic call of pain or panic, watched the equine ambulance finally drive up to tow the horse away. The crowd, its hum now faded to an uneasy murmur, started to dissolve. I stayed behind, balanced there on the ends of my sandals until my toes went numb, pinned by the quicksilver drama of hopes so immediately uncapped and washed away.

Charismatic's career-ending, but not fatal, injury meant a glorious upset for 29–1 long shot Lemon Drop Kid, named for a character in a Damon Runyon story. Fate shifts in seconds, fragile as a foreleg, and to forget this is to leave all of racing behind. Horses break down, jockeys take a hoof to the heart, gamblers lose fortunes they never even had. It's a landscape bound together by a fraternity of hope, but also by heartbreak.

I will always feel a poignancy at the track—a note of May-May, her vibrancy, which is lost and can't be recovered. At seventeen I couldn't absorb such a loss, so I drew a circle around it and stepped outside into something dry and manageable. At thirty, I've finally learned to balance what's gone with what was left behind. Alongside that emptiness there resides a willingness to take risks, to live a life that is authentic and rich and full. You don't get one without the other.

I understand this now. My seduction is complete.

Part 1:

THE STARTING GATE

Chapter One

TRUST:

The Horse of Course

M ay-May fell for Thoroughbreds the same way I would eighty years later—fully, sweetly, and without hesitation. It happened to me in her living room, kneeling on a square of plum-colored carpet. For May-May, that love first came via a cowboy dream, roaming the plains of the Wild West.

When May-May was eleven, her grandfather, soured by a post–Civil War South that had emerged as a paper cutout of its former splendor, bought a several-thousand-acre ranch outside the frontier town of Fort Collins, Colorado. The entire family piled into a private railcar and clickety-clacked their way from the new northern money of the Carnegies and Rockefellers to a land where rumor had fading cotton fortunes tripled by raising longhorn cattle.

May-May's grandmother insisted on uprooting the entire contents of their Spesushi Island plantation. The train churning along the transcontinental tracks towed behind it cargo cars laden with Queen Anne tables, china washbasins, and six four-poster beds. Her grandfather reserved one car only for his horses. Those horses were his pride, four hearty stallions with broad chests and high hindquarters, and a single fourteen-year-old mare, a former racehorse named Madame Queen. She was the one female May-May's grandfather deemed tough enough to survive the thorns and rattlesnakes of Colorado. She was also the only Thoroughbred of the lot.

Thoroughbred horses are a particular breed, like golden retrievers or Black Angus cattle, and throughout their three-hundred-year history they've existed for one reason only: to win races. Their most desirable qualities are those of any premier athlete: speed, agility, and the kind of perfectly proportioned bodies that can run river-fast without shattering. Along with such practical facts travel some highly indeterminable variables. The swiftest runners are those with the lightest bodies, leanest muscles, and longest legs, a makeup more characteristic of foals than their full-grown ancestors. Along with those juvenile physical qualities, Thoroughbreds have maintained a few other fragments of the child. They tend to be playful, moody, skittish, and temperamental, easily distracted and even more easily bored. They're expert at flouting authority, permanent adolescents straining at any parental hand. May-May's grandfather bought Madame Queen to breed her, hoping to infuse his heftier carriage horses with some of her whip-speed and fine-boned beauty, and Madame Queen proved pure Thoroughbred indeed. She boasted near perfect conformation—legs arrow-straight from shoulder to knee to ankle, muscular haunches to propel her forward, a neck that rose from her shoulders at just the right angle to balance the weight of her body as she moved. She was also a holy terror.

Madame Queen belonged to May-May, not as a gift or even a privilege, but because eleven-year-old Mary Stuart—who'd cut her riding teeth on a series of unruly ponies—was the only one who could stay atop the mare's back. In Maryland, their relationship had been limited to afternoons marking off the well-known confines of Spesushi Island, but in Colorado all that would change. While the boys carried pail lunches off to the one-room Fort Collins schoolhouse, May-May and the other granddaughters spent each morning in the nursery under the eye of an imported governess. Afternoons were their own, provided they didn't mix with the undesirable local children. For once, May-May harbored no interest in defiance. Every day at two o'clock, she donned one of her brother's oversize flannel shirts, slipped through the split-rail fences surrounding the family's log house, and darted across the dirt road to the barn and Madame Queen. A few minutes later, they were saddled up and set free.

Wandering those Colorado prairies, May-May and Madame Queen forged the sort of trust necessary for survival. When May-May lost her way during night rides through the sagebrush, Madame Queen raised her nose and led them home. When Madame Queen twisted a delicate ankle in a gopher hole, May-May swung off the saddle to walk them the seven miles back to the ranch, then packed Madame Queen's leg with homemade poultices every day for a week, drawing off heat and letting the injury heal. During the stark summer heat and lightning storms, May-May slept outside Madame Queen's stall as the horse bucked and spun and lashed out at the walls, a handful of her high-strings finally snapping loose. In the summer they would disappear overnight, May-May bedding down in the old settlers' cabins that dotted the property, then ducking into the schoolroom the next morning to await the inevitable booming voice of grandfather.

"Mary Stuart."

"Yes, sir."

She would shuffle off to his paneled office and sit in one of the imported high-back chairs with her feet dangling just above the ground. He didn't smack her with the wooden rod propped in the corner. Such punishment was saved for the boys. He would simply ask:

"Have you disobeyed me?"

"Yes, sir."

"And will you do so again?"

"Not if I can help it."

The two of them had fought the same battle too often for him to insist upon anything further. By that time he knew, maybe even admired, May-May's bent for rebellion. For all his rigid opinions, he made no move to clip those first green shoots of self-confidence. Instead, after a few months, he began to develop urgent business requiring his attention elsewhere on the property, always disappearing on those very mornings May-May slipped in at dawn with Madame Queen.

MAY-MAY'S FAMILY stayed in Colorado for only two years, a wedge of frontier heaven that slammed shut when her grandfather's fresh fortune didn't manifest itself and he grew bored with the wide-open plains. As they packed up to return to Baltimore, a neighboring rancher offered to buy Madame Queen. May-May's grandfather, pleased of any way to lighten the load, gave the man a sweet deal. As the family crowded into a wagon waiting to depart for the train depot, May-May lingered outside Madame Queen's stall, kissed her on both eyelids, and promised to return soon.

Though she never made it back to Fort Collins, the bond May-May and Madame Queen formed on those prairies bred an independent streak that would color her entire life and later come to color mine. We used to sit in her living room and exchange Thoroughbred tales, May-May weaving ten Madame Queen adventures for every river Grey Lady and I forged or fallen log we headed over instead of around. Each August, I'd erupt through her front door to relay my newest Montana adventures. I'd bubble over with accounts of raucous barrel races and herding a renegade calf back into its fold. And each August, May-May's thin fingers and still faintly southern drawl would reach out to slow me down. She would make sure that for all the rush I gleaned from this break-neck urge to give myself over, I was also absorbing the more subtle relationship evolving underneath. To know this creature meant to commit myself wholly, because a horse senses anything held back at all.

We would sift through details: the filigree of white hairs on Grey Lady's flank; the way she could slide effortlessly to the right when I'd only had time to think the direction, but not yet give it; the day her shoulder muscles first relaxed instead of tensing when she knew I was aboard. I could feed Grey Lady information without speaking, the same way a jockey draped over a racehorse's shoul-ders could make him swing wide or tuck in close to the rail just by sliding his hands up the horse's neck and clucking his tongue. And I learned to read the information she was feeding me: a droopy lower lip meant relaxed and happy, an ear cocked that something had caught her interest, a wrinkled nose that something irritated her, and a raised tail that something was making her mad as hell.

Grey Lady was never shy about communication. One time, she and I were negotiating a threadlike swampy trail up the side of a gorge, swaying along slowly with me bent forward in the saddle to take the weight off her back legs. I could feel the gentle rock of her shoulder sockets each time she took a step, and I'd slipped my feet out of the stirrups, liking how my loose legs shifted with the easy back and forth of her stride. As we neared the top of the ravine, I noticed the haunches of the horse in front of us begin to tremble as his hooves were sucked into the mire. I had a sudden image of Grey Lady's front knees buckling and both of us tumbling into the riverbed below. I grabbed at her mane to steady myself. In the instant I stopped trusting her, Grey Lady halted on the lip of the hillside, dropped her left shoulder and dumped me hard onto the ground. When I stood up, she was waiting patiently, one ear pinned back and the other cocked forward, not angry but a bit annoyed that my doubts had gotten in the way of our day. It was as if my skin turned transparent whenever I swung up into the saddle, all systems in my body pumping straight through into hers. Horses filled me up in a way nothing ever had before.

May-May and I could continue those back-and-forth tales for hours, as she reached back eighty years for the precise curve in Madame Queen's neck or the rhythm of her hooves on the Fort Collins river rock, and I entertained visions of becoming a Montana rodeo queen. Our romances became intertwined. By the time we flipped on the television for the late-summer races, May-May would have reminded me exactly why the horses had come to call on us both.

THERE WAS never any question as to May-May's opinion on Thoroughbreds. She placed them somewhere just our side of divine. They are horses boiled down to their essence—sensitivity, elegance, and a touch of something impossible to tame. From the beginning, May-May impressed upon me that a Thoroughbred's charisma stems from something far more complex than merely the quality of its flesh. Their existence requires a deft balance of strength and vulnerability. They are in part seething power, averaging roughly five and a half feet tall from shoulder to hoof and twelve hundred pounds, with a stride twenty-four feet long. They have hearts weighing anywhere from nine to fourteen pounds, and lungs capable of taking in a liter of oxygen per minute while walking and sixty liters when stretched out at a full gallop. Their body temperatures run high as their tempers, hovering just above a hundred degrees.

The alignment of muscles, bones, and tendons threading a horse together seems almost too perfectly designed for forward momentum, a bit of nature cast as art. In the sixteenth century, Leonardo da Vinci, in his quest to plumb the mysteries of the human body, filled his notebooks with sketches and studies of the anatomy of the horse. Later, scientists would discover that horses are so optimally designed to support their own weight that they actually expend less energy in standing up than they do in lying down. All horses are, literally, built to race. When they still roamed wild, running provided their sole hope of escaping predators, and they could reach speeds as high as seventy kilometers an hour. Cheetahs, the swiftest animal, can gear up to a hundred kilometers an hour, but they tire after only a few seconds. Horses can keep going, covering eighty kilometers—back-to-back marathons—in four hours' time. They can run like this because of limbs that are incredibly long and light. Over time, their toes have evolved to comprise a full third of their leg length, making their knees the equivalent of the human wrist and their hooves like four giant fingernails. Horses are forever standing, running, turning, and dodging on tiptoe. These elongated toe bones, called the cannon bone or shin, require only the sparest of muscles and no tendons at all to support them, making them featherlight to lift. The heavier muscles, those that supply the force to propel a horse's body forward, reside way up in the shoulders and haunches. Those muscles work like pendulums to swing the lower limbs backward and forward, and don't need to be lifted at all.

In Thoroughbreds, where lightness of foot is the most desirable of qualities, such a speed-centered build is at its most refined. Their legs are proportionally longer than almost any other breed—so much so that occasionally their back legs will strike their forelegs when unfolded at a run—and their hearts are proportionally larger. Even the composition of their muscles, a blend of long, slow-twitch fibers that contract slowly but waste little effort and short, fast-twitch fibers that move instantly but demand higher energy output, are perfectly balanced for a lightning pace with minimal strain. When they set foot on a racetrack, they are potential skyrockets, each one exquisitely and delicately wired.

Despite such aerodynamic design, Thoroughbreds are vulnerable. With any chance misstep, those featherweight shins and ankles can buckle under the half-ton weight they're supporting. Injuries are common—broken sesamoid bones, torn suspensory ligaments, chipped and swollen knees. Even hooves regularly crack and bruise under the stress of constantly beating the ground. Though Thoroughbreds race pressed just inches from one another, their vision is designed for just the opposite sort of existence. Horses' eyes are the largest of any land mammal, positioned at the sides of their heads and capable of scanning a near 360-degree circle in search of predators. Those wide-spaced eyes mean they catch most of their surroundings in uniocular instead of binocular vision, with minimum depth perception. They rely mostly on shadow and movement to pluck an object from its background. Such focus on distant danger has also made them naturally farsighted. Anything that draws too close becomes fuzzy and potentially threatening, be it a person, a saddle lying on the ground, or the same striped track railing they've thundered past hundreds of times before. Thoroughbreds, with their already skittish tempers, are especially prone to such skewed visions. Many race with blinkers to block out the distraction of a horse ranging up alongside, or with shadow rolls, woolly bands run across their noses, that mask the ground and prevent them from shying at the play of light flitting over the track.

Most tantalizing of all Thoroughbred qualities is their blood, thick with more hemoglobin than any other breed. That blood isn't just mythically but literally hot, their large hearts pumping more oxygen and swelling the red blood cell count to far above that of a quarter horse or a Shetland pony. Before Mendel unlocked the mechanics of gene theory in the mid-nineteenth century, many breeders believed this blood carried the qualities of speed and stamina like a river might carry along loose leaves and sticks. When a horse impregnated a mare, it was thought, his blood intertwined with hers, and even after the foal was born, some traces of that stallion lingered inside her. The mare became liquid, an ever-changing entity.

As a kid, I spent hours dreaming up what properties might be suspended in that blood, what mysterious alchemical mix could create such consummate speed and poetry. According to the veterinary manuals I would drag out at the public library, there were no magic properties, only oxygen, hemoglobin, red blood cells and white packed a little denser than they might be in a less awesome example of the species. This Thoroughbred blood provided my earliest chemistry lessons, an introduction to the idea that potential explosion might lie in the combination of properties individually benign. I found comfort in this proof that everything didn't require a logical explanation. Sometimes you could just sit back and let nature spin straw into gold.

THE FIRST known Thoroughbred ancestors wind back to North Africa and the eastern Mediterranean, where horse heads, whips, and chariots appeared etched into Egyptian monuments as early as 1500 B.C. Horses had arrived in Egypt with the Hyksos, nomadic conquerors who swept south from Syria and Palestine, waged battle from horse-drawn chariots, ruled the region for just over a hundred years, and then inexplicably departed, leaving little else behind. In the ensuing centuries, the land of Crusaders and jeweled turbans came to embrace the horse with a near holy reverence. On desert nights, horse traders brought animals into their tents, fed them dates and cups of sweet wine, played them music, and slept alongside them like children. It was believed that horses required as much care for their spirits as for their physical selves, and that sweet temperament could be absorbed like heat through the skin.

Word of these fine-boned creatures, boasting speed and stamina far superior to the thickset ponies to the north, spread across the European continent. The horses themselves soon followed. Future chariot racers were exported to Homeric Greece, Byzantium, and ancient Rome, where they gave birth to the Circus Maximus. But those bloodlines that would form the Thoroughbred headed the opposite direction, rolling east across the Sinai Desert and into Arabia.

According to Arab legend, in the first century A.D., at the heart of the Sahara, a filly was born to a horse tamer called Ishmael. She carried noble blood, the stamp of a stallion possessing a broad nose, strong limbs, and the most highly prized of qualities, an untamed rebel nature. When Ishmael's filly first raised herself from the sands, her knees buckled and she fell to the ground. Ishmael's men murmured that she would be too fragile to follow the caravan. They spoke of having her killed, but Ishmael refused to destroy any foal born of royal blood. He swaddled the day-old foal in goatskins, slung her over his shoulders, and carried his precious load home across the desert. Ishmael's filly went on to produce a legion of strong, long-limbed daughters, but her twisted legs never straightened, and she came to be known as the Crooked One. Her progeny gave birth to a line called the *kehila,* meaning purely or thoroughly bred.

Arab horsemen continued to refine the light bones and cracking speed of their mounts, but it wasn't until the seventeenth century that their influence made its way north to England, where it formed the cradle of Thoroughbred racing. Up through the reign of Henry VIII, the British racing steed had been fashioned after "the great horse," a robust creature bred to carry fully armored warriors into battle. It was Henry himself, with his fervor for conquering sport of all kind, who first imported a handful of sleek Arab horses from Spain and North Africa. Soon Arabians became a desired quantity in every royal stable and dozens were shipped across the Continent, the fruits of traveling merchants or the spoils of war. Around 1700, three especially potent stallions arrived in England to replenish animals sacrificed to the War of the Roses. Every Thoroughbred alive today descends from one of these three.

The first of the imports was the Byerley Turk, a massive and elegant warhorse captured in 1688 by Captain Robert Byerley during the siege of Vienna. Byerley, a British officer, rode the stallion in a series of skirmishes, culminating two years later in the Battle of the Boyne. When the fighting had finished, he shipped his horse home to begin a lucrative career at stud. The second foundation stallion, the Darley Arabian, was purchased in 1704 by the British consul stationed in Aleppo and sent as a gift to his brother in Yorkshire. Sixty years later, a descendant of the Darley Arabian would sire a chestnut colt called Eclipse, born during the eclipse of the sun. Eclipse became and remains the king of racehorses, winning every contest he ever ran, never once touched by whip or spur. When he retired, he went to stud pulled by a cart swathed in cloth banners and decked with rubies and pearls.

The third, and most elusive, of these taproot sires was the

Godolphin Barb, so labeled because he resembled horses found off Morocco's Barbary Coast. Rumors flew about his origins. Some speculated he'd been raised in the stables of a Tunisian prince, or once led a string of horses driven by the king of France; others that he'd been discovered pulling a water cart through the streets of Paris. The only details known for sure were that a wealthy Englishman called Edward Coke found the Barb in France in the 1720s and bought him on a lark. Back in Britain, Coke sold him to the second Earl of Godolphin, who put the horse to work breeding new additions to his budding racing stable.

In order to be considered a true example of the breed, every Thoroughbred in the world today—whether running at the Sha Tin racecourse in Hong Kong; Prairie Downs, Iowa; or the Kentucky Derby—must trace its lineage back to one of these three stallions who, by fluke or design, made their way across the English Channel.

The entire sport exists because of them.

FROM THE start, May-May took care not to let my budding fascination with racehorses slip into anything like complacency. For my first Kentucky Derby, we were simply viewers, caught up in the poetry of motion and emotion. By the following year, she expected something more. The Kentucky Derby is the first of three races— the Derby, the Preakness, and the Belmont Stakes—that comprise the Triple Crown, horse racing's version of the World Series. It lures every prodigal three-year-old runner in the country. The second time around, we prepared to align ourselves with the individual players.

Every Saturday that winter, May-May and I drove across the floating bridges spanning Lake Washington to a downtown newsstand and returned home with copies of the *Daily Racing Form* hugged under our arms. The *Racing Form* is a tabloid-style newspaper whose curlicued red banner runs under the headline "America's Turf Authority Since 1894." It is racing's sacred text, published 365 days a year. The first few pages are always articles, rundowns on high-profile races or any simmering scandals, but such prose just serves as wrapping paper, best torn through quickly to get at what's inside: the racing chart on every horse running that day.

A Thoroughbred's chart is its full history condensed into a single rectangle—racehorse concentrate. It reveals age, color, birthplace, breeder, jockey, trainer, sire, dam. It tells the particulars of the last ten races: the pace at the first quarter, the halfway point, and the top of the stretch; how far ahead or behind the horse came across the wire; even terse commentary providing clues as to personality and destiny—drew clear, flattened out, finished full of run, weakened in the stretch. At first, each chart just seemed the most cryptic sort of code, as impenetrable as the Chinese lettering on our neighbor Mrs. Li's boxes of imported almond cookies. Information came via symbols and abbreviations, and I constantly had to check the "Guide to Reading the Charts" buried in the *Form*'s back pages. But within a few months, I had the language mastered. It was my first initiation into the Thoroughbred fold.

By late February, the *Racing Form* had begun to monitor every blossoming three-year-old who might prove a candidate for that May's Kentucky Derby. May-May and I began to monitor right along with them, searching out a runner with whom to ally ourselves come spring. Their charts were still tiny, more of a fat line than a rectangle, since most had raced only three or four times. Every young colt, and the occasional filly, who pulled off an exceptional victory earned special mention on the *Form*'s three-year-olds-to-watch list. The commentary on each came laced with phrases like "ran greenly" and "veered in the stretch," letting me know they were still figuring out this racing thing, too.

"Is there one of them you think you like?" May-May would ask every weekend as we studied the results. They all seemed brilliant to me, but I would scramble for the right choice, for blistering times or flashy colors or jockeys who'd ridden as hell-bent as I might have. My favorite changed every week, often once or twice in the same day.

Repeatedly, May-May would reject not my choices but the reasons behind them. Most of all, she questioned my slippery version of confidence. In her mind, a relationship to a racehorse had to be full throttle or not at all. And even as May-May urged my impatience with the world surrounding me, she began to foster a slow-blooming patience with myself.

"Don't chose one until you know," she kept insisting. How was I supposed to know if a horse spoke to me, if one satiny coat or noble lineage contained that essential mix to rise above the rest?

Developing a system for picking horses is a core part of becoming a racing fan, a mark of character and commitment. Hard-core gamblers, known as "handicappers," make their selections via a complicated interplay of facts and statistics. In choosing a Derby colt, they will factor in the times of his previous races, whether his sire and dam excelled at the Derby's mile and a quarter distance, the percentage of Derby winners who've held his same post in the starting gate (unlike human running races, horses start in a straight line; those posted on the far outside have to make up extra ground, those posted next to the rail risk getting stuck there and spending the entire race trapped behind other horses), plus numerous other variables. Some more eccentric handicappers have been known to measure race-day wind velocity and analyze soil samples from the sand-clay mix covering the track. They tend to hold off selection until the last possible moment, forever on the alert for fresh developments that might shift the tenuous balance of a race. Such complex systems have a way of becoming a full-time pursuit.

More casual fans take a more casual stance, aligning themselves with a horse because of his name, his liquid eye, or because he won last time so why shouldn't he do it again. (This last method was especially unhelpful for the Derby, where most of the horses had won impressive races. That was how they'd made it to Churchill Downs in the first place.) May-May's system fell someplace in the middle, relying on instincts brewed over a lifetime spent with horses. She largely ignored external factors like post position and the condition of the track surface, and focused solely on the runners. As I got to know Thoroughbreds, she explained, they would begin feeding me signs about their character and desire to win.

"What kind of signs?" I insisted.

"You'll see."

The only thing I saw from the get-go was that nobody knew anything for sure. Trainers, owners, jockeys, and other supposed experts all catered generously to superstition. They came to the races toting lucky socks, lucky ties, lucky hats, and lucky friends. Some had developed their own code of laws to live by: Never buy a horse with one white sock, kill a cricket in a stall, change a horse's name, or eat peanuts in the stable. Horseshoes hung over barn doors, always with their ends facing upward, to keep the stable's luck from running out.

Given the ticklish nature of Thoroughbreds, it's no surprise that superstition has a long tradition at the track. In Elizabethan England, a lauded sportsman named Nicolle Dex used to consume nothing but white wine for three days before his horses raced. In seventeenth-century France, aristocratic owners developed a fancy for replacing their horses' usual feed of oats and grain with two to three hundred raw eggs two days before competition. Over in Ireland, it was the owners themselves who ate the eggs, but only an even number of them. For the Irish jockeys, it was considered bad luck to eat any eggs at all.

By the twentieth century, racing had absorbed the benefits of the Industrial Revolution and bounding leaps in scientific knowledge, but insiders still hadn't made much headway in unlocking the vagaries of luck. In the 1940s, one of the most prominent owners, Colonel E. R. Bradley, attributed a long winning streak to giving all his horses names starting with the letter *B*. He also attempted to aid a horse with especially poor vision by fashioning him a king-size pair of spectacles. One of his contemporaries, a New York bookmaker named Barney Schreiber, opted to flatter an even higher power. He named every horse he owned after a priest. Even the Kentucky Derby wasn't immune. In 1963, the winner, Chateaugay, raced with a chicken bone tied to his bridle for luck.

If such experts couldn't unlock the whims and fancies of a winner, how was I, an eight-year-old novice, possibly supposed to manage?

"Don't worry about picking who will win," May-May told me. "Just find the horse who speaks to you."

Beyond this, she refused to offer an opinion. She would provide the tools and a few pearls of experience, but I couldn't fall in love using someone else's heart. The faith, and the decision, had to come from me.

MAY-MAY FELL for her first Triple Crown contender in 1915, the year she journeyed to Churchill Downs to watch the Kentucky Derby in person. The object of her affections was a filly called Regret. A filly had never won the Derby, and—especially given the fact that Regret hadn't raced since the previous August—many doubted her ability to fight against the boys. Studying photos published in the Maryland papers, May-May thought she recognized something in the filly, a shared bent for breaking new ground. At twenty-four, May-May had already split from that Baltimore society which had set out to mold her from childhood. She'd shunned a marriage proposal from the son of a shipping tycoon in favor of liberty, hours free to frequent lectures on Margaret Sanger's battle for birth control and to follow the slowly snowballing effort to win women the vote. She'd gone to work as a surgical nurse at Johns Hopkins Hospital, assisting doctors in developing the earliest X-ray machines, and she spent hours studying gray sheets of film that stripped away a person's exterior to expose what lay beneath. Looking past the fat white stripe running down Regret's nose and the wide flare of her nostrils, May-May honed in on something else. She caught a thread of that willfulness required to shake free of expectation.

Regret's owner, Harry Whitney, ran his filly in tribute to his brother-in-law, Alfred Gwynne Vanderbilt, who'd sunk with the *Lusitania* after a one-two punch from German torpedoes the day before the race. The war in Europe had spread across the ocean, foreshadowing a bloody end to the decade. Even the racetrack felt the onset of gravity as thousands of Thoroughbreds bred for amusement were shipped overseas instead to serve as cavalry horses in the British army. These somber notes only seemed to fuel the gaiety at Churchill Downs. The public was on a pleasure hunt, searching out all means of temporary escape from an unavoidable future, and that year forty thousand people hotfooted it to the Derby. May-May and her brother, Robert, decided to take a train across the snow-dusted Allegheny Mountains to join the reveling crowd.

They arrived in Louisville on May 7, the afternoon before the race. Early the next morning May-May hurried into her silk dress with its black lace overlay and pinned on a pale yellow hat that the railcar soot had turned milky gray. With all carriages and motorcars booked weeks in advance, she and Robert wended their way to Churchill Downs on foot. While Robert downed mint juleps and courted potential clients for his employers, the Norfolk and Western Railroad, May-May staked out a spot along the rail and awaited her first glimpse of Regret. She didn't bother to visit the newly installed pari-mutuel betting machines, since she and Robert had already laid a heavy side wager on the race. Robert, an avid duck hunter who'd taken May-May into the backwater of Spesushi Island when she was fourteen and taught her to shoot a silver dollar off a tree stump, put his money on a precocious colt called Sharpshooter. For May-May, the only choice was Regret.

By that time, May-May was not only well practiced in Thoroughbred conformation—the broad chest, powerful stomach and shoulder muscles, and straight line from shoulder to knee to ankle that delineate a potential Mercury—she'd also developed a more refined second sense. She knew to look for an aura of barely collected energy, the promise of something extra held just in reserve that might boil over once a horse hit the track. Racehorses are unpredictable, sticking to form only when it suits their fancy. Often it's just in those final moments before a race that they make the choice whether to embrace or disdain it. They transmit this part of the message in intangibles, a language composed of sideways struts, the prick of the ears, the warmth of the air surrounding them. The signs are always there, emanating; it's just a question of whether humans can make the corresponding leap from analysis to instinct.

May-May watched Regret prance into the paddock, her neck bowed and chestnut coat aglow, watched her toss back her head, messing the neatly braided bits of mane, as jockey Joe Notter hopped aboard. She found the desired lick of flame. Only then, fully confident that Regret would come out fighting, did she join Robert in their clubhouse box to watch the race.

May-May's instincts and Regret's incandescence came through that year. The filly sprang from the starting gate and gushed speed for the full mile and a quarter. She won by two lengths, never allowing the fifteen colts in the race to slip ahead by even a nose. After Sharpshooter dribbled in third, Robert paid out from the bundle of bills tucked into his breast pocket and told his sister to buy herself a clean dress. Instead, May-May held onto her winnings for an entire year, stowing them in a jade-colored keepsake box on her dresser. The next summer she wagered her full windfall on Regret once again, as the filly took on another string of colts in New York's Saratoga Handicap. This time she finished dead last.

"What happened?" I demanded the first time I heard the story, struggling to absorb this double betrayal of May-May's intuition and Regret's once flawless speed.

"I don't know," May-May replied. She explained that Regret was a racehorse—living, breathing, temperamental. Her ingredients were fluid, always arranging and rearranging, and sometimes the order came together wrong.

"Did you ever bet on her again?"

"Of course. And she came back to win."

That night I sat on my bed with all the articles and pictures of the Kentucky Derby contenders spread out around me, picked up the first page of the first magazine, and started over again from scratch. In attempting to construct my flawless Triple Crown horse, I'd skipped one of the core ingredients altogether. I hadn't allowed him room to live and breathe.

REGRET'S GLORY and May-May's willingness to risk everything on her provided me with that extra tablespoon of faith required to play fast and loose with my own instincts. By March,

I'd made my choice, and once I tumbled, I tumbled hard. I siphoned
my heart into a showman, a smashing chestnut colt with a thick
white blaze and that same inborn radiance I imagined May-May
had spotted in Regret. He was called Alydar.

Once I'd settled upon Alydar, I began to study up hard. I
combed through the *Racing Form, Sports Illustrated,* and *Blood-
Horse* magazine, and clipped out every mention of him, right down
to the Washington State–grown hay he ate for breakfast. Everything about Alydar bespoke something almighty, from his loose-
jointed stride to the electric temper that once spurred him to kick a
groom in the chest, breaking four of the man's ribs. He'd been
bred and raised by one of Kentucky's most illustrious stables, the
bluegrass gem Calumet Farm. Even his name had royal connections; his Calumet owners had christened him after a lady friend
of Prince Aly Khan who used to sweep into a room trilling, "Aly,
daahrling . . ." He'd already collected a string of victories in exotic-
sounding races—the Champagne, the Flamingo, the Bluegrass—
and the few times he'd lost he'd done so by just a neck or a nose.
His gutsiness grabbed at me, leaving no question of stepping aside.
Mine was all childhood crush. When the Kentucky Derby rolled
around that first Saturday in May, a piece of me would spill right
out onto the track.

Alydar came with more than just snazzy devil's-red-and-blue
racing silks, adopted from the Calumet baking powder logo, and a
nail-biting style of dropping far behind the other horses and then,
in the final stretch, roaring up the outside with a shotgun burst of
speed. He came with a rival, an ace California front-runner called
Affirmed who had lost only two races in his life, finishing second
both times to Alydar. He'd also beaten Alydar three times out of
five.

May-May readily backed my devotion to Alydar. She liked his
classic pedigree—he was by a premier stallion named Raise A
Native out of a mare called Sweet Tooth—and the near perfect
lines in his conformation. Most of all she admired his clear appetite
for winning races. Some horses might run fast but lack heart, giving up as soon as another horse pokes his head forward to chal-

lenge. Alydar was an inherent leader, a characteristic that could be traced back to a time when horses roamed wild and only a choice few managed to define themselves as head of the pack. Horses' relationships revolve around dominance and submission, around knowing where they fit in the hierarchical structure of the herd and then trusting that this structure won't splinter. When Alydar rocketed to the front of a race, he was following that inborn impulse to dominate, and other horses could hear the echo of a primal battle. Clinging to instincts that once would have meant survival, lesser animals refused to pass him by. In racing parlance, Alydar had class.

Horses convey class to one another instantly, via subtle shifts in carriage, tiny movements of head, ears, eyes, teeth, and hooves. In the moment when two Thoroughbreds come alongside each other on the track, both are sending messages as to which one of them will eventually back off. What made the rivalry between Affirmed and Alydar so potent was that they possessed the same unbreakable level of determination. They could be counted upon not to give in, to believe in victory right up to the very last shaving of a second.

ON DERBY day, I arrived at May-May's condominium wearing new Nike tennis shoes with a shiny Calumet-red swoosh. When I bent down to kiss her, I spotted a matching devil's red silk ribbon tied around her hair. I flipped on the television and seesawed the antennae until Churchill Downs showed up only slightly wavy around the edges. Affirmed and Alydar were already on the track, looking equally sharp-edged and polished.

"What if he loses?" I asked, my nerves gunning as the group trotted toward the starting gate. The post positions were assigned by lots, and Alydar had drawn number ten, near the outside of the course, which could be good because he wouldn't get squeezed by the other ten horses oozing onto the track, but could be bad if he faltered at the start and got stuck far outside on each of the wide-sweeping turns. Affirmed would break from post position two.

"If he loses, we start thinking about next year."

Next year seemed impossibly far off. I knocked three times on the wooden coffee table, the only thing I could think to do for luck. Then the starting bell sounded, and they were off.

The horses popped from the gate like a line of colored champagne corks, and in those pivotal first steps, something went horribly wrong. Alydar fell out of sync with the pack, his feet scrabbling to find purchase in the deep, cuppy dirt of the track. Having lost crucial seconds, he slid further and further back until he was seventeen lengths behind Affirmed, already sizzling near the lead. I didn't know that I could stand to witness his humiliation. I reached out to punch the power button off, but May-May grabbed for my wrist.

"He's going to lose," I objected.

"Let him run his race."

May-May held on to my wrist as we watched, as the gap slowly narrowed between Alydar and the rest of the field. Then, as they rounded the far turn, Alydar rediscovered his speed. In a heartbeat, my bias shifted back in favor of hope. It was as if the film of Alydar's race started turning a gear faster than all the other horses, an untapped vein of determination—of class—catapulting him past each member of the pack until only Affirmed remained. Affirmed refused to fade. Both horses rocketed towards the finish stretched full out, Alydar digging in his feet and continuing to make up ground. But there were too few seconds and too much space. At the wire, it was still Affirmed, ahead by a length and a half.

As the television cameras flipped back to the announcers, I collapsed onto the couch. I'd never gone from so full to so empty in my entire life. Now it was me clinging to May-May's wrist, too squeezed of emotion even to cry. I knew I would be back two weeks later for the Preakness, and then again for the Belmont. Alydar had held up his half of the bargain, running like wildfire. All that was required of me was to continue to believe.

Alydar lost the Preakness to Affirmed by a neck, then the Belmont by a nose, each race delivering my eight-year-old self another hammer blow. For years I would file Alydar's Triple Crown journey under the heading of losses, of broken hearts from which I could and did recover. Something more ephemeral lingers there now. I remember how, even from seventeen lengths behind, Alydar wasn't cowed by the prospect of defeat. That faith in himself, far more than wins and losses, in the end delineated a champion.

EVERY SPRING for ten years, May-May and I selected and succumbed to our favorites for the Kentucky Derby. Occasionally we won—on a long-shot gray named Gato del Sol and a colt called Spend A Buck who carried the race by five full lengths with Angel Cordero aboard—but more often we were also-rans. Before long, it stopped really mattering. After the race, we would eat Aplets & Cotlets, mull over Regret and Alydar and all the others, and begin speculating about next season. By the time my father arrived in his Chevrolet station wagon to pick me up, I'd be lost in that someday spring when I'd make my own pilgrimage to the Derby.

Five months after I turned thirty, eighty-five years after May-May watched Regret crush fifteen colts wire-to-wire, it was finally my turn. In the past few years, I'd started picking Derby favorites again. I'd relearned the intimate nature of falling in love each spring. And I'd grown tired of waiting. That year my Derby pick would be specially weighted. On the first Saturday in May, I would finally walk through the turnstile at Churchill Downs. I was going to the Kentucky Derby.

How do you pick a Derby horse? For all my years at the track, I still don't have an answer. May-May handed me some key elements, but never a formula, and the method I've cobbled together keeps changing from year to year. It's a fluid combination of knowledge and taste, longing and instinct, an interlacing of May-May's opinions and my own. I don't play the handicapper as I tried to in college, analyzing the percentages and probabilities, distilling the Thoroughbred to something flat and calculable. Instead, I still follow May-May's advice: Don't look for the horse I think will win, just the horse I want to. This is all about heart's desire.

The fall before my Derby trip, I eyed the two-year-old colts as they began their racing careers, searching out a horse who seemed able but not precocious. I was looking for the first bubbles of ability, a horse more akin to a slow fuse than a single stick of dynamite, one that could save his peak performances until the following spring. I wanted a horse with courage, connections, and promise, and I'm always open to a little sentimental tug. By February, I'd found the full package in an understated gentleman called Captain Steve.

Captain Steve's trainer and owner, Bob Baffert and Mike Pegram, had won the Kentucky Derby with a long shot named Real Quiet the year I watched from Radio Shack, and I had my hopes their luck might unfold one more time. But Captain Steve lured me with far more than just connections. I liked his flexible running style, how he could spend an entire race at the front of the pack or stalk the pace from farther back, then make up ground down the stretch. I liked his willingness to gun for the lead even when there was next to no chance he'd make it. Most of all, I liked his personality. He was low-key and a little goofy, a youngster suffering from a definite lack of focus. Whenever he took the lead in a race, he'd start zigzagging back and forth across the track as if bored by gaining ground the old-fashioned way. He was having fun, letting loose, and I saw promise in his erratic tilt. May-May had always steered me clear of the belief that forward momentum has to be achieved in a straight line.

From the start, Captain Steve seemed graced with an internal alarm clock set for the first Saturday in May. He captured three big races in the fall, one in California and two in Kentucky, including the Brown & Williamson Kentucky Jockey Club Stakes at Churchill Downs. I liked that he was a born traveler, and that Brown & Williamson made the pipe tobacco my grandfather used to smoke. I even liked that, as the season unfolded, it became clear he hadn't yet buckled down to serious competition. He ran two big late-winter races, finishing third in both the Santa Catalina Stakes and the Louisiana Derby. This daisy chain of near misses slotted him further and further down in the media polls, each length lost allowing for another tendril of doubt. To me, this holding back only heightened Captain Steve's allure. I grew convinced he was teasing us, balancing on the cusp of what he might accomplish once that wrapped tornado broke open.

Those newspaper opinions ultimately cemented my relationship to Captain Steve. They generated a whiff of the same righteous anger I'd felt at eight when public opinion abandoned Alydar for Affirmed. It seemed unfair to expect perfection, to judge so absolutely on each brushstroke instead of stepping back to view the entire canvas. The more the reporters focused on the glitches, the faster I fell for the Captain and his late-blooming confidence. Where they spotted cracks, I saw the ticktock of potential.

That February I met Captain Steve in his stall on the backstretch of southern California's Santa Anita Park racetrack. It was the first time I'd ever encountered a Kentucky Derby contender face to face. I'd come west ostensibly to spend a few days with his trainer, Bob Baffert, but there was definitely an ulterior motive involved.

As with any professional athlete, every racehorse has a trainer—hired by its owner for a flat daily fee plus a percentage of any winnings—who handles the infinite details involved in preparing a Thoroughbred to run. Trainers design a workout schedule, determining how heavily each individual needs to trot, jog, or gallop every morning to keep muscles tuned but not taxed. Lazy horses are pushed, natural runners simply maintained, and the high-strung given an outlet to exhaust their jangled nerves. Trainers choose which races their charges should enter, sorting the class horses who will compete for high-purse stakes from low-level runners who stick to claiming races, in which each entrant is automatically put up for sale. They become expert at catering to fickle tempers, juggling horses who grow bored without frequent upheavals in their routine with those who threaten meltdown if schedules are altered at all. They keep a constant eye out for injury, any slightly cockeyed gait that might indicate sore muscles or strained tendons, and for the more elusive mental souring that happens when a horse burns out on the stresses of the job. They book the jockeys, manage the barn staff, summon the vet, instruct the blacksmith, and generally oil every gear that runs the slimmest chance of rusting up. Then they worry because, no matter how brilliantly they perform their jobs, success comes down to the horses, and Thoroughbreds are anarchists at heart.

Captain Steve's main man, Bob Baffert, was one of the most successful in the business, his horses pulling in upwards of $15 million a year. He'd taken contenders to the Derby for four years running, winning twice, and I had no question that the Captain's somewhat erratic leanings were in extremely gifted hands. At Santa Anita, Bob Baffert was king. His shock of white hair and daffy sense of humor had made him a media darling, perhaps the closest thing the sport had to a Michael Jordan or Bobby Valentine. When he spoke—whether to recommend that a jockey who failed a drug test get a second chance or to suggest smaller hamburger buns at the track's FrontRunner restaurant—things happened. Spending a few days alongside him provided a crash course on who's who in southern California racing. If they didn't stop to shake hands, swap one-liners, congratulate or commiserate with Bob Baffert, they probably weren't anyone at all. Given my position at the right hand of the sovereign, I never did mention I'd also come to see somebody else.

I searched out Captain Steve the morning after I arrived. As I stepped up to his stall, I felt nervous, as though I'd been invited to eat breakfast next to a movie star and hoped I wouldn't say anything dumb. We spent a few easy minutes feeling each other out, he snuffling up my coat sleeves for hidden carrots or Jolly Rancher candies, I rubbing his muzzle and keeping my fingers clear of bared teeth. He was chocolate brown, with one crooked white stocking reaching halfway up his left hind leg and a thin white stripe barely a trickle down the center of his nose. He didn't look flashy the way Alydar had, but endearing and solid. His was a quiet sort of confidence, and I suspected that if he won the Derby he would do so not with trumpet flourishes but in an honest, workmanlike fashion. When I was eight, such understated style would have disappointed, but no longer. I'd learned to separate substance from its jazzy backdrop.

I dropped in on Captain Steve every morning for five days. Most horses get daily exercise to keep muscles toned and nervous energy in check, but all that week the Captain had been stall bound, save an hour each morning spent walking a circle in front of the barn. One rear hoof had bruised ever so slightly when the blacksmith nailed in a new pair of shoes, creating a nearly imperceptible limp, and Bob Baffert was taking no chances with his spring prodigy. Kept to the confines of the barn, the lackadaisical Captain Steve had started pacing the front of his stall and demanding attention from anyone who passed. He liked to hang his head over the doorway with his tongue lolling out, hoping someone would come along and tug on it. Once, after I'd delivered a few yanks, he changed his mind and latched his teeth onto my coat. It took a three-minute tug-of-war to work my way free.

When I arrived for my good-bye visit late on a Sunday morning, he was turned around, scratching his nose on the far wall of the barn. I leaned against the nylon webbing guarding the door to watch him, and he twisted his neck toward me, hearing or just sensing an arrival. His ears swiveled back, as if pondering irritation, then cocked all the way forward. He maneuvered a tight half circle in the straw and ambled over to me, pushing his lip up my empty sleeve and letting a puff of warm, hay-scented breath escape onto my wrist. Then he just stood there for a few minutes, resting his muzzle in the palm of my hand.

After that, I was a goner. Head over heels.

IN THEORY, it goes against May-May's philosophy to have a second choice for the Derby, to grow fickle and siphon off even an atom of that whole-scale belief. But May-May's first rule about rules was that they should regularly be broken. So, though there was no question I'd tumbled hard for Captain Steve—his goofiness and composure and lolling tongue—that same week I decided to pledge ever so slightly divided loyalties. My runner-up was a small dark colt called The Deputy, bred in Ireland and imported from England, where he grew up running on grass instead of dirt. I'd always fancied horses from foreign countries: Ireland, France, Argentina, Brazil. I envisioned them carrying something exotic, a drop of Godolphin Barb or The Crooked One, into the mix.

The Deputy's allure came from a higher premium than just European lineage, or even the eye-swiveling way he sliced past the competition to win the first race he ever ran on dirt. It came from his trainer. For only the tenth time in the 126 years of the Kentucky

Derby, that trainer—Jenine Sahadi—was a woman. What I knew of Jenine came secondhand, since she operated solely on the West Coast. She had a reputation for a hair-trigger temper and the ability to win big races, bigger than any female trainer in the country. She'd set a new bar for women in 1996 when her horses earned more than $3 million, ranking her twelfth in the nation. With The Deputy's arrival on the Derby scene, my curiosity had been piqued.

I met Jenine during that same trip to Santa Anita, having convinced one of the *Racing Form*'s beat reporters to let me accompany him to her barn. Bob Baffert's kingdom is just inside the main gate onto the backstretch—including a parking spot for his black BMW and a gate guard who, on his off-hours, volunteers for runs to the car wash. Finding Jenine required winding our way into the center of a maze of shedrows. We reached her about ten, just as the last horses were filing home from their morning workouts. As we approached, I could see her framed in the arched doorway of her barn watching one of her charges get a bath. She wore work clothes, dirt-smudged jeans, and a baggy green sweatshirt, had a Diet Coke in hand and round sunglasses pushed atop lots of long, loose dark hair. Business came first and was dispensed with quickly. She refused to hand over any information about The Deputy, save that he was healthy and training well. Predictions were out. Racetrackers don't venture them often; to augur success is to place it in the air early enough that it might be snatched away. Even the word *Derby* got her a little fired.

"I'm not even thinking about Kentucky. There's too much that can happen between now and then."

"Any ideas at all?"

"Nothing. I'm not going to jinx it." She took a swig of Coke.

"I'm just wondering . . ."

"I said leave it."

A small tirade on the pressures of the press followed, and I got the feeling we were about to be asked to leave altogether, but my reporter friend backed off and the steam release evaporated. We moved on to track gossip, tossing around plenty of non-Derby speculation, and eventually Jenine relaxed. We were leaning against the wood wall opposite the open door of her tack room. Inside I could see tidy rows of bridles, bandages, vitamin supplements, and boxes of the red wine she adds to her horses' feed to mellow any lingering racetrack stress. Everything was neat, well swept, homelike. A groom passing by even offered us each a powdered doughnut. She kept us twenty minutes with stories about the dinner party she'd thrown the night before, all of it punctuated by a throaty laugh, but later my reporter friend said he could tell the coming Derby whirlwind had her wound up. Usually she was an open book with the press.

Having a serious Kentucky Derby contender places any trainer on red alert, dodging journalists, critics, and the occasional crisis of faith, and no doubt Jenine knew to have her trigger cocked early. She'd been deflecting blows since she started training horses in 1993, aimed first at her well-connected background—her father bred racehorses and ran a top-notch Thoroughbred sales operation—then later at her tempestuous romance with the Peruvian trainer who helped her set up shop. If she'd developed a reputation for being prickly, defensive, and even flat-out rude, perhaps it was understandable. Things haven't changed so much since May-May's day. A woman doesn't have it easy at the track, especially when she's pressing against the top ranks; especially when she has a journalism degree from USC in a place that tends to value experience over book learning; and especially when she used to work in the Santa Anita public relations office alongside another highly suspicious breed, management. In just a few weeks, Jenine would enter a very public fracas with Bob Baffert, storming out on a press conference when he made a joke about The Deputy's jockey being the one who'd trained the horse.

"Thank God my horse has class," she announced to the gathered media, "because there are a lot of people here who don't have any."

"I was just trying to have a little fun," Baffert responded. "She hates me. She hates my guts. She hates everyone."

Jenine rubbed people. I liked that. I liked that she was young—

just thirty-seven—outspoken, and tougher than tire rubber, defying the static-crackle of nerves by chain-smoking cigarettes and popping emerald green bubble gum. And then there was her horse.

By the time we left her barn that morning, Jenine had softened enough to lead us over to meet The Deputy. Thoroughbreds aren't cute and cuddly like riding-school ponies or backyard saddle horses. That hyped-up energy which sends them jetting around the racecourse can curdle offtrack, making them more likely to snap than nuzzle. I once met a groom with two useless fingers and a purple half-moon scar running the entire width of his palm, courtesy of a racehorse who objected to having his mane combed out. I always approach with caution. The Deputy was a tenderheart. He reached his head all the way out of the stall so I could scratch the base of his mane and leaned his black-satin muzzle against my chest. His ultra-petite build formed lines so dainty I imagined his legs must shiver like saplings under the pummeling they took each time he ran. My second Derby horse in two days. Delirium.

He studied us while we departed, gazing all the way down the length of the shedrow as if in contemplation of some meatier question. Though scientists say most of a horse's ample brain is devoted to coordinating its four limbs to walk, trot, and gallop, I could've sworn we'd triggered some dormant strain of intellectual curiosity. Jenine told us that when The Deputy reached the track each morning, a time when most horses grow obsessed with jigging and yanking against the bridle, he loved just to stand still and observe the world streaming past.

"He even likes to watch the tractors," she boasted, like a parent bursting with the news of their three-year-old learning to read.

We walked past a clutch of empty stalls on our way out, floors swept clean of straw and cobwebs gathering in the doorways. I discovered later that despite having won back-to-back million-dollar Breeders' Cup races in 1996 and 1997 and now training a Derby-bound colt, Jenine hadn't quite caught on with California owners. She was constantly scraping for enough runners to fill up her barn.

No female trainer had ever won the Derby. Not Mary Hirsch, the first woman to hold a trainer's license in 1937, or Shelley Riley,

whose horse Casual Lies skidded in at second in 1992. I was definitely torn. I amended my vision of a dream Derby, the one where
Captain Steve broke free from the pack in the final hundred yards
and cruised solo across the wire. Now I pictured him and The
Deputy pasted together the entire length of the stretch, a duel so
tightly knit it was only in the final fragment of a second that one
nose jutted itself forward. If that nose were chocolate brown with a
narrow white ribbon, I'd be celebrating. If it were dark and European, I wouldn't be too disappointed, either.

CAPTAIN STEVE and The Deputy both had one prep race left
by the time I'd fully and absolutely settled upon them as my men,
the mile-and-an-eighth-long Santa Anita Derby. Come early April,
the two of them plus four other California Triple Crown contenders would all get ready to rumble. For each, this would be the
race before the big race. The perfect scenario meant victory under
90 percent effort, that extra bit yoked back, then funneled into 110
percent at Churchill Downs. I was back in New York by the time
they ran, but all morning I felt wingbeats from those same butter-
flies I used to get before each Triple Crown prep race as a kid. It felt
good to be invested. This I've realized: I'm a romantic. I like hope.
I like feeling a fraction more alive.

The Fox TV broadcast began at five, but I had the television on
ten minutes early, glancing every few seconds at a muted baseball
update to make sure I wouldn't miss the changeover. By the time
the cameras switched over to the track, the horses had strutted
through the paddock tunnel and onto the course, each one coupled
with a rider aboard a lead pony—a staunch, placid non-Thorough-
bred who walked alongside to soothe them in those last frenzied
minutes before a race. I surrendered to the elastic bounce of muscles and the glitter of sun off buffed coats.

The track announcer called three minutes to post, then two,
then a countdown by seconds. The bell rang, the doors flicked
open, the horses gathered themselves and leapt. Captain Steve
broke clean, flashing red-and-yellow silks as he surged into fourth
place crouched just behind the leaders. The Deputy jumped for-

ward and settled right ahead of him in third. They kept up a gentle, rolling pace down the far side of the track. The jockeys held their mounts tight, conserving a few grains of speed to unleash in the final furlongs. I remembered to exhale, and we shared a brief, rhythmic pocket of calm.

As they swung into the homestretch, momentum shifted. The jockeys released those kept notches, whips switching and reins pulled wide, sending forth the signal to cut loose. Each dropped low in his saddle, and their bodies stretched and bent in rhythm with their mounts. Strumming down the straightaway, Captain Steve started his usual bob and weave. Then all of a sudden the wanderer found his focus. He dug into the track and lunged forth with a gigantic burst of speed. But ahead of him, The Deputy was already soaring, and he'd left no grace period for wandering minds. He flattened out his body and thrust that elegant little head forward, hooking the leader—a colt called War Chant—then drawing on something more and shooting ahead. Captain Steve kept gaining, but that conscious choice to get down to business had come too late. The Deputy, to-the-bone professional, shoved his ears back and came first across the wire like a glossy black bullet.

It was a premier performance, and I felt a rush of pride for this delicate fellow who a month earlier had pressed his nose against my chest. The camera followed The Deputy into the winner's circle and zeroed in on his head. Usually a horse looks mustang-wild after a race—mane tangled, nostrils flaring, and veins popping like he's hooked some primal urge. The Deputy just looked red-eyed and exhausted. The effort he'd put out was enough to break your heart.

Then the camera angle widened to include Jenine Sahadi. She'd just become the first woman trainer ever to win the Santa Anita Derby, and behind her a flock of still photographers pointed and clicked like mad. She planted a huge, smacking kiss on The Deputy's neck.

"I'm so proud," she cooed. "I'm so, so proud of you."

The following day, the front page of the *Racing Form* trumpeted

Jenine's chance to become the first female Derby winner. I recalled her cautions against tempting fate, but I cut out the article anyway and pinned it up on my bulletin board, the same way I used to do with Angel. I only wished May-May could have been there, to see how ideas and opinions and patterns of flight can change.

Chapter Two

REWRITING THE RULES:

The Front Men—Trainers and Owners

Though she never had the chance to flex her skills on the backstretch of a racetrack, May-May had an instinct for training horses. Her most visible successes were Countess Highland and Dr. Rhythm, the pair of washed-up American Saddlebreds she transformed into trotting champions in the 1930s. But the true triumph of her training career came a decade earlier, from a creature who never made it within a hundred miles of a racetrack. He was a crossbred packhorse with turned-in knees and a square chin he carried too high in the air, as if to announce his stubbornness to the universe. He came to May-May unbroken and unrefined, as part of a deal struck with a retired fur trader in New Mexico in 1920, the year she spent as a trapper along the Mexican border.

When the First World War bumped to a close, May-May faced the prospect of an ordinary nursing job and a ring of uninspiring southern suitors. Her grandfather had died two years earlier, leaving her a small window of financial independence. Every grain of her resisted being angled into a fixed and permanent heading. She'd been too thoroughly captivated by the anything-goes atmosphere of the races, and by the electric energy generated by the onset of the Jazz Age. Women clamored for the vote, bootleggers and speakeasies blossomed in the cobbled Baltimore streets, and May-May wanted her own slice of such daring. She had Robert question his racetrack connections, but he couldn't turn up anyone interested in hiring a thirty-one-year-old society spinster to gallop their horses or oversee their barns.

As May-May debated whether to accept a senior nursing position at Johns Hopkins Hospital, she received an unexpected invitation from her godmother, Aunt Wee. Wee had shipped out to Las Cruces, New Mexico, the previous year and set up a tiny but flourishing trading post specializing in East Coast luxuries like cotton fabrics and rolled cigarettes. Her letter urged May-May to venture cross-country for a visit. Within four days, May-May had packed her trunk and bought a train ticket, unsure whether she would ever return. She equated Las Cruces with Colorado and still craved that open landscape she and Madame Queen had devoured. If she couldn't establish herself along the backside of a racetrack, the uncharted Southwest seemed a promising runner-up.

When May-May arrived in the spring of 1920, Las Cruces was still frontier territory, its renegade character largely shaped by the nearby Mexican border. There were few women around and even fewer ways for a female to make a living. Trailblazing was the word of the day, and May-May plunged in at once, setting up shop as the first female fur trapper in town. She bought a string of traps from a retired Spaniard, and he threw in the only horse he had remaining, a feisty two-year-old colt who'd never been under the saddle. The locals hooted with laughter, one promising to spit-roast and dine upon his own hat if May-May caught a single critter. Plenty of tough women had passed through town—rumor once had Calamity Jane shooting up the ceiling of a nearby bar when they refused to serve her a drink—but none of them stuck around more than a few weeks. Life in Las Cruces didn't lend itself to feminine ways. But after years at the racetrack, May-May had grown expert at shrugging off the odds. She called the horse Rattlesnake, because she figured he should know about his craftiest enemy right off, and ignoring the wisecracks, she set about transforming them both into working trappers.

Beginning with that birthday pony on Spesushi Island, May-May had nursed a fascination for reaching into a horse's mind. She'd discovered early on that horses, like humans, didn't conform to a single set of rules. Instead, she tuned her senses towards picking up the messages wrapped in their individual behaviors. If a horse flared angry, she looked for something inflicting damage, a cut hoof or a bit of the bridle chafing against an ear. If he turned nervous, she sought to soothe what frightened, the drip of water in a dark barn or the way a shadow fell across his face each time she raised the saddle to his back. The relationship hinged on give and take, each interaction leaving its mark until eventually horse and human had composed a mutual trust. In the case of Rattlesnake, it was a question of doing so quickly and leaving as few loopholes as possible behind.

Confining herself to Aunt Wee's fenced-in backyard, May-May devoted long, solitary days to Rattlesnake—draping herself over his back, stroking his belly with her hands, sliding under him with the girth of an unwieldy western saddle. He was a fighter, seemingly convinced that saddle, bridle, or May-May herself would surge up to smote him the way a snake might rise out of a dried-up riverbed. His instant reaction to anything new was to rear up on his hind legs and lash at May-May with well-aimed hooves, once catching her cheek and leaving behind a crescent-shaped scar only centimeters from her right eye. May-May refused to grace Rattlesnake's panic with even the slimmest measure of support. Horses learn by memory and repetition, a simple chain of action-reaction unclouded by human precepts like logic or imagination. History has primed them to pair external cues with the approach of danger: the crack of a twig with the scent of a predator, dampness rising off the grass with a thunderstorm. Such associations take hold quickly, good as well as bad. As long as May-May offered nothing that inflicted damage, eventually Rattlesnake would learn to stop expecting harm.

May-May spent a week working up to climbing onto Rattlesnake's back, and another either hanging on tight as he bucked and danced, or flying through the air when his will to defy her surpassed her own will to hang on. He demanded reservoirs of patience and nearly all her waking moments. She swabbed iodine on the cuts he acquired kicking out at rail fences, and tossed buckets of water over his steaming back. Progress was painfully slow. Occasionally, some of the other trappers would lean against Aunt Wee's gate and watch May-May work, laying bets among one another on how long it would take for Rattlesnake to snap one of those female bones right in half.

A bit of that doubt crept into May-May's mind as well—though she refused to admit it even to Aunt Wee—a worry that Rattlesnake would prove too tenderhearted and unpredictable for navigating the desert. Come dawn one morning, she wandered out to the backyard with a bridle slung over her shoulder, prepared to wait out his usual flurry of high-speed figure eights. She let herself through Aunt Wee's back gate and leaned against one of the fence posts. Rattlesnake, who'd raised one wary ear to monitor her approach, pivoted toward the far end of the yard ready to erupt. He took a step or two backward, then changed his mind and trotted forward instead. He stopped with his chest flush to May-May, who was still leaning against the gatepost, and cautiously touched his nose to her shoulder. May-May reached up to stroke him, and he lowered his head even farther, until they stood together cheek to cheek.

Rattlesnake proved a colt loyal to his convictions. Once May-May had earned his favor, he never once asked for it back. Each dawn May-May would swing a canteen over her saddle horn and pack a .32 Colt revolver onto her hip, and together they'd gallop off into the desert. On Saturdays, she would stride into the town trading post and hand over a bundle of fox and muskrat pelts, accepting a wad of paper bills in return. One starry evening the entire town, May-May and Rattlesnake included, gathered to watch one of its most vocal residents spit-roast and swallow most of a battered tan buckskin hat.

For months, May-May and Rattlesnake trekked the New Mexico desert, seemingly invincible. Then, a year after she arrived in Las Cruces, a band of Mexican entrepreneurs stole May-May's entire trapline. Twice she tried replenishing her stock, hiding traps in gutted-out bushes and along arid riverbeds, but the fresh competition proved too clever for outfoxing. Eventually, she took it as a sign to depart. She retired Rattlesnake, and the bit of herself she'd poured into him, to Aunt Wee's backyard stable and answered a newspaper ad for nurses in the copper-mining town of Kennicott, Alaska. In Kennicott she went on to become the first woman to ride packhorses into a series of glaciers, helping to set up tents, fry bacon, and talk racehorses with adventure parties made up of Guggenheims and Whitneys.

I once asked if she'd ever considered taking Rattlesnake with her, but she instantly shook her head.

"He must have missed you," I insisted.

She laughed. "He belonged to Las Cruces, never to me."

It was the price you paid for standing cheek to cheek with a wild thing.

THE SHAKY alliance between humans and horses stretches back nearly six thousand years. Before that, the two species merely coexisted. Cro-Magnon cave artists in Spain and Lascaux, France, often painted separate figures of horses and people, but never a partnership between the two. When we finally did come together, it wasn't as conqueror and captive but out of the mutual need to survive. By 4000 B.C., climatic changes wrought by the end of the Ice Age meant horses were nearing extinction all over the globe. They had evolved perfectly to suit their niche—the spare, sweeping grass-lands that had once covered much of the earth's landscape—but as temperatures warmed, lush forests began to replace the plains. Horses emptied out of North America, crossing a land bridge into western Europe, then pushing farther and farther east in search of exposed pastures. The largest pocket of these equine ancestors—chunkier, shaggier, and shorter-legged than their modern descendants—collected upon the open tundra of the Ukraine.

Their closest neighbors, the human inhabitants of the nearby forest steppe, had reached a similar crisis point. Early attempts at clearing land for farming had driven their primary game, wild boar and red deer, deep into the woods and out of hunting range, and food grew perilously scarce. Wild horses were one of the few animals still in proximity. For awhile the Ukrainian people tried hunting them, but the equine's muscular build and diet of low-quality forage made for poor eating. Then, somewhere along the line, one of those humans ventured a terrific leap of the imagination. Somebody had the idea to climb aboard.

The first known domesticated horse appears to have been more idol than conquest. His burial site, uncovered in the Dereivka region of the Ukraine north of the Black Sea, contained the massive skull of an eight-year-old stallion, skeletons of two dogs, and a collection of clay figurines. It also held two pieces of antler tines with holes bored through the centers, perfectly shaped to serve as cheekpieces for a bridle. Analysis of the beveled enamel coating the stallion's back molars showed steady wear consistent with carrying a bit between his teeth. Though the Dereivka people had already successfully domesticated cows, sheep, and goats, to align themselves with wild horses took a different sort of bravado. These creatures were stronger, faster, and far more volatile, with muscular jaws and large, flat hooves capable of inflicting immediate damage. It was unclear what practical use this "cult stallion" served, if any, but his ritual burial bespoke a connection still steeped in veneration.

The formation of that horse-human alliance would eventually crack open the world. The Dereivka people donned knives and

spears and began chasing their prey into the dense forests. Settle-
ments expanded, homes grew larger, and artwork became more
elaborate. Journeys that had taken several days were whittled
down to a few hours, and once isolated local tribes began to trade
and travel. Copper ornaments and rock carvings indigenous to the
Ukraine spilled over into Europe. Within a thousand years, the
equine population had swept back across the Continent, through
Hungary, Romania, and into the West, where images of horses
began appearing on petroglyphs and etched into decorative vessels.
On their end, for the first time ever horses had a secure source of
food, shelter, grooming, and protection from predators. The
species, which for thousands of years had flirted with extinction,
gave way to a population explosion that today has reached the 60
million mark.

Those first Dereivka horse tamers couldn't have foreseen the
impact or even the success of their grand experiment. Boarding
that cult stallion seems a simple act of curiosity, giving in to the
constant temptation to know the unknown. Despite the thousands
of years we've had for refinement, that first coupling couldn't have
been all too different from what it is today—uncertain, intimate,
awe-inspiring, fringed by an otherness neither half can quite com-
prehend.

SINCE ITS very beginnings, training horses has been an impre-
cise science. In 510 B.C., the Sybarites of the Roman Empire taught
their most gallant warhorses to rise on their hind legs and dance to
certain tunes, hoping to court the favor of the gods. Spies from
neighboring Crotona witnessed these wartime festivities and so
carried a full measure of flute players alongside them into battle. As
fighting commenced, the players struck up a tune and the impecca-
bly trained Sybarite steeds rose onto their heels, sending the warriors atop them tumbling to the ground. As their good-luck charms
danced before the enemy, the Sybarites were destroyed.

In seventeenth- and eighteenth-century Europe, the earliest racehorse trainers were little more than ill-paid stable grooms responsible for combing out a horse's tail and carrying its feed bucket, as

well as rounding it into racing shape. Instructions came at the most practical level. An early British racing manual advised that all fat horses needed eight to ten weeks of training to prepare for a race, and all lean ones only six, offering no advice for dealing with temperament in any form. Horses seemed to thrive more by luck than due to any expert treatment, existing on erratic diets of moldy hay, raw eggs, and rich licorice-flavored sweetmeats dipped in butter. Many suffered through long, twice-weekly training gallops over rock-hard ground that taxed muscles rather than built them up and often led to crippling injuries before a horse even reached the track.

As aristocracy's fascination with the game grew, the job of training racehorses began to take on its own luster. By the early 1800s, owners demanded more of their trainers than just a high capacity for physical labor. Success required sensitivity to the animals under their charge. In nineteenth-century England, the most gifted trainer was a passionate Yorkshireman and former jockey named John Scott, who became known as "the wizard of the North." Horses belonging to the wealthiest men in England came under his tutelage. He ran his racing operation like the general of a small army, employing a string of stable lads to carry out his orders. Abandoning the wisdom of the day, which advised training all horses identically, Scott designed individual diets and workout regimes adapted to each animal's strengths and weaknesses. Every day, he climbed aboard a mount of his own and followed his charges out onto the moors, shouting detailed instructions to each lad about how fast to exercise a horse or how thoroughly to rub him down afterward. He was also fiercely private, at one point importing a pair of American-bred hounds specially trained to track runaway slaves. Each morning, he released the dogs onto the moors surrounding his stables. Within the hour, they'd treed any tipsters come to spy on Scott's horses in the hopes of some inside information they could sell to gamblers back at the track.

In North America, breeding and owning racehorses was a rich man's game from the start, but training required only a shrewd business sense and a fine hand with the horses. In 1750, the first self-styled trainer to set up shop in the British colonies was an Irish immigrant named John Leary, who also served as jockey aboard all his charges. Later, in the 1830s, training would provide one of the few portholes through which black men, both slaves and newly freed plantation workers, could piece together a career. Though owners knew how to spot fine horses from a distance, training them was a detail game. Black farmhands possessed firsthand knowledge. They were the practitioners, schooled in icing a horse's hind legs to keep its muscles tight, feeding it curdled buttermilk to rebuild intestinal bacteria after colic, or just spending half an hour whistling over a stall door to get a high-strung filly to relax.

Though horses still had to race under the names of their white owners, black trainers dominated the East Coast competition for almost seventy years. One of the most famous of these horsemen was a former slave and ex-jockey named Ed "Brown Dick" Brown. In 1877, Brown led a colt called Baden Baden to victory in the Kentucky Derby under a seventeen-year-old black rider named Billy Walker. They were the second black trainer-rider team to take the Derby in its first three years. By the turn of the century, Brown was one of the richest trainers in the country, black or white. He developed a reputation for parading about the paddock in a tailored herringbone suit, walking stick in hand, flashing a $75,000 bankroll long before the present-day marriage of big money and sports.

But no matter how honed their skills or powerful their self-conviction, such black trainers faced social tides that would eventually prove stronger. By the turn of the century, the breakup of the Old South—fueled by poverty, lynchings, and the night rides of the Ku Klux Klan—began pushing black men away from rural racetracks and into more urban environments. In 1908, racial tension in the sports world detonated when the success of black boxer Jack Johnson prompted race riots across the country. By this time, training Thoroughbreds provided its stars not just with money but social prestige, and the elite class didn't welcome any dark skin into the mix. A number of successful black trainers moved overseas to England, France, Russia, and even Poland, where a more liberal mind-set allowed them to continue their careers.

Back in the United States, the growth of the sport had left behind its share of casualties, victims to opinions still cemented in the Old South. To this day, black trainers are a rare commodity at most premier tracks. What's left are misty recollections of other people's recollections. There was a time when conventions parted long enough to provide minority horsemen with a taste of something more.

AS A child, I was slow to warm to the complex role of the trainer on the racetrack. These characters, briefly glimpsed amidst post-race celebrations, always appeared too dour, too tense, too unsung. Held up against the pop and sizzle of the jockey's life, their romance was more elusive. I came to see them like ancient map-makers, their lives consumed in charting the unknown territory of each new horse. They operated in the realm of tiny details, ever alert to what each one could signify; when a lazy ankle meant serious injury, an untouched feed bucket signaled fever brewing, or a flicker of unexpected speed in the morning boded brilliance untapped. There were bits of shared knowledge—feeding regimens that built stamina or mud poultices to soothe sore muscles—but most of the time trainers struck out on their own. The most skillful navigators shifted variables constantly—altering diet, racing schedule, or even the music played in the barn—in the hopes of balancing the remarkable energy circling inside their charges.

It was May-May who finally brought me around to the supreme worth of the trainer, painting their labors—far more than anything executed by jockey or owner—as responsible for what came to pass on the track. Her first mention of legendary trainer John Nerud came the way May-May's track stories always arrived, via a Thoroughbred. This time, it was a powerhouse called Dr. Fager, the best sprinter of the century, who—running in the late sixties—swatted down track records like so many flies buzzing around his tail. In May-May's mind, Dr. Fager was one of the most magnificent ever. He possessed everything she cherished in a racehorse: brawn, elegance, charisma, and a natural, well-oiled stride. He ran through pain and injuries, on grass or dirt, strange tracks, deep tracks, wet tracks, dry. He ran because nature so clearly intended it and because he so clearly craved the ride. And he ran because of John Nerud.

Dr. Fager's story began in the late 1950s, a full five years before his birth, when Nerud fell in with the head of the Minnesota Mining and Manufacturing Company (makers of Scotch tape), W. L. McKnight. The two first met the way most racetrack collisions take place, on the coattails of chance. McKnight needed a new trainer for his small, mostly losing string of Thoroughbreds. A friend of a friend suggested John Nerud.

The fifty-five-year-old Nerud was a track veteran, an elfin ball of energy whose wealth of opinions had long ago earned him the nickname "the Mouth That Roared." He was also an old-fashioned horseman through and through. His equine schooling had started in childhood, growing up on a Nebraska cattle ranch, and he'd ascended the racetrack ranks from the bottom up, working as a rodeo jockey, a stable groom, and a trainer for hire. Along the way, he'd developed a simple philosophy: whenever possible, follow the natural rhythms of the horse. When his charges came up tired or irritable, instead of pushing them Nerud prescribed long vacations on Kentucky horse farms where they could roll in clover and remember why it was they loved to run. While other trainers experimented with trendy medications, he still had his vet hand-mix "leg paints," usually a blend of oil of wormwood and white thyme laced with alcohol that was brushed on his horses' legs to keep muscles cool and tight.

Nerud's old-school ethic didn't always jibe well with the fifties, an era enamored of the newfangled in everything from rocket ships to credit cards. He employed patience with his horses—waiting out strained tendons and cracked hooves for months or even years if required—but an increasing impatience with owners who cared little for rest and reflection, eager only that their horses run often and win. By the time McKnight came around, he, too, was looking for a change.

McKnight scheduled a brief meeting with Nerud, brief because he had only one question.

"Can you beat this game?"

Nerud answered without hesitation. "Yes I can."

McKnight nodded. "Alright then, write me a plan."

Nerud knew what McKnight expected, to buy a handful of young colts and aim for slightly higher-caliber races, the usual steps toward climbing the racing ladder a rung at a time. For years, Nerud had been harboring a grander scheme. He wrote up not just a business plan but a full-blown fantasy, asking McKnight for $3 million and pledging his own life savings to build the most elite racing operation in the land. Their farm would be based in northern Florida, where a layer of limestone just under the soil provided nutrients to knit strong young bones. They would breed and raise every horse themselves, letting foals romp in open pastures, breaking them to saddle, bridle, and rider on the farm, then personally delivering their plum prospects to the track. Should McKnight assent, it would be the equivalent of a client asking his new broker for stock tips, only to wind up creating his very own Fortune 500 company. Nerud presented his vision to McKnight and waited. Two days later a hand-delivered letter arrived at his door:

> *Dear Mr. Nerud,*
> *You may execute your plan.*
> *W. L. McKnight*

McKnight gave Nerud five years to prove himself. Nerud began immediately, constructing a mini racing empire under the shingle Tartan Farms.

Four years into their partnership, Nerud and McKnight bred their mare Aspidistra, a solid but unremarkable racer from a solid but unremarkable gene pool, to a little-known stallion called Rough'n Tumble. They wound up with a strapping bay foal. Nerud named the colt after the man he esteemed most in the world, the brain surgeon who'd saved his life following a serious riding accident. From the start, Dr. Fager was every trainer's precocious dream child. He devoted all his waking hours to galloping across the Florida fields, building long muscles, a hearty constitution, and a love for running as hard and fast as he pleased. When he arrived at the racetrack at age two, he already moved as if he'd caught hold of the wind. He didn't need human interference in order to travel faster—just a trainer with enough sense to fill his monster appetite, wrap his aching legs, then stand back and let that genius blossom on its own. So Nerud designed the gentlest of training regimes to keep his miracle horse happy, morning workouts just challenging enough to maintain muscle tone without jostling that inborn rapture for speed. Speculation buzzed as to what the colt might do if really pushed, but Nerud just closed his eyes, held a divining rod over his horse, and listened. The message coming back was always the same: I want to run.

Dr. Fager didn't disappoint. He claimed his style, jetting to the front of the pack then refusing to give way, and became undisputed master of pretty much anything he tried. He didn't care how far he ran, what sort of surface lay under his hooves, or whether the state flags flying over the finish signaled New York, California, or Kentucky. He suffered from chronic colic, pain so fierce he would sometimes bang his head against the side of his stall the night before a race. Come afternoon, even that didn't matter. He was headstrong and impetuous, seeking to dominate everything he touched. If a jockey tried to slow him down a bit to conserve speed for the finish, Dr. Fager yanked the reins right out of the rider's hands. He knew what to do and nobody could tell him otherwise. Nerud was wise enough not to try.

At age four, his final year at the track, Dr. Fager was named Champion Sprinter, Champion Grass Horse, Champion Handicap Horse (handicaps are races in which runners carry varying amounts of weight according to their ability), and Champion Horse of the Year. He earned more than a million dollars, and set track records, national records, and a world record for the mile that stood for twenty-nine years. When his spectacular career ended, John Nerud took his wing-footed wonder—now insured for $2.5 million—back home to Florida, where he would be bred to a string of mares citing ancestry far more impressive than his own. He even bought Dr. Fager a full membership at the local golf club.

Though never known as the modest sort, Nerud always refused to accept credit for Dr. Fager's brilliance. He simply thanked whatever good fortune had twined their paths. His greatest success had been a combination of luck and one of most subtle training skills of all. He'd known when to step out of the way.

IN THE mid-1960s, a few years after his prodigal son had retired, John Nerud happened to glance outside his Tartan Farms cocoon long enough to spot *Sputnik,* McDonald's cheeseburgers, and the nuclear bomb. He decided technology had finally advanced far enough that he might use it to his own advantage. The time had come to develop a synthetic racing surface. Like many trainers, Nerud was fed up with his horses running poorly and getting injured because the real dirt surface at any given track was too deep or sandy or wet. He'd tired of switching to special horseshoes tailored to the various track surfaces, risking bruised hooves and tender feet with each visit from the blacksmith. So he hired a chemical engineer. Backed by the ever-willing W. L. McKnight and his 3M Company, they tinkered with various formulas until they wound up with an artificial grass possessing the perfect balance between density and give. Now all they needed was a track on which to test it out.

One summer afternoon, Nerud bumped into the owner of Florida's Tropical Park. The man let drop he was interested in selling the track. Scenting opportunity, Nerud picked up the phone and informed Mr. McKnight he'd found the perfect arena for debuting their state-of-the-art racing surface. The single catch was McKnight's part of the bargain, a speedy few million dollars to purchase Tropical Park. McKnight, of a similar day-seizing mind-set, agreed to the deal.

Nerud lay his experimental grass on the inner circle of the track, dubbing the invention "Tartan turf," then stepped back to watch the entire sport revolutionized. But between track officials, never high on innovation, and trainers unwilling to risk their prize commodities on some harebrained scheme, the idea didn't fly. Nerud nudged and cajoled, but to no avail. People found the concept plumb crazy. Eventually, Nerud was forced to let his brainstorm fade to black. Energy unflagged, he moved on to Tartan Farm's next generation, and to what were sure to be brilliant new master plans. A decade later, he helped launch an unprecedented, multi-million-dollar fall racing festival called The Breeder's Cup that would lure runners from all over the globe. Meanwhile, according to Nerud, someone else spotted his creation, someone whose vision extended beyond just the racetrack. On the heels of the 1965 invention of Astroturf, they adapted that undesirable artificial surface for use in other sports venues. Then they sold Nerud's sliver of genius to stadiums all over the world.

Hearing such a story, it would be easy to register the biggest missed opportunity of a lifetime. But that would mean you were approaching from the wrong angle, concentrating on fortune or reputation. That would mean you'd forgotten to view the universe through the telescope belonging to John Nerud, the trainer of the fastest sprinter in the land. While others were busy sizing up humans, he focused only on racehorses. When life didn't unfold to suit the Thoroughbred, Nerud just left it behind.

Now in his nineties, John Nerud continues to tweak the racing landscape. Though he no longer actively trains, he's fully enmeshed in a new venture, a Thoroughbred breeding farm centered in upstate New York. I've met him several times around the Florida tracks, where he still spends much of the winter, or in the summers out at Belmont Park. He hops from paddock to stands as if fueled by an invisible power line strung from spit-and-polish shoes to plaid sports coat to full head of fluffy white hair.

"I thought you were supposed to have retired twenty years ago," I once teased him as we stood side by side watching a particularly feisty colt being saddled.

"Miss Mooney," he replied, lifting his voice to allow any nearby owners or trainers the benefit of his seventy-plus years of Thoroughbred wisdom. "There's one reason I've made it at the racetrack. I never let anyone tell me what I was supposed to do."

THROUGH MAY-MAY I learned to value those old-style "hay, oats, and water" trainers like Nerud, underdogs with pure hearts and salty personalities who could never be swayed by television cameras, waving dollar bills, or anybody's party line. They were the definition of the rugged spirit, men—and the occasional woman— who devoted their lives to clearing the path between a Thorough-bred and the track. Then, when I was in my mid-twenties, I became aware of a different sort of rule bender blazing his way down the horizon. Though I was barely following racing at the time, this guy proved impossible to miss.

Bob Baffert is a prematurely white-haired irreverent, possessing a *Hee Haw* sense of humor and near genius eyes for horses. He has Wild West origins, rooted in the bush tracks of Arizona, which run counter to every fusty drop of blue blood still anchoring the "sport of kings." From the start, he took positive glee in dumping conventions on their backsides. He overturned silver trophy cups on his head in the winner's circle, laced his victory speeches with crude jokes, and spoke his mind before he had time to regret it. He seemed convinced there was a way to enjoy life and achieve at the premier level. I was intrigued. As my own life advanced like molasses, I took vicarious pleasure in the coming of this unlikely outlaw. I began to believe that if he could recast his role, there just might be hope for me as well.

I first latched onto Bob Baffert in 1997, when I watched from a friend's couch in New Jersey as he nabbed his first Kentucky Derby with a horse called Silver Charm. A year later, I stood in a Radio Shack on Sixth Avenue and saw him pull a Churchill Downs repeat, this time with a serious underdog named Real Quiet. The next morning, I bought a *Daily Racing Form* at a newsstand on Bleecker Street, searching out background on Baffert and his long-shot triumph. I found one of racing's fairy tales.

Two years earlier, Bob Baffert and one of his owners, Mike Pegram, had visited a Kentucky horse sale looking for bargains. At a time when most top trainers focused on runners price-tagged at a million or two, they plucked out a yearling colt for only $17,000. Real Quiet's legs were cockeyed, and his chest so underdeveloped that viewed from the front he nearly disappeared. Baffert nick-named him the Fish after those wafer-thin tropical fish that are all brilliant colors and stripes sideways but nearly nonexistent face-to-face. Real Quiet's first home was a Kentucky farm where he was broken to saddle and bridle and tested around a small training track. He was long-limbed and gawky, requiring extra time to gather himself and get moving. But once in motion, he displayed tinges of something, an ingrained swiftness and easy, loping stride. At two, deemed ready to try racing, he boarded a horse van and bumped across the Kentucky byways to his future port of call, the Churchill Downs racetrack.

Under the tutelage of Baffert and his Kentucky assistant, Real Quiet went through mock morning contests alongside more experienced horses, practice breaks from the starting gate, and race-day schooling sessions in which he circled the saddling paddock amid shrill voices and the slap and flutter of consulted programs. His preparation was impeccable, but two-year-old horses are still children, their muscles waiting to fill out, their bones soft and their attitudes just forming. Real Quiet, submerged in all the gangling confusion of adolescence, launched his career with loss after loss. The jockeys aboard him came away blinded by frustration, but Bob Baffert saw something else. Flashes of speed lit up the track when all the pegs miraculously fell into place. He brought the horse across the country to his stable headquarters in California, rubbed his palms together, and prepared to work a little magic.

There is only so much a trainer can do to improve a Thoroughbred's physical capability. Advances in sports medicine that have redefined human athletic competition, reducing muscle fatigue and cranking up aerobic output, have had little effect at the track. Unlike people, horses are already optimally designed to operate at top speed. Breath, stride, and the heart's capacity to pump blood are ideally balanced by nature to turn in the fastest possible times. Compared to human runners, horses require remarkably little conditioning to stay in shape. Their morning exercise usually consists of an easy mile or two gallop, layered by some days of working—running hard over a set distance, usually less than a mile—and others of walking or light jogging around the outside edge of the track. A common error among inexperienced trainers is to push a good horse too hard in the mornings so that, come race day, he's drained before he even starts. The most gifted touch is a light one. As long as a Thoroughbred eats well and doesn't get injured, genetics usually take care of the rest.

More often a trainer's edge comes from psychological tinkering, successfully generating a relaxed and focused racing mind-set. Young stallions like Real Quiet can be particularly puckish, flexing that instinctual impulse to test the social hierarchy and ensure it won't break out from under them. They play status games—gazing off into the distance and refusing to acknowledge a human presence, or nipping and kicking at anyone telling them what to do. Baffert had experience trumping such neophytes, having spent his early career years taming the adolescent impulses of studdish young quarter horses. He set about capturing Real Quiet's dancing attention span and honing it down to gate and wire.

He noticed Real Quiet kept backing away from the hooves of other horses and tossing his head each time he spotted a clod of dirt flying up from the track. So Baffert fitted him with blinkers, hooded eye patches that kept his gaze aimed at the finish and closed out everything else. Real Quiet won his next race by three lengths. Next, he began preparing the horse to expect the unexpected, sending him to races in New Mexico and Kentucky, testing him at different distances, in contests that took him around one turn of the track, contests that took him around two. As those four erratic limbs began to collect themselves, Baffert noted that Real Quiet had ingrained stamina. The longer the race, the more confident the colt grew. He was a classics horse; classics as in the Belmont, the Preakness, and the Kentucky Derby.

Baffert laid out a fresh road map, this one leading straight to Churchill Downs. He chose unconventional prep races, contests that would offer Real Quiet enough challenge to spark his competitive edge, but not so much that he was worn out chasing down his rivals. The two traveled to San Francisco to run through inches of mud in a rain-soaked Golden Gate Derby. Baffert refused to change Real Quiet's shoes to ridged "jar caulks" that would better grip the track for fear they might dig too deeply and twist one of the colt's already crooked knees. Real Quiet stumbled across the finish line dead last, making it clear to everyone else that he belonged miles from the Triple Crown. Baffert stuck by his instincts, which still hollered that Real Quiet was the real thing, a pile of gunpowder in wait of the proper match. Come the first Saturday in May, the pair of them lit up the sky.

I drank in the details of Real Quiet's saga—a shaky misplaced colt taken in hand, an outsider whipping the pants off the establishment, a renegade horseman unwilling to be confined or defined. Two weeks later, I watched him garner a confident, long-striding victory in the Preakness. By the time the Belmont Stakes rolled around in early June, I was hooked.

That year I watched the Belmont on the floor of my Greenwich Village apartment. I started out seated Indian-style in front of the television, but by the final stretch of the mile-and-a-half race I was on my feet, cheering Real Quiet as he snagged the lead and stayed there, dangling furlongs and then yards from the Triple Crown. A heart-skip from the finish, another horse appeared, a razor-sharp rival called Victory Gallop. Both animals battled hard, but in the end it was Victory Gallop who edged his nose out in front. It was Alydar all over again and every piece of me knew it. As Real Quiet crossed the wire, Bob Baffert and his crooked colt rolled me out of my adult rut and back into the races.

TEN YEARS before Real Quiet's star performance, Bob Baffert had debuted on the Thoroughbred racing scene convinced he had nothing to lose. He had a devil-rider past, harking from the tiny Southwest border town of Nogales, Arizona, where his father raised cattle and a ragtag bunch of quarter horses that ran at local tracks. Baffert spent his teen years as a jockey on backwater racecourses rife with mariachi bands, illegal gambling, and even the occasional shoot-out.

The Southwest has its own brand of racing history, starting from the 1660s when Spanish settlers crossed into Texas with prized Andalusian horses, which were promptly stolen by local Indian tribes. Some Indians learned to ride instinctually, imitating what they'd seen of the Spanish invaders. Others were schooled by bands of mixed-race comancheros who dealt in illicit horse trading, or by Spanish missionaries who employed them as vaqueros, or range cowboys, to patrol their open lands. These hunting tribes—the Comanche, Apache, Cheyenne, and Arapaho—soon developed a full-scale obsession with horse racing.

Far from the well-ordered two- and three-mile competitions conducted on eastern tracks, the Spanish-influenced Southwest was all about bravado. In *correr al gallo* races imported from northern Mexico, riders tore across a length of range with live roosters tied underneath them, pecking at the horses' bellies as they ran. In Texas, they would hang a goose with a greased neck upside down from a tree limb. The winner was the first rider to gallop past and snap off the goose's head. A California variation featured chickens buried up to their necks in the sand. Riders flew by at a flat-out run, plucked the chickens free, and finished waving the squawking birds through the air.

In the coming centuries, the loss of identity threatening these same Indian tribes seemed to fuel their bent for racing—and for heavy gambling. In the 1870s, Comanche chief My-la-que-top challenged the entire U.S. Cavalry garrison stationed at Fort Chadbourne, Texas, to a match race—his woolly-haired, thick-legged pony against their finest Kentucky-bred mare. Both sides tossed down fistfuls of money and, discarding the club he used as a whip, the Comanche rider took off bareback at a dead run. He soon left the cavalry's Kentucky lady paddling through half a mile of dust. In the final yards of the race, the brave flipped around on his pony and taunted the cavalry audience with both free hands.

Bob Baffert grew up in a southwestern horse culture still colored by this brave new world sensibility. After outgrowing the job of jockey, he followed his father straight into the family business, training quarter horses. In Arizona and neighboring New Mexico, quarter horse contests—so dubbed because the breed's early burst of speed made them ideal for brief quarter-mile races—flourished everywhere from Podunk tracks to stadiums. A dozen years after sending out his first runner, Baffert reached the pinnacle of the training profession. But he didn't stay there long. Quarter horse races are short, straight, and bereft of strategy. There is only one style of running—fast—and Baffert had a bent for forging fresh angles that rusted up quickly under such limitations. Despite more than a million dollars earned in his final years as a quarter horse trainer, he was ready for a fresh belt of adrenaline. He longed to plunge into the rarefied world of Thoroughbred racing and knock it permanently off-kilter.

WHEN BOB Baffert decided to cross over into Thoroughbreds, he left much of his small-town baggage behind. What he carried forth he chose carefully—a uniform of cotton shirts and pressed blue jeans, a taste for tequila, and a backslapping best friend and business partner named Mike Pegram. Baffert met Pegram while training quarter horses at California's Los Alamitos racetrack in the eighties. A kindred freewheeling spirit, Pegram had parlayed street smarts and a rural Midwest background into a lucrative string of McDonald's franchises in Washington State. He owned a few quarter horses and wanted to buy more. More important, he knew how to swallow disappointment without eclipsing his bounteous appetite for a hell of a good time.

The two started acquiring quarter horses together, and when Baffert got the Thoroughbred itch, Pegram offered to finance the first few ventures. Their initial purchase, a $32,000 gelding (a male horse that's been castrated, usually because he's far too ill-tempered and libidinous to control) named Hidden Royalty, arrived at the barn with a cracked shin. A few months later, they sold him for just over $12,000. With Baffert's livelihood dependent on a 10 percent cut of the purse money his horses earned, prospects had taken a definite downward turn. Veterans of the sport advised him to return to quarter horses, saying Thoroughbreds were too tough and too sophisticated a game. Baffert dug in all the harder.

In the next five years, Baffert rebounded from Hidden Royalty with a career trajectory that would've sent any average head whirling. He and Pegram visited small horse sales, buying up cheap animals with minor physical flaws and below-average pedigrees. Baffert carted them home and, pulling on those decades of horse knowledge, tinkered with their quirks and power sources as he later would with Real Quiet. The strongest candidates proved awesome, and he sent them out to swipe first-place finishes in expensive races. Soon, other owners came calling, the sort with extra millions leaking from between their fingers, and Baffert's barn at Santa Anita filled with the most elite company. In a single circling of the board, he landed on both Boardwalk and Park Place. His partnership with Pegram continued, a steady pulse underscoring the lurching excitement of the big time. Theirs was a different angle of ascent—not jet-fueled by seven-figure purchases, but a slow, even climb. In 1998, it culminated in what every racing partnership covets: a $17,000 colt called Real Quiet and a victory in the Kentucky Derby.

Anyone can own a racehorse, no prior knowledge of the sport required, but they rarely prove sound financial investments. The guaranteed payback comes in the form of glamour and prospective glory. Past owners rosters are call lists in high-profile names like Leland Stanford, Averell Harriman, Fred Astaire, Diamond Jim Brady, and Verne Winchell, the Donut King. In the first few years of the nineteenth century, president-to-be Andrew Jackson ran Clover Bottom, one of the most prominent racing stables in Tennessee. Also an avid gambler, Jackson once lost an entire wardrobe full of suits when he couldn't scrape together enough cash to meet a racing bet. When he reached the Oval Office, he secretly kept a tiny stable in Washington, D.C., designed by celebrated architect Robert Mills and publicly registered under the name of Jackson's private secretary. At the turn of the century, dance hall sweetheart Lillian Russell, in keeping with feminine sensibilities of the day, owned a string of Thoroughbreds under the alias "Mr. Clinton" after her hometown of Clinton, Iowa. Some owners were devoted to the game; others amassed racehorses as accessories. But no matter how enormous their bank accounts, they all wound up chasing the same thing: a little piece of the hope.

Women left their first major imprint on the sport through ownership, wealth and some social standing being the only prerequisites for entry here. In the 1930s, the leading Thoroughbred owner was a Virginia socialite named Isabelle Dodge Sloane, whose jockeys all wore snow-white racing silks decorated with royal blue crosses. A few years later, candy heiress Ethel Mars amassed a top-level racehorse collection under the label Milky Way Stables. She named one of her finest fillies for the popular chocolate bar Forever Yours. Self-made millionaire Florence Nightingale Graham, better known as cosmetics queen Elizabeth Arden, kept her flock of runners swathed in perfumes and body lotions, regularly bathing their joints in vats of her "eight o'clock" cream. Her stable help reportedly organized a covert side industry, bottling the cream and reselling it to humans for a dollar a jar. In 1947, Elizabeth Arden won the Kentucky Derby with a horse called Jet Pilot. She also developed a reputation for discarding trainers as frequently as used tubes of lipstick.

Strained relations between owners, who control the purse strings, and trainers, who possess the knowledge, have always been known to snap on a regular basis. Owners accuse their trainers of assuming near dictatorial control, withholding information about a horse's health and prospects especially when something threatens to go wrong. Trainers claim their human clientele are compositions in unrealistic opinion, one win sending visions of the Kentucky Derby dancing through their heads. When a horse's record begins to slip, an owner's first move is often to fire the trainer and start over. Distrust is imbedded in the grain.

The fluid owner-trainer friendship running between Bob Baffert and Mike Pegram—each leaning back to pull the other a rung up the ladder—is a rare thing at the track. Perhaps some clue to their mutual success lies in the fact that neither of them had to go it alone. It can take such steady contact, someone who believes in you full stop, to nail down self-confidence. Such relationships nurture the freedom to walk just the other side of the line.

ONCE YOU'VE won the Kentucky Derby two springs in a row and captured millions of dollars in races year after year, the headiness has no choice but to settle. In just a decade of training Thoroughbreds, Baffert upset a string of records—for millions earned, numbers of races won—until the boundaries he was bursting through became those he'd set himself. He could no longer sneak his way into the Derby with a $17,000 underdog. The year after Real Quiet's reign, his potential Triple Crown stable came up empty, and he was forced to conquer a different kind of odds, those which dictate shooting stars will level out. Part of the law of prodigies is that eventually they reach adulthood.

By the time we met, Bob Baffert was no longer plain renegade spirit, his most precious skill polishing diamonds without cleaving away too much of the rough. Success can't help leaving its fingerprints behind, and Baffert, in his late forties, didn't come away unmarked. He'd made some discoveries since his quarter horse days—about Thoroughbreds, but about humans, too. People require a different type of massaging. Despite his aw-shucks beginnings, Baffert proved masterful at this as well. He'd learned to soothe and succor those millionaire owners just as skillfully as he did their horses, spending race-day afternoons in the Turf Club restaurant instead of mingling with his on-track buddies, perfecting the art of taming his own ego to capture someone else's.

He made a conscious effort to woo the media—watching himself on screen, carefully crafting a seemingly spontaneous persona, then practicing it in front of his bedroom mirror. The media embraced his exuberant personality, his willingness to cut loose, and his gift for one-liners, and the Baffert interview became a regular feature on network racing broadcasts. He cottoned to the flavor of fame—sprawling back in his black leather office chair to watch videotapes of his interviews, laughing at his own cleverness when quotes appeared in the *Daily Racing Form*. He was also self-aware.

"Reading your own words as newspaper headlines can be dangerous," he told me. "It's easy to fall into that movie-star trap. You start believing what you say means a hell of a lot more than it actually does."

Navigation took on a new subtlety. It required figuring his way around the man who wants to do right, but not quite as much as he wants to do well. Stakes and profile had risen. This time around he had something to lose. Captain Steve's Kentucky Derby would call for a different sort of man.

CAPTAIN STEVE'S stall at Santa Anita is two doors down from Baffert's office. Every morning when he's led out toward the track, the Captain passes walls draped with the memorabilia of his predecessors' Derby triumphs—Silver Charm's grass-green-and-yellow striped silks, the red-and-gold colors of Mike Pegram and Real Quiet. Framed winner's-circle photos line the office walls. There is no puritan lack of pride on display here. Baffert is a man who can and does hoot and holler.

That unconventional bone is echoed in the tools of his trade: a cell phone with a glittery Stars and Stripes faceplate, funky lavender-tinted sunglasses, and a daily dose of coffee spiked with Equal and a shot of Reddi-Wip—a concoction the track kitchen has dubbed "the Baffert Special." Such off-the-cuff spirit infuses his barn as well. It's the antithesis of the military-style operations run by many trainers, base camps in which horses' daily feed is delivered on time to the minute, straw bedding packed tightly enough to bounce quarters, and the general shows up at 4:30 every morning to crack the whip. At Camp Baffert, the occasional stray bandage is draped over a railing and the printed workout schedule for the next day hangs cockeyed on its rusty nail. The leader himself is apt to stay up for *The Tonight Show,* then amble in somewhere around 7:30 or 8:00. It's as if details have intentionally been softened to preserve a hang-ten mood.

Forty of the hundred-plus horses Baffert trains are stabled at Santa Anita in an old wooden barn with peeling paint and a pepper tree planted outside the front door. The overflow goes to stalls at Los Angeles's other major racetrack, Hollywood Park, or to his East Coast contingent in Kentucky. His staff is handpicked, loyal, and—hitting that high point on the Baffert value scale—knows how to have fun. Most of the anxiety Baffert claims he's rejected seems to have taken up residence in his always-on-the-move assistant, Jimmy Barnes, whose head houses encyclopedic stores about the needs, records, and shortcomings of each horse in the barn. In the mornings, when Baffert is trackside and Jimmy stuck at home base, the two communicate via walkie-talkies hitched to their belt loops. A constant flow of information crackles back and forth as to which horses are working and how far and fast they should go, plus the daily business of choosing jockeys for races and races for horses, and generally keeping everyone mellow and pleased.

The barn foreman, Bhupat Seemar, Baffert's third in command, keeps track of bridles, saddles, leg wraps, shadow rolls, blinkers, and all other manner of equipment as the horses come and go. Bhupat belongs to one of India's wealthiest racing families, and his uncle, Satish Seemar, trains for a sheik in Dubai. He came to California expressly to work under the great Bob Baffert, to store up trade secrets, then carry them back halfway across the globe. For a while, one of Baffert's exercise riders—employed to pilot the horses through their morning workouts—was also an import, a pale and skinny aspiring jockey from England named Glenn. Though a diligent rider, Glenn was painfully timid around two-legged folk, and Baffert couldn't resist teasing, testing, and generally giving him a hard time. After a few months, Glenn's resolve turned to jelly. He choked, kept messing up Baffert's instructions, and eventually had to return home.

One evening when I'm visiting in February, I wander back to Baffert's stable at the tail end of the race day. The air around the barn is celebratory even though two out of three horses who ran that afternoon lost. Baffert kicks back, cracking wise and chugging beers. This is steam-release time, a contrast to his morning rhythm, which is pace, circle, dodge, greet. Horses poke their heads out of their stalls and sigh heavily into the dirt, as if longing to come out and play. Sprawled in a tooled leather director's chair with REAL QUIET stenciled on the back, a can of Coors Light in his hand, Baffert is clearly in his milieu. He stays late, far later than anyone needs to, joking and reminiscing.

Around dusk Roberto, one of Baffert's grooms, shows up, having heard the boss was looking for him that afternoon.

"*Sí, sí!*" Baffert calls out, slamming down his empty beer can.

Though he speaks Spanish, picked up as a kid in Nogales, he switches over to English so everyone can share in what's coming. "Man, you're in serious trouble."

Roberto's face loses its hangdog smile.

"Go get it," Baffert tells Jimmy, who's hovering at his elbow. Jimmy disappears into the stable office and returns holding a laminated winner's-circle photograph.

"Look at this." Baffert holds out the picture for all of us gathered around to see.

There's Roberto, holding the horse's lead shank and mugging for the camera for all he's worth, arms spread wide like an Ethel Merman finale. If you look hard, you can just pick out the face of the winning horse behind one of his outstretched palms. Everyone tenses for a moment until Baffert lets loose a whooping laugh.

"Man, what were you thinking?" The groom shrugs and relaxes, officially off the hook. Baffert shakes his head.

"What the hell were you thinking?"

He seems more envious than angry, as if he wishes he'd thought of pulling that one himself.

AN OPERATION the size of Baffert's usually has multiple angles all operating at the same time. Still-forming two-year-old colts and fillies arrive at the track plump with nerves, anticipation, and a little residual baby fat, as trainer and animal ready themselves for mutual exploration. Baffert sends them out to the track each morning and watches from the grandstand for details that will translate into style. He sifts those with the instant acceleration suited to sprinting from those who harbor a slower-building power that lends itself to mile-plus route races. He works them alongside more experienced runners to suss out their natural tendencies, noting which newcomers hunger to run in front from the get-go and which like to hang back, then pass down the stretch. Some horses prefer always to have an eye on the competition ahead of them, and they'll steal the lead only in the final seconds of a race. These are the heart-attack runners. They win just as often as other

horses, but they always do it in a last-second flurry by a neck, a
head, or a nose.

Such newcomers are stabled alongside jaded professionals, four-
and five-year-old veterans with rounder muscles and more settled
tempers, who are gearing towards six-figure stakes races that will
set them crisscrossing the country. By this time, Baffert under-
stands their quirks and preferences well. When such horses reach
the track they know what to expect, know the difference in energy
between a gentle morning work and an afternoon standoff. They
are more mature, less fickle and flighty. They would be embarrassed to execute anything like Captain Steve's joyful bob and
weave down the stretch. With them, the game shifts once again,
from education to maintenance. Now it's figuring how to put minimal strain on the battle-scarred body of an aging athlete; how to
make sure ease doesn't slip over into complacency, that they don't
shed that blind urge to run.

By spring, Captain Steve's stablemates have all begun to dim just
a bit. Baffert's focus is narrowing, telescopic, to a single straight
line. The Triple Crown. I make a second trip out west in March
and find Captain Steve seemingly unaffected by the halo descended
upon him. When I check in on him the first morning I'm there, he's
his same sweet and feisty and little-bit goofy self. The filly next to
him is scheduled to race that day, and there's a neon-yellow sign
tacked to her stall door reading DO NOT ENTER. Regulations as to
who has access to a horse on race day are strict. A trainer assumes
full responsibility for anything that happens to his runners, regardless of whether he had a hand in it or not. People are always offering horses treats, and something as innocent as the caffeine in a
chocolate bar or morphine traces in a poppy-seed bagel might be
enough to register on the drug test submitted to the first three fin-
ishers, earning the trainer disqualification, fines, or even a suspen-
sion. The only people allowed close enough to touch the horse are
the vet who will precheck her for injury, her groom, and Baffert
himself. Captain Steve keeps jutting his nose over his stall door to
stare at that DO NOT ENTER sign, tossing his head as if jealous he's

still stuck home in neutral. Pleasure would be so simple; just hit the track and go.

Baffert can't quite manage his charge's nonchalance. Pressure has escalated since the Real Quiet days. With each Kentucky Derby won comes a blanket of roses, a six-figure winner's check, and the expectation that there will be a repeat performance. With Real Quiet, Baffert was jumping off cliffs. Now he's expected to turn three backflips in the air.

When we sit in his office for a few minutes talking about Captain Steve, Baffert shows an uncharacteristic reticence, as if there is something here so precious it must be examined as little as possible. For once, the freewheeling persona is playing at low key, a Baffert redesigned. His Derby strategy is simplicity itself: Do as little as possible. Captain Steve will run against The Deputy in the Santa Anita Derby, and then move straight on to Churchill Downs.

"Plenty of horses will get screwed up between now and then," he opines. "He who stands wins the Derby."

Action by inaction. It's a shift from the man who flew Real Quiet to San Francisco to run the Golden Gate Derby in the pouring rain. Suddenly there's vulnerability poking out from behind the cocksure. He's shifted from gulping down, Pac-Man style, to a more steady rhythm of gaining ground yard by yard.

It's a tricky business, this training horses, one that fosters more paradoxes than revelations. The days I spend with Baffert are cloaked in secrets, so that at times I feel as if I've joined ranks with a master spy. He continually wanders off for private phone calls, whispered consultations with vets, jockeys, and even fellow trainers. He can't explain exactly what it is that makes him such an expert horseman, except to joke that he has equine ESP. I don't press him. I think I prefer to preserve the mystery, to imagine he doesn't quite understand it all himself.

One morning, as we're making the rounds of his barn, he tells me that he's decided his job really just boils down to two factors: spotting good horses, and keeping them healthy.

"Keeping them healthy is the hardest. You watch like a hawk and try not to work them too hard. That's about all you can do. You can have the best horse in the world, but if he's hurt you've got nothing at all."

As for picking the stellar horses, he teaches me a simple test.

"A real racehorse, a winner, won't back away when you run at him. He stands his ground."

We pause in front of a scrawny filly with ribs countable under her chestnut coat. Baffert jumps at her, waving his arms in the air, and she scurries back a few paces.

"See. She's cheap." He moves on to the next stall, containing the soon-to-be-retired Real Quiet. Baffert's arms fly back up again. Real Quiet blinks and takes another mouthful of hay.

"The real ones, they know who they are."

WHENEVER I imagine what May-May might have been like as a trainer, I see pieces of Bob Baffert and John Nerud—that trailblazing sensibility and a tigerlike self-confidence even as everyone around them begins to question. There is also something missing, an inherent gentleness I noticed whenever I saw May-May alongside a horse. It was as if she faded just a bit and the animal grew brighter alongside.

Shortly after I started to follow the East Coast racing scene, a New York trainer worked his way into my sphere of vision. He didn't land with a Kentucky Derby splash the way Bob Baffert had, but arrived by way of a more subdued temperament, a steady rate of success, and horses who lit up in his stead. If Bob Baffert and John Nerud are the ultimate showmen, then trainer Christophe Clement is their perfect counterfoil, the Thoroughbred artiste.

In a universe that revolves around two-minute increments, Clement has a rare ability to slow down long enough to focus on the larger picture. His horses tend to be older, trained to evolve slowly, blossom late, and last a long time, which is why his name doesn't appear on the list of Triple Crown aspirants or Kentucky Derby winners. Horses pushed to run so hard when they are so young, bones scarcely formed, can burn out early. Their careers often end at age three or four, sacrificed to battered joints or spirits simply gone sour.

Clement is young, in his mid-thirties, the son of a famous French trainer, Miguel Clement, who was killed in a car accident when his son was thirteen. He grew up in something akin to race-track paradise, the celebrated French racing town of Chantilly. Against a backdrop of country châteaus and low rolling hills, the Thoroughbreds took hold. Racing in Europe is different from in the United States. The heritage stretches deeper: to Roman emperor Caligula, who housed his favorite horse in a marble stable with an ivory manger and his own retinue of slaves; to thirteenth-century Italy and yearly *palio* races run through the city streets toward a jewel-encrusted banner awarded as the winner's prize; to Tudor England, where Elizabeth I frequented the course at Croydon so often she required her own box, erected in 1585. Such traditions run to time spent developing a horse, with training more akin to a craft than a business deal. The racing season is shorter and the tracks more bucolic, but there is also less money to be made and less patience for experimentation. After earning an economics degree from a Paris university, Clement served his apprenticeship in Europe, under the tutelage of some of the Continent's most celebrated trainers. In his late twenties, he came to the United States for the same reason Europeans have migrated to the Americas since Columbus. There is fresh ground here, customs are still flexible, and racetracks come paved in gold.

During the spring and summer months, Clement is based in New York, but, like much of the East Coast racing colony, he migrates south to Florida during the winter. He doesn't stable at any of the three Miami-area tracks, but instead reserves coveted space at a private training facility called Payson Park. For his runners, this means horse heaven. Payson can be measured in open stretches of grass, giant sand pans for rolling, and a very untrack-like serenity. Birds chirp. Palm trees line the pathways. The sky stretches unbroken into the horizon, on most days a flawless glassy pane of blue. Since I know an owner who has horses with Clement, on one trip to Florida I wind up spending a morning at his Payson Park barn.

Clement conducts his daily business on the grass in front of his

shedrow, holding a cup of coffee in his right hand and a Marlboro
Light pinched between the first two fingers of his left. He's dressed
neatly—an Oxford shirt tucked into khaki pants, hair brushed flat
to his head with the occasional wisp catching the wind and dancing
loose. He doesn't say much, but his French accent and dry sense of
humor are enough to make me feel cosmopolitan simply standing
at his side. As soon as the first set of horses returns from morning
works, the exercise riders—most of whom have come from France
expressly for Clement's tutelage—automatically begin circling
their mounts around him like a bay-and-chestnut-colored merry-
go-round. He checks in with them as they walk past, sometimes in
English, sometimes in French, filing away any details of lingering
nerves or progressing confidence.

Occasionally he calls out to one of the riders to pause, setting
down his coffee cup and moving forward to probe a knee or ankle.
Clement's particular gift is communication, the sophisticated back-
and-forth that draws a high class of owners, but, even more important, a wordless interplay with the animals themselves. His hands
and eyes flit continuously, drinking in information. He tests joints
for the warmth of blood rushing to an injury, watches how each
animal stands and shifts, trails his hand along a neck or backside to
calm the nervous tremble of energy just beneath the skin. His fingers move quickly, dexterous and confident, the way you might
imagine those of a surgeon or a concert pianist. One horse in the
circle seems to be bothering him, and he keeps returning to her,
crouching down to slide his palm along the length of her shin.

"She is a little bit off," he explains once he's backed away, though
she looked sweet and even to me. He nods to the rider to continue,
and this time I think I notice her rolling her right hip ever so
slightly to one side.

Horses are naturally easy movers, their bodies orchestrated to
avoid placing excess stress on any one limb. When a Thoroughbred
begins operating out of alignment, it's usually triggered by pain.
Pinpointing that pain is a separate challenge, exacerbated by how
intricately bones, muscles, and tendons intertwine. A gimpy hind
foot might stem from a bruised hoof, a strained tendon, even a sore

hip or back. Sometimes the best way to trace the source is simply by pressing fingers over the coat inch by inch and waiting for some telltale flinch. Thoroughbreds' bodies are not deceptive. To someone with the proper finger knowledge, their inner workings can be read like braille.

Clement stops the filly again and goes back to her hind leg, this time tapping his fingers in an easy circle around her knee. At one point, she takes a tiny side step. Clement lays his palm flat against her flank until she stills, then presses two fingers into the muscle. She raises her hoof a few inches off the ground. Whatever it is, he's found it, and he rattles off instructions to his assistant, Bertrand, who looks like a well-scrubbed French schoolboy. Then he nods to the lead rider and the whole string begins circling once again.

When it's time for the next set of horses to hit the training track, Clement rides out alongside his charges aboard a thickset stable pony, observing, touching, testing as they go. As he rides, his body sways in perfect rhythm with the pony's amble. Only a slight hunch in his shoulders—and the ever-present cigarette—signal he has taken on an impressive load. Watching his runners glide past under navy blue saddle blankets with a gold CC embroidered on the corner, I wonder if he's actually figured out how to siphon off that anxiety usually borne by the horses themselves. The nervousness seems to have rolled out of their muscles, leaving them longer, suppler, imbued with pleasure. I want to buy racehorses just so I can send them to Clement, then watch them emerge so long, so slim, and so pleased.

Clement purposely leaves his stable small, no more than fifty-five horses, in order to keep a finger in it all. When a trainer expands to eighty or a hundred-plus runners, he's forced to turn management. He makes an automatic choice to delegate most of the hands-on work to someone else. Clement does not choose to do so.

"To me, if I were not working with each horse, that would not be training."

That evening I'm supposed to attend a Palm Beach cocktail

party thrown in his honor. I do attend, but Clement does not. He has a sick horse and opts to spend all night at the barn.

IT TAKES courage to undertake what Clement has. In a world where the prevailing energy eddies around the Kentucky Derby, he's professed that this isn't his end-all dream. He could have stayed in France to unquestioned success. Many of the horses in his American barn share his European roots—hand-delivered by way of England, Ireland, and France from European owners who carry a bit of that adventure gene themselves.

"I've been lucky," he's offered. "I know that. I got help from many of my father's clients and friends."

In true European fashion, Clement's most noted owner isn't a software tycoon or a Kentucky blue blood, but Queen Elizabeth II. In 1999, she sent him a filly called Fictitious, who runs on the grass in the States and wins.

Fictitious came to America because she was too tautly strung for the European tradition of living on farms and vanning to a different track each race day. Before even reaching the starting gate, she would break out in an energy-sapping nervous sweat. In New York, she can reside just yards from where she runs. Clement stitched up all that undid her with promenades through the paddock and past the grandstands. He sent her out to the track each morning, allowing her freedom to high-step around the outer edge of the course until the feel of dirt against her hooves and the taste of race-day air joined her permanent lexicon. She emerged cool and courtly, a credit to her heritage. It does seem fictitious, like a line copped from *Alice in Wonderland:*

Christophe Clement trains Fictitious for the Queen.

He's a trainer for my adult self, but also for my dream-weaving child.

Growing up, I rode a string of racetrack crushes, seduced by anyone's expert ability to mesh a Thoroughbred's nature with his own. Coming back to racing as an adult, I found that same awe-inspired fantasy settling over Clement. In French, his name means gentle or merciful, and sensitivity is clearly the defining ingredient to his art. He's found what the Dereivka people must have been seeking thousands of years ago when they boarded their cult stallion, and what trainers have chased after ever since. He's discovered how to marry the human and the wild.

Chapter Three

LEAPS OF FAITH:

Playing the Breeding Game

That single semester I spent at St. Timothy's boarding school when I was fifteen did manage to fulfill one of my lofty expectations. The school, rumored to have once been a Catholic convent, sat in the heart of Maryland's richest horse country. Pastures and picket fences fell away from our classrooms like the drapes of a taffeta skirt. Whenever we'd take a weekend bus ride to Baltimore or the local mall, I'd press my face to the mottled glass windows and watch breeding farms whip past. Somewhere behind those laurel hedges and colonial gatehouses, race-horses were evolving.

May-May had taught me years earlier that whatever equine wonders occur at the track are first set in motion by sire and dam. Top breeders pay hundreds of thousands of dollars in stud fees for the privilege of pairing their mare to someone else's famed stallion. They devote lifetimes to fiddling the question of how to transpose physical properties and spirit quality from one generation to the next. I knew that if I ever hoped to decipher the alchemical compo-sition of a racehorse, I would have to find my way to that germina-tion point. Over the phone, I consulted with May-May, who concurred with my extremely loose plan of action. I had to gain entrance to one of those breeding farms.

Eventually I befriended a day student named Dottie, who couldn't miss the fact that I was mad for horse racing. Dottie's aunt and uncle bred Thoroughbreds somewhere in those acres of farm-land we drove past. They ran the sort of family operation increas-ingly rare amid conglomerate-sized farms capable of investing millions of dollars in a single prospective sire. Her aunt and uncle stood two stallions, one of whom had won a big stakes race in Ire-land, and a handful of mares that they bred at home or vanned to other Maryland sires. Most of their yearlings sold at local auctions. A successful runner meant one who triumphed on regional tracks—Pimlico, Laurel, and Delaware Park—with perhaps an occasional foray up to New York. It wasn't the big time, Dottie kept cautioning me, but I didn't care. I just wanted the genesis of a racehorse.

Dottie and her parents picked me up in their Volvo station wagon one Sunday afternoon. After a circuitous half-hour drive through farmland checkered with housing developments, we finally turned off the two-lane highway onto a pitted gravel road. Clover-cloaked fields stretched out on either side of us. Halfway down, we passed a pasture of young Thoroughbreds. After St. Timothy's stables of petite Arabian show horses, they looked enor-mous, ungainly, and riotously beautiful.

Dottie's aunt and uncle were small and leathery, sporting cal-lused palms and dusty blue jeans—horse people as I knew them and a welcome refuge from Augusta's buttery leather riding boots and creased jodhpurs the color of marzipan. Dottie opted out of the tour, rolling her eyes and saying she'd seen everything a thousand times before. So I went alone to meet the barn foreman, Leo, who would be giving me "a look-see around." Leo, lean and thirtyish with a fringe of ginger hair poking out from under an Orioles cap, was waiting for me on the back steps, playing tic-tac-toe with himself in the dirt and finishing the final game—a draw—before we set out. With an accent that sounded as if he'd just dropped in from County Cork, he told me that Mooney stuck him as a good Irish name. I agreed that it was, by way of my grandfather. As we hiked from the house to the first set of barns, with me half loping to keep my sneakers even with his mud-caked canvas boots, he filled me in on how he came to be running a Maryland breeding farm.

Leo had started his career as a jump jockey at age fourteen, riding steeplechase races all over Ireland. He lasted four seasons until one of his mounts crashed into a fence, landed on top of him, and shattered his pelvis. Then he worked as a groom at a racing stable in Tipperary, an hour's drive from Ireland's famed Curragh racecourse, where he said the grass was sweeter than anywhere else in the world. He came to the United States six years later, accompanying the retired Irish sprinter Dottie's aunt and uncle had bought for stud. They offered him a job, and he accepted. Eventually, he decided that he preferred breeding to racing, watching the foals grow into yearlings, develop personalities and quirks, learn to trust humans—but not too much.

"After that, there didn't seem any earthly reason to move on," he finished.

Despite having spent the past month within giggling distance of a hundred teenage girls, this dirt-streaked Irish farmhand seemed the first like soul I'd found.

We arrived at the breeding shed, a cement room about the size of a boxing ring with a large drain in one corner for easy cleaning. It was spare and sterile, with the musty-air feeling of having been uninhabited since the breeding season ended in July. Finely carved gingerbread molding lined the doorways, and a central square of padded rubber flooring served to cushion the actual act. Leo showed me the bottles of Betadine used to rinse both horses' genitals before and after breeding, the stock of disposable surgical gloves worn by anyone handling the animals, and a thick leather cape that went over the mare's shoulders in case the stallion should decide to sink his teeth into her back for a better hold. I absorbed the clinical details and felt as if I was viewing an engineer's drawings. It seemed all system without creation, all breeding without racehorses.

We entered the shed office, a closet-sized room lined with windows onto the breeding area. It was packed with file cabinets, microscopes for ensuring the stallion's semen contained live sperm, and index cards that recorded every mating. Each card was divided into columns for rating the quality of copulation on a scale from one to five, valuations based on how easily the stallion had mounted the mare, the number of thrusts before ejaculation, and how much of his semen made it inside. If the stallion received a low rating, a one or a two, Leo usually tried to improve the odds of conception with a follow-up attempt the next day.

Occasionally, Leo told me, two horses would instinctively clash. They got within yards of each other and started to donkey-kick and bare their teeth, at which point—despite the cost in returned stud fees—he always gave in to nature and pulled them apart.

"You can force things all you want, but when they've taken unkindly there isn't much point."

"Because she won't get pregnant?"

"She might, she might not. Some people say foals who come into the world that way are cursed," Leo explained, seeming to accept the folk wisdom as readily as he did the data stowed on his office index cards. "I can't see how it's fair to do that to any living thing."

On the way out, he led me past an isolated stall at the rear of the barn where they kept the teaser, a hopped-up quarter horse who spent his days in unconsummated foreplay, nuzzling, nudging, and titillating a mare to the point of readiness before the stallion took over and finished the job. The closest he ever got to any action was when he was allowed to jump atop a maiden mare so Leo could get a sense of how she would react to having the real deal on her back.

"Some of them don't take to love too kindly. If she's going to start kicking and screaming, I want to know about it beforehand."

Almost in afterthought, he pointed out a boarded-up hole on an outside wall of the barn. He explained that a stallion had kicked straight through it in his impatience to get to the mare he sensed and scented on the other side.

Both of the farm's smaller enclosed paddocks held a single stallion, isolated because he would have greeted any companion with the hooves and teeth necessary to guard his personal turf. Leo's Irish stallion ambled forward—slow and deliberate to let us know our meeting up would be entirely on his terms and not at all on ours. I realized I hadn't considered the physical changes that came from leaving the racecourse, from a prime athlete retired. His coat had thickened and a bull-like crest of muscles rose above his shoulders, highly developed by the lifting, thrusting, and coupling that now made up his days. But the rest of him had spread until he was just staunch and solid. His stomach drooped, and the etched musculature blended back into his chest as if someone had dragged a hand across wet clay. He bit at Leo's palm holding up a wild cherry Lifesaver, and Leo smacked him one on the nose.

"They get plenty full of themselves when they go to stud," he explained. "They know all they have to do is get fickle, and all our lives are done for."

Next we stopped beside a pasture of broodmares, who wandered over at Leo's whistle and munched on more Lifesavers he pulled from his pockets. A few of them, due to deliver in February or March, showed bellies just beginning to swell with foal. They were weighty and self-contained, stripped of that flightiness which accompanies them on the racetrack. It was as if they'd lapsed back into themselves, all-natural creatures bereft of the sculpted muscles and frantic energy that comes of human engineering. What lingered were the basic elements of conformation, a dished Arabian nose or one slightly splayed front foot, and that ever-present charisma.

We came last to the foal paddock sprinkled with more broodmares, most of them already pregnant again, and their young. September was too late for newborns. For racing purposes, all Thoroughbreds are given a universal birthday. Whether born in February or August, every runner turns a year old on January first. Competition is gradated by age, many races restricted to just two- or three-year-olds or conditioned to allow younger horses to carry fewer pounds. When late babies first come to the track, young physiques still forming, those few months of lag time can prove a serious disadvantage. Mares are bred most heavily in early spring, February and March, with the season tapering off by late July. Foals arrive eleven months later.

Most of Leo's brood were already five or six months old, their gangly limbs just beginning to fill out and days spent flexing their independence by trotting away from their mothers and nipping at each other's shoulders and flanks. In a few weeks, the oldest of the lot would be weaned and moved to a separate pasture. There was only one baby among them, a product of the tag end of the season who would probably fall so far behind his contemporaries he wouldn't even touch a racecourse until he'd turned three.

"He's our keeper," Leo told me as we leaned against the gate. Horses so young didn't have a prayer of drawing any reasonable price at auction, so this one would just stick around and race in Dottie's aunt and uncle's name. "He'll be struggling until he's three or four, but he's sound enough. He might turn around into a real racehorse."

He was roughly a month old, caramel-colored with a peach fuzz coat and legs spindly as tent poles. When we arrived, he was nursing, his nose invisible in the hollow under his mother's belly. After a few minutes, he stepped away and began trotting back and forth alongside her. He sped up a bit, then started teetering, as if still trying to figure out which way his knees folded and unfolded. Just when he seemed to have all four straightened out, the whole thing buckled and he crashed down belly-flat, his chin taking an exaggerated bounce off the ground. I winced, but Leo laughed.

"That's how they do it. Just keep trying until it works. Another week and he'll be galloping circles."

I kept watching him, all scraggles and wobbling, trying to morph the image into three years down the line. It was like looking through frosted glass, making out vague outlines of things to come: a willful temper, long silky ears, knees that looked straight and true.

"Could be a Derby winner," I said to Leo, who'd taken off his Orioles cap and was rumpling his thinning hair.

He grunted. "More likely he never makes it to the track." Then he surprised me with a huge grin that revealed two gleaming gold teeth on the bottom row. "But, by God, we keep chancing it. We'll keep on chancing it until the day we die."

Leo wandered off soon afterward, back toward the stallion paddocks and more pressing duties. I kept hanging over the fence until the sun slipped down and streaked the sky pale pink and vermilion, until Dottie's parents wanted to leave, and the whole family came out to find me. Even as I watched their silhouettes advancing through the uncut grass, I made no move to meet them. I didn't want to go, didn't want to substitute St. Timothy's for this Thoroughbred place where you never knew what was going to happen the next time you tried to trot off. Where you kept on chancing it until the day you died.

BREEDING HORSES has always required a certain strain of creativity. As far back as 200 B.C., Iberian horsemen left their mares outdoors all night long in hopes that they would turn to the west wind and became impregnated by it, giving birth to foals blessed with galelike speed. Arabian horses of noble ancestry wore their lineage in gold lockets strung about their necks, talismans meant to carry greatness on to the next generation. Arab horse traders and later those in Elizabethan England inbred their animals as closely as possible, often mating stallions back to their own daughters, in an effort to re-create something diamond pure. Since its origins, breeding has hinged upon chance—isolating the qualities of a brilliant runner, pairing together two horses in possession of such qualities, then adding crossed fingers and prayer.

Though the British had generations of experience with warhorses and draft animals, the notion of breeding purely to race didn't take hold in England until the 1500s, when Henry VIII began to import agile, lighter-framed Arabians from Italy and Spain. His two most valuable stallions, valued at 100,000 ducats apiece, were a gift from Ferdinand of Aragon. Ferdinand's contemporaries choked over such generosity, blaming the Spanish king's madness on the aftereffects of an aphrodisiac dinner his young second wife, Germaine de Foix, had fed him two years before. Henry set about creating a "noble studderie," crossbreeding Arabian speed with domestic draft-horse stamina, then staging contests against the neighborhood landed gentry. He passed a number of official edicts to prevent the weakening of these freshly fashioned bloodlines, including one which outlawed breeding any mare who measured less than fourteen hands, or fifty-six inches, tall.

Racing caught on as a sport in the coming century, the number of racecourses in England doubling from the 1660s to the 1700s. Theories and folk wisdom soon developed around the secret to putting mare and stallion in the proper state of mind to generate a champion. In 1614, breeder Gervase Markham advised his contemporaries to feed their mares clarified honey stirred into new milk, then "with a brush of nettles all to-nettle her privy parts and immediately offer her to the horse." British horsemen also began recording their breeding experiments. They noted particular nicks—crosses of bloodlines or individual horses—that repeatedly produced high-quality animals, and attempted to reproduce them by tracing the history of proposed sires and dams. The information proved muddy at best. Horses' names were often misspelled or repeated from generation to generation, and their ages not reported at all.

In 1688, the first of that trio of taproot stallions—the Godolphin Barb, the Darley Arabian, and the Byerley Turk—arrived in England from the Arabian desert, originating the three bloodlines that would directly evolve into the Thoroughbred racehorse. Their dominance helped breeders—largely wealthy peers or offshoots of the Royal Stables—start to refine those physical qualities that produced the swiftest and soundest runners. Ideal conformation included elegant heads with wide nostrils to enhance airflow and long necks, desirable for stretching out first across the finish. Breeders denounced flaws such as the "cock-throttled" head and neck, joined at an abrupt angle that constricted wind through the throat. They carefully studied horses' legs for any of a multitude of tiny imperfections—toes turned in or out, offset knees, hooves unusually large or small—that might make an animal prone to injury.

To breed a racehorse with perfect conformation was exceedingly rare, especially when numerous stallion owners bent the facts about their horse's lineage, neglecting to mention a propensity for lameness or inventing a celebrated ancestor in the hopes of collecting a higher stud fee. By 1752, such general disorder reigned that a group of nineteen sports-minded noblemen—among them a royal duke, five regular dukes, a marquess, five earls, a viscount, and a baron—established an organization designed to provide racing with consistent rules and a general seat of authority. They dubbed themselves the Jockey Club, jockey at that time signifying either the owner or the rider of a racehorse. As their first order of business, they arranged for a special coffee room to be built in their honor at Newmarket racecourse. Until its completion, they gathered regularly at the Star and Garter tavern in town to discuss methods of diverting fraud and regulating race conditions on the country's tracks.

Among its widespread duties, the Jockey Club began to compile *The Calendar,* an extensive printed record of every race run in England in a given year, including each horse's owner, trainer, jockey, and pedigree. Such documented pedigree information was an immediate hit. Demand rose and, in 1790, the club authorized its Keeper of the Match Book, James Weatherby, to draft a separate document devoted to charting the bloodlines of all the Thoroughbreds in Britain. The document, titled *Introduction to a General Stud Book,* traced each horse back multiple generations, providing proof that it had indeed descended from one of those three Arabian patriarchs. As information was updated and adjusted with each yearly reissue, the *Stud Book* became racing's law of the land. Only two hundred horses, roughly a hundred mares and a hundred stal-

lions, could prove ancestry pure enough to be officially labeled a
Thoroughbred. Those animals descended from cloudy parentage
earned the name "cocktails"—because of their well-mixed breeding—and were banned from racing at royally sanctioned tracks.

From the moment such newly baptized Thoroughbreds crossed
the Atlantic, breeding in America took on a decidedly capitalistic
bent. An 1806 Maryland newspaper advertised stallion seasons at
the bargain rate of $22 a mare, or the equivalent in bricks, beef, or
whiskey. In New York, monthly sales of young horses took place at
an auction house on the corner of Fifty-fifth Street and Seventh
Avenue. By the 1850s, the sport had worked its way across the
continent to California, where stud farms set their rates in ounces
of gold dust. The American breeding business, not yet bound
together by a central set of rules, soon began to suffer the same
inaccuracies and untruths that had plagued its English counterpart.
In 1873, a Kentucky-bred former Union soldier named Colonel
Sanders Deweese Bruce got hold of the latest edition of the British
Stud Book and began crafting an American version. He eventually
produced a six-volume genealogical epic, tracing horses all the way
back through their European bloodlines. He published it as the
official *American Stud Book*.

With such extensive pedigree information finally on record,
breeders on both continents considered it only a matter of time
before they pieced together all the elements necessary to design the
ideal racehorse, one capable of winning at any distance, on any
track. The most desirable physical characteristics were continually
charted and refined, but the intangible aspects—that perfect balance of speed and stamina, that turbulence in the blood—seemed
impermeable to human intervention. Men of science toiled and figured, tossed out theories and mathematical formulas. The prophe-
sied superhorse refused to materialize.

Then, on the cusp of the twentieth century, just as Planck's discovery of quantum physics unleashed the concept of atomic energy,
an Italian horseman named Frederico Tesio decided to focus upon
an even more elusive power source—the Thoroughbred. Tesio,
too, was a scientist, but he was also a philosopher and a mystic. His

goal was enormous: to breed the quintessential racehorse. His dictum was unprecedented:

"To discover new facts, however interesting they may be, is of scant value if we do not find the laws which govern them as well."

FREDERICO TESIO had long been intrigued by the combination of horses and the unknown. As a young man, he sought adventure as a steeplechase jockey riding in jump races all across Europe. During the off-season, he explored South America on horseback, learning to break broncs on the Argentine Pampas and befriending locals—from gaucho cowboys to a nomadic tribe of Cacique Indians—with the common language of horsemanship. He led a mounted expedition through the interior of Patagonia, journeying from the Rio Negro to Punta Arenas equipped with only one tent and two native guides. The party herded forty horses—thirty-nine stallions, and one mare to keep the stallions from wandering off—and lived off local game, including llamas and Argentine ostriches. Tesio navigated the treeless prairie like an ancient ship's captain, guided only by a compass and the Southern Cross of stars.

In 1898, Tesio decided to abandon his roaming in favor of a single stationary pursuit. Spurred by his passion for Thoroughbreds, he purchased a farm at Dormello on the banks of Lake Maggiore in northern Italy, and set about accomplishing what had defied centuries of breeders before him. He would create the perfect runner. He fashioned Dormello after the environment that nourished horses in the wild, leaving his pastures untamed because irrigation forced the grass to grow too quickly, diluting its nutrients. His horses rollicked across open grasslands, near heresy at a time when Thoroughbreds were still considered delicate creatures best blanketed and confined to box stalls. In winter, he heeded the animals' natural inclination to migrate south by shipping his colts and fillies to a Roman country estate owned by an obliging marchese.

From the start, Tesio fashioned a boutique operation, daily laying his hands upon each animal. He refused to employ trainers or stable managers who might insert themselves between him and his brood. He read extensively—not just racing histories, but ancient Egyptian scrolls, books on evolutionary science, and the biochemistry of human fatigue. Determined to shed all previously assumed knowledge and approach the world from scratch, he called to mind the great Italian thinkers who'd come before him— Leonardo da Vinci penning his codex and Galileo charting our course around the sun.

Tesio's first major experiment began in 1906 when, after ingesting a fellow train passenger's copy of Mendel's genetic research on sweet peas, he grew fired by the idea that such discoveries might apply to Thoroughbreds. If racehorses could be honed down to standard combinations of inherited characteristics, the same way Mendel had divided his plants into short and tall, then it would be simple to breed any number of them to order. Tesio needed only isolate one dominant trait, some genetic master signal that separated the strong runners from their recessive counterparts, and he would have the key to engineering a bevy of streamlined racing machines.

Tesio dove into genetics as fervently as he'd accosted the Patagonian hillsides, beginning with an attempt to determine how the most visible of physical characteristics, equine coat color, related to skill on the track. His research took several years. His conclusions were sweeping.

Surveying the range of colors, from bleached gold to near midnight, he whittled the palette down to just two:

1. Bays (B), reddish brown to black with dark manes and tails
2. Chestnuts (Ch), yellow-colored with manes and tails to match their coats

Since gray horses were always born as either bays or chestnuts before their coats changed, he discounted their adult coloring as a disease of pigmentation.

After condensing data on every Thoroughbred ever recorded in the English *Stud Book,* Tesio announced bay the dominant color in a ratio of four bays to every one chestnut. Extrapolating from the

experiments of French chemist Paul Fornier, he attributed the B
gene's precedence to the fact that hairs of the red color family, when
placed inside a high-frequency electronic conductor, gave off a
greater wavelength of light than the yellow Ch hairs. In nature, the
small always gave way to the large.

Next, Tesio drew upon a line from an obscure Indian verse
poem stating that "if they ask you which horse is the best, answer
that it is the bay," and upon an Arab folktale that spoke of chestnuts
possessing speed and bays endurance. He concluded that bays came
equipped with the stamina gene, winning most often at longer distances, while chestnuts were stamped by speed. After years of tabu-
lation, a jubilant Tesio turned to the British racing *Calendar* to test
his theory. He examined more than a century of winners from five
classic English races run at four different tracks, varying in length
from one mile to two and a half. He found every result imaginable—chestnuts that dominated at two and a half miles, bays that
flew wire to wire in sprints, chestnuts and bays beating each other
by a nose—but he found no correlation whatsoever between coat
color and speed. Bays won races of all distances in the exact same
ratio they existed in nature, four to one.

Victory didn't hinge upon a single law of genetics. Only upon
the infinite laws of chance.

UNDAUNTED, TESIO chalked up this initial failure to his own
hastiness. Upon reflection, he deciphered a less tangible but perhaps even more compelling message in his results. His experiment
proved that the qualities comprising a prime racehorse were not
passed from one generation to the next like individually wrapped
packages along a genetic string. They were the result of chaos, one
inherited characteristic acting upon another, acting upon another,
in endless combination. Capturing the ideal patterning depended
upon guiding affinities, not engineering certainties. Tesio, the
philosopher, had always been far more at home in the realm of possibility. His emphasis shifted. He decided that the key to harnessing
Thoroughbred power lay in knowing all there was to know about

their history, their intelligence, their chemical composition, and their souls. No detail was too trivial, no tangential question unrelated to the whole.

Early in his career, Tesio had assumed that speed and stamina were separate genetic traits, just like a bay or a chestnut coat. The more he probed these two qualities, the more he came to realize they were entwined in something greater, concluding that to attempt to isolate one from the other would be "like trying to draw a line where cold ends and heat begins." Racehorses operated under the same guiding principles as the universe: all movement, from the molecule to the star, depends upon speed extended over time. The secret to a premier runner lay not so much in his physical makeup as in the conflagration of his energies. A nervous current pulsed through the best of them, like a battery rigged to a lightbulb, triggering that fierce will to win.

Tesio wasn't the only turn-of-the-century breeder to believe Thoroughbreds operated upon impulses ungovernable by modern science. In 1907, a former British jockey, Colonel Hall-Walker, met with considerable success matching sires and dams according to their horoscopes. But for the most part, Tesio's contemporaries found him eccentric. They stuck to the treatise that physical con-formation was the surest route to racecourse domination and con-tinued to pair horses according to leg length, musculature, and heart size. Dismissing such tunnel vision, Tesio followed the leads of other revolutionary thinkers of the century, most notably Ein-stein and his theory of relativity. Matter—whether an atom or a racehorse—was all highly concentrated energy, motion inseparable from the forces that generated it.

Tesio conducted further research in which he examined the parentage of English Derby winners stretching back 152 years. He discovered that counter to expectation, the most tireless runners—those that had trained hard and raced season after season—rarely produced a brilliant second generation, at least not until years after the end of their racing careers. Their foals, though often physically near flawless, lacked the driving force that had launched their par-ent to victory. Tesio concluded that racehorses contain a limited amount of energy. If that energy were spent on the racecourse, there would be none left over to pass on in the breeding shed. Nature operated on the basis of ebb and flow, her overarching theme to maintain a universal balance. For each generation of brilliance, she demanded payment in terms of a second generation of rest. Tesio compared his theory to the interplay of human minds in which geniuses, however potent, rarely pass on their stratospheric intelligence to their offspring. In an Einstein, a Michelangelo, or a runaway English Derby winner, the energy allotted has already been too fully spent. Tesio's newest dictum was a humbling one:

Only nature can reign supreme.

TESIO CONTINUED to experiment. He imported animals from England and France, injecting untested catalysts into tired Italian bloodlines. Eventually, his offbeat theories bore rich rewards, earning him the nickname "the Wizard of Dormello." Thoroughbreds he'd bred and raised won the Italian Derby twenty times in forty years. The most golden of these, a colt called Nearco, notched a fourteen-race winning streak, including the Grand Premio di Milano and the Grand Prix de Paris, run only six days apart. Nearco proved an exception to Tesio's hypothesis on equine genius, and, once retired to stud, he became the taproot to a Thoroughbred dynasty.

Near the end of his life, Tesio published a slim volume entitled *Breeding the Racehorse,* all his ruminations and experimentation condensed into a little more than a hundred pages. Its frontispiece showed a photo of Tesio as an old man with sunken cheeks and a body lost inside a rumpled overcoat, his mouth propped open as if on the verge of voicing some fresh inspiration. He devoted an entire chapter of the book to castigating the onset of technology in favor of nature, most particularly the concept of artificial insemination. Tesio believed that horses, like all animals, were tuned to radiation produced by their environment. They possessed a sixth sense that could lead them to water in the desert or alert them to the earliest rumblings of earthquakes and sandstorms, signals that man with his "advanced" dependence on seismographs and barometers could no longer read. Combining genetic building blocks without the accompanying emotional motion meant ignoring this deep internal pulse. In Tesio's opinion, it was the surest path to excising the essence from the breed.

He cited a story about an acquaintance of his, an eccentric Neapolitan breeder named Cavaliere Ginistrelli, who owned a topflight filly, Signorina. Once retired from the track, Signorina gave birth to several lackluster foals before Ginistrelli permanently relieved her of her broodmare duties. When she was seventeen, he received an invitation to mate his aging lady with a fashionable English stud named Isinglass. Ginistrelli decided to accept. As he was leading his mare down Newmarket High Street towards her intended, they met up with an unremarkable stallion called Chaleureux. The two horses halted nose to tail, inhaled deeply, and refused to move another step. Proclaiming it instant infatuation, Ginistrelli—less a businessman than a romantic—gave over to the murmurings of the heart. He abandoned the arranged marriage with Isinglass and bred Signorina to her far humbler chosen suitor. Their love child, Signoretta, became one of the greatest racing fillies in British history, winning the 1908 Epsom Derby at odds of 100–1.

Ginistrelli's contemporaries accorded Signoretta's success to the occasional dominance of blind luck. Tesio believed the love match proved something more. Science and reason could never replace "the arrows of the equine cupid." Breeding a true racehorse required something only nature could furnish—a rush of sexual pleasure that shaped itself into exceptional energy. For once, Tesio had no empirical research to back up his radical convictions. He had romantic tales like that of Signoretta, and the hard fact that as yet no artificially produced Thoroughbred had proved brilliant on the track—a truth that holds to the present day. Most of all, he had concrete faith in the invisible, in a smoldering that could travel all the way onto the track.

TESIO CONTINUED to be consumed by the study of heredity, raising thoroughbreds in the grasslands of Dormello until his death in 1953. In the end, he defined breeding as something "the course of which no force can alter except disease and which no force can halt except death." He might have cringed at the contemporary intersections of science and nature. Today fillies are often filled with hormones to suppress their sexual cycles on the racetrack, then, once they reach the breeding shed, injected with counterdoses to keep them in a near constant state of heat. Since foals born earlier also race earlier, broodmare stalls might be flooded with extra light in January and February to jump-start the breeding season by simulating an early spring.

On her chosen day, a mare is usually vanned to her partner's home base a few hours prior to copulation. Her tail is wrapped to prevent its coarse strands from cutting the stallion's penis, and her front two feet are often hobbled together so she can't shift or kick in the midst of the act. The teaser moves in for a quick round of foreplay, the nosing and nuzzling executed through a window to a neighboring stall. If she's too slow to unwind, a stable hand might also apply a last-minute dab of K-Y Jelly. Between hormone shots and internal palpation, vets can precisely pinpoint the moment of ovulation and so determine if the odds of a successful first consummation are high. Ultrasound technology takes only twelve to fifteen days to verify whether a mare is pregnant. If not, her owner can breed her back again and again.

A stallion's preperformance schedule is a bit less daunting, just warm water or a mild disinfectant splashed over his genitals to keep things sanitary. If his high-testosterone existence has made him aggressive—inclined to bite the mare or his handlers—he dons a cagelike wire muzzle that covers nose and mouth. It can take as many as five humans to guide a stallion through a single mating: one to hold him by the head, a second to hold the mare, two more to pull back her tail and lift her rear leg for easier access. The fifth person then steps in to direct the stallion, as if he might not know where to go. In recent years, stallions have started to operate under increasingly demanding schedules. Many regularly serve six months in America, covering as many as three or four mares a day, then are shipped to breeding farms in the Southern Hemisphere—where the seasons are reversed—and repeat the job during the flip side of the year. Whereas once a full calendar meant at most eighty or ninety mares, now a stallion might top out at over three hundred. The strength of his libido has become nearly as important as the length of his pedigree.

One of the most cutting-edge horse-breeding trends is embryo transfer, technology capable of generating offspring from mothers who can't carry to full term or of producing a multitude of foals from a single mare in a year. The donor mare, brought into heat courtesy of heavy hormones, is artificially inseminated with sperm supplied by an absent sire. Seven days later, the fertilized egg is flushed from her uterus and caught in a microfilter. The embryo, still the size of a pinpoint, is picked up under a microscope and, moments later, injected into the uterus of a recipient mare capable of carrying a baby to full term. The recipient, also laden with hormones to synchronize her gestation cycle to that of the donor mare, becomes an unknowing—and most likely quite confused—surrogate parent. From there the breeder can only wait, praying the recipient mare's body will take to immaculate conception. A healthy donor might be bred back to another stallion and spend the winter carrying a second foal of her own.

As yet, embryo transfer can only be used to breed Thoroughbred mares to quarter horse stallions, producing progeny that will run in quarter horse races. Artificial insemination is still illegal in Thoroughbred circles, for fear that a single mare producing five or ten foals a season will dilute the selling market upon which the breeding industry depends. In August 2000, an embryo transfer yearling, the offspring of top quarter horse stallion Royal Quick Dash and top Thoroughbred mare First Mirage, sold at public auction for $225,000. First Mirage, who suffered from a crippling hoof disease called laminitis and from toxic metritus due to an earlier failed pregnancy, died six months after the procedure. Her owners counted themselves lucky to have salvaged some final profit from their crumbling investment, Tesio's concept of nature requiring a balance sacrificed in favor of a quicker rate of return.

Even the terminology has changed since Tesio's day. Once upon a time, "a lover" meant a Signorina or a Chaleureux, a horse who savored the heat of passion and heeded the drumbeat of the heart. Now it's a derogatory label, used to describe stallions who take their own sweet time with the ladies, who like a bit of flirtation, a bit of pleasure before consummation. Who want to slow down business long enough to keep the spark alive.

I'VE VISITED all variety of horse farms since that long-ago afternoon with Leo. Though commerce has streamlined much of the breeding industry, slow remains the guiding pace in just a few places. It's still the speed along Bowman Mill Road in Lexington, Kentucky, where Mill Ridge Farm sits tucked between low backwater hills. This is boots-in-the-mud country, sensuous and tactile, maintaining the illusion of being untouched by human hands. Great green tree limbs form a latticework over the road, and dandelion fuzz bobs through the air, mixing with gnats and flies and bumblebees. It's the sort of place that would grow wearisome were you not enamored of the scent and touch of horseflesh. As you slip past miles of raw wood fencing, past fields loosely sprinkled with horses, the farm's scope seems limitless. But Mill Ridge is only a thousand acres, rather average as far as Kentucky breeding operations go. On my first visit, just a few days before the Kentucky Derby, I coasted down the driveway, past polite little signs reminding humans to pull aside for any horses coming the opposite direction, and knew I'd crossed over. This was Thoroughbred terrain, with people just necessary adjuncts.

Mill Ridge houses 175 broodmares and stands four stallions, the most valuable of whom is Gone West. He's a sixteen-year-old soot black former champion with three ragged stockings and a droplet of white on his forehead (according to Tesio, markings that descend from snow-white Arabian ancestors). Gone West contains prime genetic material. His sire, Mr. Prospector, fathered so many champions that any list of them just ends with the word et cetera. His dam, Secrettame, was a daughter of Secretariat, perhaps the greatest racehorse ever, an athlete akin to Martina Navratilova or Tiger Woods, who won the Triple Crown with thirty-one track lengths to spare. Gone West's own progeny have won classic races and sprint championships, repeatedly flaunting that lick of divine energy, and he is listed among the top fifteen sires in the country. The breeding business is financially matrilineal, foals becoming the property of the mare's camp and not the sire's. The owner of a broodmare pays a flat rate, a stud fee ranging from several thousand to several hundred thousand dollars, to couple with a given stallion. A booking to Gone West costs $125,000. His offspring sell for as much as $3 million.

Gone West spends most of his nonworking hours in his own paddock, free to gallop and preen and consider his responsibilities. On my way into the farm offices, I paused to admire him, and he stopped grazing long enough to glare back at me. He was a bruiser, less exquisitely muscled than when he'd raced but dense, well-grounded and wreathed in a sense of his own importance. I thought I could spot the generations in him, as if millenniums ago a Spanish mare turned her fertile self into the west wind and Gone West was what had come to pass. After a moment, he grew bored and with a dismissive sweep of his head turned and loped off, his oiled gait still nursing ripples of the track. He left behind an impression of high back and fluttering tail—a creature who did whatever he damn well pleased. Hooves thumping over the grass of his farm, his domain, a thousand acres he graciously shares with its human residents. Nature as Tesio intended it.

I WANTED to visit Mill Ridge in part because breeding is the initial point of heat, the catalyst to all future Thoroughbred combustion, and in Kentucky, "the Thoroughbred Capital of the World," that heat catches like kindling. But mostly I went to meet its owner, Alice Chandler. Alice has inhabited the breeding business for more than fifty years. She's known racehorses since she measured head-high to their bellies. I knew her only by reputation, but that reputation was for a woman who believed in Thoroughbreds as wholly as Tesio did, in unpredictability and wizardry and chance.

She met me in the hallway of Mill Ridge's low-ceilinged wooden office building, stretching out both hands and greeting me as if spotting an old friend. She's seventy-four, but if I hadn't known her age from a newspaper article about Kentucky's leading business-women, I might have easily knocked off twenty years. She combined silk and lightning as they seem to only below the Mason-Dixon line: blue jeans, coral lipstick, cropped blond hair under a baseball cap, and an undisguised frankness of opinion.

"If you breed horses," she said straight off, ushering me into an office furnished in more raw wood and montages of racing photos, "you have to love them with every grain of your being." As she spoke, a mare traipsed past the open office window, her backside brushing against the screen.

"I've known I would do this since the day I was born."

Alice's Mill Ridge hours are swallowed up by such conviction, by stallions and mares and foals, birth, conception, animal magnetism. She flows between it all trailed by two Jack Russells, Brady and Fast Eddie, who take to the world at a fast waddle. Breeding Thoroughbreds is hard and dirty work and—if you think in terms of sure things and solid investments—not rewarding work at all. Her hands are callused, with crescents of dirt under unpolished fingernails, and lines and spots etched in by the sun. The seat next to me on the couch was filled with coiled lead shanks and dog toys leaking their stuffing. Her desk held no files, no empty coffee cups or clutter—no sign that its owner spent much time sitting behind it at all.

In 1486, an English breeding manual contained an excerpt from Dame Julia Berners, opining on the ingredients necessary to brew a solid racehorse:

> *A Goode hors sulde haue XV propretees and condicions.*
> *Off a man boolde prowde and hardy.*
> *Off a Woman fayre brestid faire of here & esy to lip upon.*
> *Off a fox a faire tayle short eirs with a goode trot.*
> *Off an hare a grete eygh a dry hede and well reunyng.*
> *Off an asse a bigge chyne a flatte lege and goode bone.*

For women, Dame Julia proved a high point. In the ensuing centuries, the breeding industry was only slightly more accepting of female participants than the racetrack itself. Occasionally, a hobbyist would generate a Thoroughbred of note. In 1885, Mrs. Harriet Brown's Tecumseh won the Preakness Stakes, and in 1924, Mrs. R. M. Hoots bred and ran Kentucky Derby winner Black Gold. Such flashes of competency were considered more the chance fruit of someone's pastime than a legitimate business. Even when the first female names appeared among lists of top money earners in the early 1940s, success tended to fall to wealthy widows—Lucille Wright-Markey of Alydar's Calumet Farm or Greentree Stable's Mrs. Payne Whitney—who gained access the same way many of the earliest women broke into politics. They employed large staffs and walked paths paved by their husbands' reputations. The independent operators, the Alice Chandlers, are rare.

CREATING A racehorse hinges upon something earthy and instinctual. It's blood and sex and the scent of damp hay in a foaling barn, a family spark jumping from generation to generation. So perhaps it's fair to say history did come down, at least partly, in Alice's favor. Thoroughbred bloodstock is in her blood. Her father's father owned a second-place finisher in the Derby, and her great-great-uncle on her mother's side was the original bluegrass horseman, Daniel Boone. But to find the risk-taking bone, that compulsion to work with unstable elements, one need travel back only a single generation.

"You could go twelve lifetimes and never meet a man who loved horses like my daddy," she offers. "Every stitch of Mill Ridge is here because of him."

Alice's father, Hal Price Headley, was a legendary horseman in a land that sets high standards by its legends. In the early part of the twentieth century, he played patriarch to his own breeding estate, Beaumont Farm, churning out champions at a regular clip. More important, he captained a group of wealthy racing men who gathered in 1936 to create Lexington's Keeneland racecourse—a rarefied, not-for-profit track built entirely of native limestone, and deemed even before its first race "the Royal Ascot of the South." In the Thoroughbred-mad world of the bluegrass, Hal Price Headley's role in Keeneland would forever ensure his legacy. Imagine someone today orchestrating a state-of-the-art football stadium in the heart of Green Bay or Dallas.

Alice was the fourth of four Headley daughters, erasing her father's longtime hope for a son to inherit Beaumont. But it was clear from the start whom she took after. She was headstrong and fearless, going on the lam at age four to sleep in the barn under the hooves of her pony. She spent her early years tramping the Beaumont pastures hard on her father's heels.

"If my toe wasn't under his boot, I was lagging," she laughs. "He was so strong, and he never once told me to hold back. If I could've gotten hurt, he sure didn't let me know about it."

Hal Price rubbed that boot in the dirt and erased any lines between boys and girls, should and shouldn't, can and can't. He called her Al. He taught her horse sense and common sense and what to do when nothing made any sense at all. Every year, Alice helped him start out the yearlings, the first human to climb on their backs, get pitched off into fence rails and barn walls, then climb back on again. She rode anything she could get her legs around, hunters and jumpers and retired racehorses that flew across the countryside knocking against tree limbs and fallen stumps.

As Alice grew older, her stubbornness flared into rebellion, chafing even at her father's formidable bit. She married young, at eighteen, had two children, and got a divorce. She married a second time in her mid-twenties, to a man for whom the family business meant Southwest Supply Company, a pipe and oil-field parts provider based in Houston, Texas. They moved away from Beaumont, taking up residence on the sere rim of the desert Southwest. Alice spent a decade in Houston, had two more children and no horses, slid into some facsimile of normal life, and hated every suburban kitchen and drop of crude. Each time the phone rang, she longed for it to be her father, to drink in details of new foals and two-year-olds taking fresh to the track. After she'd been away ten years, Hal Price finally asked, "When are you coming home, Al?"

"I told him, I'm coming right now," she recalls. "It didn't take me longer than a heartbeat to get out of there."

Within months, she and her family had packed up their station wagon and navigated the country's rural highways back to her roots. The adult Alice fell in with Beaumont as readily as the child had, working in the breeding shed and foaling barns day after day, consuming and consumed. She'd found rapture, then she'd found Texas, and never again would there be a choice between the two. That was when Hal Price bought a bit of land lost amid the winding back roads of Lexington, 286 pristine acres perched on the far side of the tiny town airport, well clear of the land developers creeping across the county like rust over a broken-down pickup. He held the acreage untouched. He figured one day Al would be ready to branch out on her own.

In his prime, Hal Price Headley had purchased a ten-thousand-acre spread in Georgia where he could fill his leisure time as fully as he did his working hours. Every winter, when the breeding business slowed to simple maintenance—mares incubating foals, stallions recouping their eloquence, Kentucky sheathed in snow and ice—he would pack up his buddies, hightail it for the Peachtree State, and spend months hunting, shooting, and having a southern "grand old time." By the time he'd reached his late sixties, life still full to straining, his heart began to send signals that it might have been stretched beyond capacity. In 1962, his ailing health brought him home from Georgia in early March. Kentucky greeted him with dogwoods and pale sunshine. The yearlings were being prepped for auction in September, Beaumont was rolling in its own good fortune, and its working bloodlines now extended from Hal Price to Alice—now single again—to Alice's fifteen-year-old-son, Michael, who spent weekends and summers learning the farm.

Hal Price's other darling, Keeneland racetrack, sat only a few miles from Beaumont, allowing his young horses to experiment and grow tipsy with racing confidence just a hop-skip from home turf. The track was lodged below a cliff of honeysuckle, which by March of that year had exploded into a riot of creamy white blossoms. One warmish late morning, Hal Price towed Alice and Michael down to Keeneland, accompanied by a collection of promising two-year-olds with exercise riders aboard. He spent hours sending one horse after another flying down the stretch, dashing back and forth along the honeysuckle bank with a clock-face stop-watch dangling from his neck. He called out times to Alice, who jotted down the numbers, watched the sweat drip down his fore-head, and knew—as she knew about mares laboring long or foals arriving weeks before schedule—that this was not good.

When they'd finished, Alice and her father sat together in the tack room under a tangle of reins, bits, and bridle straps. They compared times and mused about possible futures, which early bloomers to sell, and which late developers they might want to keep and race in the Beaumont silks. Then, in the middle of a list of runners, Hal Price stood and excused himself for just a moment. The barn was silent save a few tussling hooves and the rustle of muzzles against hay nets. In the emptiness, Alice heard the latch swing shut on the tack-room door. She knew she'd been locked in.

Hal Price walked the length of his shedrow, pausing at each horse to rub a cocked ear or hand out some loose grain. He made his way up one side then down the other until he'd reached his grand-son. Michael stood in the doorway of the final stall, holding a flighty young filly on a length of lead rope and watching his grandfather because his grandfather was the sort of person you couldn't help but watch. Hal Price paused and asked for his arm, saying he wasn't feeling too well. In the second it took Michael to unplug every inborn, ingrained instinct that you never unhand a lead rope and turn a horse loose, his grandfather collapsed at his feet and died.

IT'S A core tenet of the breeding business: The end of one thing is always the start of something new. Hal Price's death destroyed Alice. At first, what he'd left behind looked to her like dust and rubble, the shards of her own foundation. In truth, something more remained. She had 286 acres, and the chance to go it on her own.

In addition to the land for Mill Ridge, Hal Price left Alice a handful of start-up horses, including a broodmare called Attica who he thought one day just might throw a promising foal. But the horse business was laced with promises and just mights, most of which came to nothing at all. Eventually, Alice decided to begin again because the pain of movement didn't seem quite as unbearable as the pain of standing still. She didn't possess a wisp of knowledge untouched by her father. He became Mill Ridge as surely as he'd been Beaumont.

"He was on every stick and blade of grass," she recalls. "There were times when I didn't think I would survive it. Every day I woke up and told myself, 'Let's just make it through another one.' "

And every day, somehow, she did.

Alice set Mill Ridge into motion with a few broodmares and a staff of four local horsemen unorthodox enough to work for a woman. She borrowed money from her mother to build barns and split-rail fences, and padded the trickle of income that came off selling her first foals by boarding other people's mares in her empty stalls. She did everything she possibly could on her own. In the winter, she woke up with the 4:00 A.M. ring of the alarm clock and spent the next eight hours working frozen fingers warmed only by horses' breath. When she went back to the house for lunch, she would run a bath and eat her sandwich neck deep in steaming water, her body doing its best to thaw before she started all over again, wielding lead shanks and pitchforks until the stars came out overhead.

"After all those years, I thought I'd know exactly what to do. But running a farm is like learning to drive. You don't have a clue what's going on until you get behind the wheel."

Everything felt new—each mare teased to readiness, each knee and ankle tested for joints smoothly aligned, each virgin muzzle cleared and guided to its mother's teat. When a pregnant mare colicked, Alice would spend all night sitting outside the stall on a hay bale making sure she didn't lie down and roll, flipping her uterus or adding another twist to her convoluted gut. When there was nothing more she could physically do to help, Alice would pray to God or her father or anyone listening to keep them all alive and healthy, at least for the first few seasons.

Not every obstacle came by way of nature. It was 1962, the age of Camelot and *Leave It to Beaver,* and Alice inhabited a South predating legalized civil rights. The female of the species was considered too sensitive, too instinctual for running a hard-labor business.

A woman of class, even Hal Price Headley's daughter, didn't belong in a breeding shed. One afternoon, an old acquaintance of her father's ambled into the farm office, and found Alice dirt-stained, shivering, and perilously near the breaking point. He advised her to stop struggling so hard.

"You ought to take on something better suited to a woman of your position."

"Like what?" Alice demanded, half hoping he could provide an answer.

"Like arranging flowers."

"And where the hell am I going to get the money for the flowers?" No white knight rose up to offer her a ride.

It took factual evidence finally to open minds, to raise the possibility that in an industry revolving around animals who sense every wisp of impure intent, sensitivity and instinct might even count as assets. A few years down the line, Alice bred Attica, that broodmare Hal Price just had a feeling about, to a stallion called Sir Gaylord. The result was a precocious colt named Sir Ivor. Alice sold Sir Ivor, and his new owners packed him off to England. In 1968, as a three-year-old, he became the first horse bred by a woman to win Britain's royal race of races, the Epsom Derby.

BREEDERS ARE picky about the quality of mares they book to their stallions: the higher their percentage of successful progeny, the higher their stud fees can climb. By the early eighties, Alice's bloodstock had earned a spot among the equine elite. She sent one of her resident mares, Rullah Good, down the road to Calumet Farm and a midspring session with Alydar, who'd just launched his stallion career. A baby girl arrived eleven months later, a filly as perfectly formed as her father with straight legs and a tiny fluttering tail. But her eyes, twin pearly gray pools, registered nothing at all. She had been born blind.

Alice's breeding agreement with Calumet contained the usual "live foal" clause, promising to recompense the entire stud fee if the foal couldn't stand and nurse on its own and had to be destroyed. Odds were this one wouldn't survive beyond a few days, that Rul-

lah Good would reject her deformed infant or the young filly herself would wither inside her permanent black hole. Even so, when
Alice phoned the Calumet offices, she told them she wanted to try
to save the foal, to preserve the baby and the bloodline.

Calumet kept their coffers sealed and wished her Godspeed.

Alice named the filly Begum, after the title customarily bestowed
upon an Indian queen. That spring, the leggy chestnut foal became
the center of Alice's Mill Ridge universe. She fenced off a special
paddock for broodmare and baby, digging a trench around the
inside edge so Begum wouldn't tangle herself in any loose fencing.
She removed the water trough and every rock big enough to trip
up tiny hooves, then hung a bell around Rullah Good's neck so
Begum could locate food and warmth whenever she pleased. As
with most animals whose predomestication lifestyles didn't permit
lingering in the nest, foals will imprint upon a mother figure soon
after birth. Their minds are most malleable then, making instant
and lifelong associations regarding pleasure and danger. During
those first crucial days, Alice spent hours standing nearby, accus-
toming Begum to the smell, sound, and touch of what she would
depend upon for the rest of her life: a human presence.

Begum grew up evincing little of the royal grace of her name.
She could be all sweetness when the mood struck, but more often
she turned impatient and surly. She had a serious dose of her father
in her, Alydar's unwillingness to give in or give way.

"She knew her own mind," Alice remembers, "and no person
was about to change it. I think she was just plain angry about being
born in the dark."

She bit at any human breeze swirling past. She kicked and paced
and balked. To ease such brooding, Alice housed her in a special
paddock central to all the farm doings. Each time Alice came in or
out of the office, she could slide past Begum's gate and deliver some
whispered confidence or just a waft of straw and boot leather. The
following spring, Rullah Good was bred back to another stallion
and slipped gently out of the equation. Alice and her filly turned
mother and child.

When Begum herself was ready for breeding, Alice began with baby steps, pairing the mare with one of the farm stallions she scented daily just the other side of the fence. Her first baby, a colt, arrived whole, sighted, and beautiful, though he had to be whisked off to a nurse-mare when Begum nearly trod on his sapling legs. The next year, Alice stepped out a bit farther, loading Begum onto a horse van and taking her to a stallion at a nearby farm. Another perfect foal arrived, was snuffed and licked by its mother, then carried off to a surrogate parent. Step upon cautious step, Alice continued, keeping each season secure and simple.

"I never asked for more than the queen bee wanted to give."

Alice's dedication came to fruition in Begum's offspring, winners of stakes races and parents to further champions who scattered bits of Alydar from Kentucky to California. The reward came even clearer in the view outside Alice's office window for nearly fifteen years: a mare radiating contentment, loping lazily around the paddock she knew down to its every rut and stone. When Begum died at age fifteen, Alice dug a hole and buried her in the backyard.

"From the start, if there was a chance to save her, I figured it was my job to take it," she explains. "Mill Ridge isn't a numbers game."

Mill Ridge is simply racehorses.

THE FARM has matured gracefully in the forty years since Alice began. Nature still prevails, but it's not as simple to preserve essence of Thoroughbred as it was in Frederico Tesio's or Hal Price Headley's day. Science has brought benefits—ultrasound tests that help monitor a healthy pregnancy or indicate early signs of trouble; a neighboring veterinary hospital, which means Alice no longer has to sit up nights monitoring a colicky mare. The modern world can also prove invasive. These days a horse's fine-tuned senses must go to work instantly, filtering out carbon particles, exhaust fumes, and stress. Lung problems are more common, brittle tempers more likely to snap.

Mill Ridge does its best to move at an earthy pace, with overgrown fields and foals taking to the outdoors just hours after

they're born. Alice refuses to send any of her stallions to do double
duty in the Southern Hemisphere, handing Gone West and his colleagues a prescription for six months of lollygagging instead.

"It's too hard on them not to rest," she explains. "They need that.
Horses are nature, and nature is cyclical."

One of Alice's less prominent stallions is an ankle-socked bay
called Valiant Nature. He tends more toward the fickle than the
fertile, usually impregnating only about twenty mares a season
instead of the desired fifty plus. She books the ladies to him spar-
ingly and brings each mare on his schedule to the farm a few days
early, just as she first begins to go into heat. Mill Ridge boards her
free of charge, palpates her ovaries daily to feel for the peak of ovulation, then mates her with Valiant Nature at the moment success
seems highest in the stars. If things don't click the first time, the
mare might be bred back again and again. Each contract contains a
live foal clause, obliging Mill Ridge to return the full $7,500 stud
fee if Valiant Nature doesn't rise to the job.

For many breeders, such effort would hardly be worth the questionable payoff. But fording such uncertainty is no longer so much
a choice for Alice as a way of being. Valiant Nature comes from a
rich, underexplored bloodline, one she doesn't want to see die out.
His grandfather was a European stallion called Ribot, a product of
the unspoiled grasslands of Dormello. Fruit from the mystical
elixir of Frederico Tesio.

FOR THE youngest horses dotting Mill Ridge's pastures, life is
devoted to long gallops, play fighting, and hatching a highly prized
cockiness. But such sweet time too is cyclical. At some point after
their first birthday, Alice's yearlings—and all their neighboring
colts and fillies—must start to prepare for the future. Most begin by
leaving home, their breeders offering them up for sale at yearling
auctions. Horses are prepped for such sales like fashion models
styled for the catwalk. Several months of easy exercise, an hour of
walking or light jogging each day, lend definition to their waifish
bodies. High-protein feed supplements—and in some cases

steroids—melt baby fat and chisel in lines of premature muscle. Though still too unformed to support a rider, they're acclimated to the close quarters of a stall and to the rush of human hands and voices. They undergo rounds of meticulous grooming—hooves clipped into half-moons, coats buffed, manes picked clean of any unruly hairs. Once a week they might even get a hose bath in Lemon Joy dishwashing liquid, known for imparting a particularly glassy shine.

The yearling auctions are harsh spotlights, the tiniest conformational flaw reason enough for buyers to look elsewhere. Occasionally, corrective surgery is done on crooked limbs to boost a horse's desirability. A procedure called periosteal elevation encourages twisted legs to grow straighter by slitting the periosteum, the elastic tissue covering the bone, on the weak side of the limb. Before Bob Baffert plucked Real Quiet from that Kentucky horse sale, his knock-knees had been partially straightened by a contraption of screws, staples, and wires inserted to pull aside the growth plates covering the joints. Once Real Quiet's bones had successfully lengthened and connected face forward, he underwent a second operation in which the hardware was removed. Such untested yearlings can sell for anything from several thousand to several million dollars, the market price based on conformation, bloodlines, and a mountain of guesswork. From there, they cross over into the realm of serious investment. Farewell bluebells, clover, and alfalfa. Hello grit and bones of the track.

I love two-year-old races. Colts and fillies have spent the past six months immersed in the highest learning curve of their existence. They've ambled innocently onto yet another farm, and wound up in weeks of racing boot camp. Trainers specializing in such pre-track preparation drilled them in the straps of bridle and saddle against their skin, the weight and shift of a person atop their backs. They practiced flowing into and out of a starting gate, and tearing down a training track without swerving into the horse pounding along next to them. Endless hands explored their joints, probing for signals that everything continued to grow straight and true.

They discovered that mischief and stubbornness, curiosity and rest-less energy are all good things, and that by doing what they love most, running and racing and roaring about, they get nothing but praise and more opportunity to explode. They acquired things—their first pair of shoes, a regular groom, and a single detail which will forever define them. Each of them finally has a name.

Thoroughbreds' names are an essential part of the racing flavor. A name can help determine a horse's future, grace it with dignity or arrogance, archness or impenetrability. Before it's permitted to race, every runner must be registered with the Jockey Club. Its ancestry is checked and cross-checked, and its identity officially cemented with a number tattooed to its inner lip. Since no horse can run without one, the new owner also submits a name. The Jockey Club's naming committee adheres to strict rules. Nothing can run longer than eighteen characters (spaces included, numbers spelled out), giving birth to concoctions like Grits'nhardtoast and Thistyranthasclass. Nonsense words must be accompanied by a convincing explanation. A horse can't be named after a famous person (except with permission), a famous racehorse, or any horse—runner, stallion, or broodmare—still on active duty in the sport.

Before the onset of the official *Stud Book,* horses often ran under their sire's name, "Daughter of Hautboy" or "Son of Pul-leyne's Arabian," and tradition still dictates an allusion to the parents and their bloodlines. In the 1860s, a stallion called Dangerous fathered five fillies—Merciless, Relentless, Regardless, Remorse-less, and finally Ruthless, the most gifted runner of them all. One-upmanship, ever present at the racecourse, dictates a name should be clever and preferably a bit risqué. Jockey Club officials lean toward the straitlaced, but, as with the Hollywood censors and screwball comedies, it only takes a bit of imagination to outfox them. Alfred G. Vanderbilt Jr., one of the leading owners of the forties and fifties—an adventurer who rode big-game safari with Ernest Hemingway and took to the African plains in a twin-seater behind lady bush pilot Beryl Markham—had a particular gift for circumventing the official eye. Among his portfolio:

Polynesian + Geisha = Native Dancer
Ohsay + Low Cut = Ogle
Cold Reception + Low Cut = Décolletage

One of his favorite creations arose from pairing that same racy muse Low Cut with a stallion called D'accord. Vanderbilt came up with Tit for Tat. The Jockey Club turned it down flat.

A name, however insipid or inspired, is one of the few concrete items a Thoroughbred possesses that first time it ventures onto a real racetrack. For a real race. The period of intensive study is over. The initial crash course has given way to a second cycle as the youngsters moved once again, this time to their permanent trainer's barn. They've eased into track culture with more mock morning starts and finishes, honing their speed in a series of practice gallops. None of it has come close to preparing them for the actual fact.

Shortly after visiting Mill Ridge, I went to Belmont one twilight spring Friday and stumbled upon a rarity: a two-year-old race at just five furlongs, in which all eight horses entered were taking to the track for the first time. The program page, usually crammed with information on earnings, prior starts, expectations met or unfulfilled, stretched clean. Each horse listed an owner, a jockey, a trainer, and the clockings of a few morning workouts. Nothing more. Gamblers hate such races, situations where all is serendipity and chance. I love them. Anything could develop. It's impossible to predict.

I watched the horses in the paddock, seven colts and one filly, all gangly and tentative. Their chests were adolescent slim, legs spidery, breath high. A few had broken out into a nervous sweat that foamed between their back legs or formed dark splotches along their flanks. Watching them was like observing a room full of preschoolers, helter-skelter energy and personalities just beginning to emerge. A few yards from where I stood, a feathery gray colt bolted when the jockey lit on his back, and sat down in a pricker bush. The jockey sailed off, a brilliant pink cottonball, and made a neat two-footed landing in the grass. The colt's groom began stroking his ears to return some tiny degree of calm. By then, all the

other horses had turned skittish in sympathy and the entire company began to dance and fret.

My attention settled on a pale-gold chestnut with two white
socks who seemed to have already designated himself the class free
spirit. Head up, ears pricked, he ignored all the gyrating foolish-
ness around him and kept advancing step after steady step. He
nearly made it to the track in perfect order, only giving himself
away at the last minute by trying to jump a shadow and getting
tangled in his own feet. Post-recovery, he strutted sideways for a
few paces, inflating his knobby ribs and reclaiming his bravado. I
went inside and bet $5 on him to win because he'd looked so poised
at first and then so genuinely stunned when that poise got knocked
off-kilter. The man in front of me bellied up to the window, laid
down a complicated series of bets, then told the clerk:

"God only knows."

It was what May-May used to say whenever we'd prepare to
watch those early two-year-old races.

"Yes," I wanted to tell him. "Exactly."

The race was chaos.

My chestnut got caught off balance when the gate opened and
stumbled onto the track, instantly dropping back a length and a
half. Ahead of him, one horse lugged in and another veered outward, their shoulders nearly colliding as both jockeys curbed their
reins, waved their whips, and went to work steering a straight line.
It took half the race for the mess to untangle itself. They folded into
the turn loosely packaged, a few swinging way wide and the others
hugging in close to the rail.

Coming down the stretch, my chestnut broke out from the center of the pack, saw daylight, and scrambled into the lead. But the
excitement was too overwhelming. He started curving far left then
farther right, tacking like a sailboat, and gobbling up extra ground.
I loved him even more as he corkscrewed past, coming in third by a
length to the hopped-up gray from the paddock and a barrel-
chested filly capable of straighter trajectory. He was Tesio in full
glory, static-crackle and exuberance, no rules in operation save
what nature had handed down.

It took the jockey a full quarter mile to slow him down and turn him around, the colt still drunk on speed, on depth and breadth and motion. I waited for him alongside the tunnel leading back to the barns, watched him skate across the dirt, breath rifling in and out. The jockey hopped off and unclipped the saddle, a two-second, two-fingered operation—one planted on the belly-circling girth to hold it down and the other flipping open the buckle—executed as nimbly as a banker stacking money or a blackjack dealer flipping over cards. He delivered a quick departing pat to the colt's shoulder. The chestnut shook his mane out and arched his neck even tighter. He seemed a changed being, the uncertainty dimmed, something else grown more luminous.

He'd set out undecided, and come back home a racehorse.

Part 2:

EARLY SPEED

Chapter Four

COURAGE:

Riding High—The Jockey's Life

T**he first live race I ever saw came a full year after my initial Kentucky Derby. May-May refused to take me to
the races right away. Instead, she waited and educated,
determined that when the time arrived I should understand exactly
what it was I saw. Throughout that first summer and into fall and
winter, I learned my earliest Thoroughbred lessons watching tele-
vised races from Florida and California, where sweat foamed on
the horses' sides even as freezing rain thudded against May-May's
Seattle windows. The following spring rolled around, and with it

came season-opening "Doo-dah Day" at Longacres Park, the same track May-May had frequented in the thirties. Buckled into her black Ford sedan with its high dashboard and pop-eyed headlights, she and I finally set out for the races.

We reached the track long before post time, breezing past the grandstands and betting windows to examine the perfect oval of the course. Half an hour before the first race, we moved on to the saddling paddock. I leaned against the fence, my arms barely reaching the second rail, and inhaled the dusty scent of straw and saddle leather. I prepared for my first real-life Thoroughbred.

He arrived looking every bit as exquisite as I'd expected—a slim, sculpted bay gelding with dark molten eyes I could've stared into forever. I watched his groom lead him into one of the open stalls, watched his trainer, fingers flying, fasten the flimsy one-pound leather racing saddle. Only when the horse began circling the paddock again, raising his head to check out his surroundings, did I bother expanding my gaze to take them in as well. When I did, I noticed another creature had entered upon the scene. Strutting through the paddock gate came a wiry doll-man cloaked in brilliant color, radiating an energy that might have sent off sparks if I'd been close enough to see. He announced his arrival by spinning his whip through the air like a baton, then popping the end of it against his boot. I twisted my head to ask May-May his name, but she only allowed for half my question.

"Watch him," she said, resting her hand on my shoulder and steering me back to face the rail.

The jockey exchanged a few whispered words with the gelding's trainer, riding instructions he might or might not follow depending on how the race actually unfolded, then gave his mount a staccato pat on the flank. The trainer bent down, cupped his hand around one pint-sized knee, and lifted. The rider popped aboard as if a string had pulled him up from the sky.

I was a practical child—no one's birthday party magician could convince me they'd drawn a rabbit from a hat—but what happened next didn't fit into any of my known forms of logic. When the jockey lit in the saddle, his earthbound elements seemed to transform. Suddenly, seamlessly, he became part of the animal beneath him. The taut little body turned lithe and fluid, knees curving into his mount's withers as if they'd been sewn together with needle and thread. As the horse stepped forward, his human weight traveled right along, their twin centers of gravity merging. Perhaps everyone else that day witnessed just a man with a strange springy gait and a head too big for his body. I saw a sorcerer. I wanted to reach up and touch him, actually lifted my fingers as if my eight-year-old arm could extend the full length of the paddock. The jockey must have thought I was waving, because for a second the hybrid creature became horse and human again as the top half raised his hand to wave back. I would've been just as stunned had the horse opened his mouth and bellowed out a hello.

Minutes later, I watched this same wizard, recognizable only by the pink and orange diamonds adorning the sleeves of his jacket, leap from the starting gate. He hurtled onto the track barely fastened to the saddle, his entire body lifted into the air like a butterfly preparing to take flight. Only his hands on the reins and the tips of both boots wedged in the stirrups still tied him to earth.

"Watch him talk to the horse," May-May whispered as the pack blurred down the track.

I wasted seconds searching for his mouth buried behind helmet and plastic goggles before I understood he wasn't speaking in words. His hands sat cocked along his horse's shoulders, reins held tight, ten human fingers somehow convincing this mass of energy to hold something back just for now. Then, as they rounded the far turn, the message changed. His arms began to pump along the horse's neck, rhythmically urging him forth, almost as if he were lifting both of them up into the air and thrusting them down again with each stride. He kept talking—head nodding, hands rolling, elbows flaring out and in—movements so minute they might have been tricks of the elusive sunlight, pumping energy from human to animal, or animal to human, or perhaps just allowing it to circle through the single entity which had become both. They shot past us down the homestretch, a smear of color and a rush of whips and straps and hooves.

By the time that horse-rider soared across the finish line, I'd decided to become a jockey.

IT'S A commonplace among jockeys that the more gifted the rider, the harder it will be to explain that gift. Racehorses occupy a universe that operates almost entirely on intuition. To think too much, analyze too deeply, is to interrupt that rhythm which flows between human and horseflesh. Too practical a mind-set might resist walking the ledge of a skyscraper three, five, nine times a day.

Race riding is arguably the most dangerous sport around. Most jockeys boast a patchwork of scars, puckered emblems that read "there but for the grace of God." Riders fall constantly. They go down when their mounts act up, when they rear in the starting gate, smashing their riders' knees and hips and heads against the metal caging, or try to bolt midrace and wind up accelerating straight into the rail. They go down when horses, hammering along at forty miles an hour, brush or clip or collide in the compressed space of the pack. They go down when their mounts go down, when they snap bones and ligaments and joints midstride. In the United States, a single year at the track averages twenty-five hundred injuries, two and a half riders paralyzed, and two more killed. The ones who are merely injured get back on and ride. They possess an unhealthy disrespect for life, a conviction that any existence worth living is worth risking on a regular basis. From the start, I found this bald defiance of the laws of nature—those dictating that Thoroughbreds are stronger, faster, and never quite under anyone's control—one of the most seductive elements of race riding. Recklessness is forever there, hardwired.

Some jockeys embody their bravery quietly, with gentle hands capable of instilling confidence in the craziest of mounts. They balance in the saddle still as a stone and take race after race "hands down," folding their whips under their elbows and coming across the finish line using nothing more than their fists rolling in time with the horse's stride. May-May always preferred such subtle style, favoring pure horsemanship untainted by fiery personality. But I was younger, more restless, and eager to be entertained. Once I'd set my heart on jockeydom, I wanted a role model steeped in show-manship and razzle-dazzle. No one dazzled like Angel Cordero Jr.

Angel—pronounced the Anglicized way with wings and halo attached instead of the traditional Spanish "On-hell"—was one of the hottest race riders in the United States for almost thirty years. Brilliant and unbearably cocky, he imparted equal doses of talent and controversy. He was the bad boy, the Dennis Rodman or John McEnroe of American racing. He threw temper tantrums and left hooks and, more than once, was accused of throwing races. He made rude jokes, cursed on national television, and never bothered hiding his ambitions. Emotions rippled through him as visibly as the muscles along a Thoroughbred's sides.

Angel was born to be a jockey. Not just because of his tiny size and enormous attitude, but because horses traversed his bloodlines. His father, Angel Cordero Sr., was a champion jockey at Puerto Rico's Las Monjas racecourse. The front door of the family's wooden house opened right onto the track. Instead of spurring his son's ambitions, Cordero Sr. questioned Angel's courage early on. Courage was the most crucial prerequisite for a Puerto Rican jock. At Las Monjas, riders triumphed by knocking other jockeys off their mounts with a well-placed kick, or lashing them in the face with a whip. They spent almost as much time down in the dirt as perched up above in their saddles.

When he was seventeen, Angel was the third of four jockeys tangled in a spectacular domino collision at San Juan's El Commandante track, which left horses and riders sprawled the entire width of the course. Though Angel came out of it with only a cut to his forehead, one of the jockeys who went down in front of him crushed his neck and nearly died. Cordero Sr. had predicted that such a brush with danger would siphon off his son's remaining confidence. As if marching to unspoken orders, Angel began to fulfill his father's prophecies. He started angling his mounts to the unfettered outside edge of the track, taking the longest and safest route to the finish line and losing his next few races by wider and wider margins. He was committing the ultimate sin. He was riding scared.

In Puerto Rico, the racetrack serves as a breeding ground for legends. Perhaps tales are still embroidered around the afternoon Angel Sr. publicly confronted his son, storming into the jockey's room, grabbing him by the scruff of his gaudy racing silks, and ordering him off the track until he'd stopped riding like a coward. Angel went home and brooded for four days before dusting off the piece of himself that would determine his entire future. That future was to race. He returned to the track possessed of a reckless courage that would accompany him the rest of his riding life. If he couldn't ride timid, he would master the opposite. He would court danger with every flick of his very active whip.

ANGEL'S NEWFOUND feistiness quickly led him out of Puerto Rico and into the big time—American racing. He arrived in New York City in 1962, nineteen years old, speaking only a few words of English, and so naive a street hawker talked him into buying a $20 share of the Empire State Building. Already an expert at timing, Angel had scheduled his U.S. debut perfectly. Racing—along with baseball and prizefighting—hovered at the forefront of pop culture. In New York, the sport had also become lucrative business, newly developed offtrack betting parlors providing a fresh flood of riches outside the reach of organized crime. The industry was ripe for stardom. By the time he'd permanently set up in the States in 1965, Angel was primed to rocket like a Roman candle.

From the start, Angel threw up a web of contradictions. On the one hand, he rode like his name, with a celestial grace that echoed the natural rhythm of the horse. And he whispered. Decades before horse whisperers came into vogue, Angel could calm his mounts with a slight feathering of his fingers and a few Spanish sweet somethings murmured into their cocked velvet ears. Once when a horse collapsed under him in the middle of a race at Gulfstream Park in Florida, Angel lay down in the dirt and massaged its heart until the vet arrived. When the doctor told him the animal had died, the entire track watched Angel roll over onto his back and sob to the sky.

For every gentle ounce of Angel's wiry body, there was a corresponding pound of the devil. He discovered early on that it simply wasn't enough to ride well. Studying other American sports, especially boxing and ice hockey, he gleaned that the public didn't want you unless you could fight. He attacked every race—no matter how minuscule the purse or second-rate the horse—on a tightrope between riding aggressively and riding dirty.

"If someone messes around with me . . . boxes me in, herds me, chases me on the fucking lead when I've got the speed and he don't have a fucking chance? . . . I'm not going to scare," he boasted to a *Sports Illustrated* reporter in the mid-eighties. "That's just race riding."

Angel exercised an extremely liberal hand with his whip. When on the move, horses instinctively give in to dominance far more readily than when they're standing still. If they begin to wander during a race, a sharp tap from a rider's whip can instantly refocus them. Hitting a horse is a practiced skill, reliant on timing and placement rather than power. Jockeys synchronize their strokes as precisely as a musician following a score, each tap delivered in time with the horse's stride. Strict rules dictate how often a rider can hit a horse, and contact is limited to the heavily muscled shoulders and backside. Angel rode that governing line as closely as he rode everything else. He excelled at "switching sticks," juggling reins and whip at forty-plus miles per hour to deliver blows to alternate haunches without skipping a stride. He would smack his mounts all the way down the homestretch, if that was what it took to get them first across the wire.

Occasionally Angel put his whip to more creative use, slashing it across the face of a rider who pressed him too close. He was notoriously rough on talented newcomers, and once slammed a cocky young jock and his horse against the inside rail of the track, just so he would know "what race riding is all about." More than a few pieces of Angel lore featured a neophyte riding in the perfect ground-saving position along the rail just ahead of Cordero. Instead of ceding such a plum spot, Angel would start shrieking:

"Get out of the way! I got a problem here! Get out of the way!"

The startled rider usually obeyed. If not, Angel helped out by reaching over to gently slap the other horse on the rear with his whip. Then he'd drive his mount straight through the hole, leaving behind nothing but a dust cloud and a devilish little grin.

In 1974, Angel captured the American racing dream, winning the hundredth running of the Kentucky Derby aboard a long shot named Cannonade. It was a sensational ride, classic Angel threading his fearless way from back to front through twenty-two other horses. The victory shed its halo when word leaked out Angel had arranged to split his prize money with two other jockeys in the race. It was as if he couldn't help himself. Somewhere inside, bravery and bravado were stuck on a permanent collision course.

Angel was the latest in a long line of brilliant race riders with an equally consuming taste for spectacle. Near the end of the nineteenth century, a reedy jock called Snapper Garrison, who strode about town in creased trousers and a handlebar moustache, had the audacity to adopt a flashy crouched-over riding style unlike anything ever seen at the track. He set the stirrups on his saddle ultrashort and rode ducked low, working his fists along the horse's neck, rather than the old way of balancing straight up and down as the horse moved in back-and-forth counterforce underneath. At first Garrison's new seat, rear thrust high and thighs pulled together like a knock-kneed schoolboy, was deemed absurd. Then he began winning races by tiny margins, his manic hands literally pushing mounts forward that final jump to the wire. Soon jockeys across the country had adopted Snapper's aggressive style, and Garrison's guiding principles still predominate today. A decade later, Tod Sloan, a champion jockey and fellow man-about-town, carried Snapper's gutsy new style across the ocean to England, where he became the contract rider for the Prince of Wales. Ever a dapper society figure, Sloan inspired George M. Cohan's musical *Yankee Doodle Dandy,* and hobnobbed with everyone from Diamond Jim Brady to the king and queen. He refused to travel anywhere without three full trunks of clothing and a personal valet to help him dress.

Off the track, Angel soon exposed his own relentless need to be at the center of everything. He flirted with TV cameras and threw punches in locker rooms, always striking first in case the fight was broken up early. Whenever he won a race, he leaped off his mount and landed two-footed in the dirt of the winner's circle like a gymnast springing off a vault. A few trainers refused to hire him simply because of his grandstanding reputation. Most would have lain across the track if it could guarantee Angel on a single horse in a single race, just to become the smallest point of light aboard his flashing comet's tail.

EVENTUALLY, ANGEL did win that attention he so craved, coming to dominate the patrician, still largely white world of racing. But his Puerto Rican roots would always keep him separate from its blue-blooded core.

Many of the earliest jockeys had been minorities, slaves bought and sold in package deals with the horses they rode, or freed men grasping at any chance to earn a living. In the early nineteenth century, one of the most popular jockeys was a four-foot-six, crookbacked field hand called "Monkey" Simon, who was rumored to have been an African prince. Prior to the Civil War, such riders existed outside the slave laws of the South, traveling to tracks across state lines even as Nat Turner's revolt had plantation owners shackling workers in their homes. The most skilled of these slave riders accepted payment in the form of freedom, and future earnings often went towards purchasing liberty for their families. Of the fifteen jockeys entered in the 1875 inaugural running of the Kentucky Derby, all but two were black.

In the 1880s, a black rider named Isaac Murphy—the son of a bricklayer killed in the Civil War—became the darling of the New York circuit courtesy of his elegant upright riding style and seemingly incorruptible honesty. Early in his career, the teenage Murphy was offered the dollar equivalent of a small Kentucky plantation if he would purposely lose a Saratoga Springs stakes race. Murphy declined. In the decade to come, he would win back-to-back Kentucky Derbies. By 1887, he earned up to twenty thousand legitimate dollars a year, making him the highest-paid athlete in the country. He rode with an exquisite sense of timing, stealing races at the wire so often that the sporting papers claimed "no man with a touch of heart disease should ever back his mounts." That same year, Murphy bought seven acres of land in the heart of Lexington and built a $10,000 house. He shelled out for diamonds to ornament both himself and his wife, Lucy, and hired a young white boy to serve as his personal valet. He soon became a frequent guest at society galas, sporting pointy-toed boots and a hand-tailored Chesterfield coat.

Less than a decade later, the thirty-four-year-old Murphy was dead of pneumonia, victim to "drinking propensities" and constant crash diets to maintain his 118-pound riding weight. The era of the black rider began to fizzle just as dramatically as it had soared. As the number of white jockeys increased, they began to gang up on their black competitors, squeezing the black riders' mounts against the track railing or kicking at stirrups to launch them from their saddles midrace.

In 1900, Jimmy Winkfield, the last of the great black jockeys, was nearly killed in an on-track riot in Chicago that broke four of his horse's ribs. He stuck things out for three more years, then moved to czarist Russia, where he spent the next decade riding for princes and barons, though never Czar Nicholas II, who was notorious for underpaying his riders. In 1921, Henry King finished an inauspicious tenth in the Kentucky Derby aboard a horse called Planet, the last black rider to have a Derby mount for nearly eighty years.

Half a century later, Angel became one of the earliest Hispanic riders to plunge a fist through that invisible wall which still kept the fair-skinned boys in the races and the dark-skinned ones carrying feed pails. His success helped shatter the decades-old logjam of prejudice, allowing for a groundswell of minority jockeys. In 1965, Angel arrived in an America on the cusp of integration, where racial equality was often theorized but still rarely practiced. Track elders claimed such concerns didn't apply to the world of sport. As the country registered a collective tremor under the onslaught of the civil rights movement, Angel's explosive persona drew these larger social issues smack into racing's center ring.

From the first time he sauntered onto a New York track, fans and fellow jockeys mocked Angel's dark skin and heavy accent. A 1984 *Sports Illustrated* article reported him fending off epithets including "bean-eater," "monkey," or just "little black mother-fucker."

"It's not for his black face that I won't ride him," one trainer was quoted as saying. "It's for his black heart."

Angel returned fire, engaging in high-volume confrontations with trackgoers offended by the presence of a Puerto Rican who rode like a prince. Racists in every crowd showered him with obscenities, crumpled programs, sometimes even empty beer bottles. Eventually, Angel became so accustomed to death threats that he asked not to be informed of them. When a brace of cops showed up to escort him to the paddock, he merely assumed another fan was plotting his murder.

AS ANGEL matured, as a man and as a rider, he began to refine his rip-roaring image. He was no less the warrior—still embracing those battle-honed values of pride, strength, and aggression—but his energy shifted from that of foot soldier to decorated general. He plumbed the art of strategy, becoming expert at discovering his rivals' weaknesses and then moving in for the kill. When he arrived in the paddock before a race, he'd enter slicing his whip through the air, sometimes taking out a flowerpot or two along the way. He'd pause alongside the most timid riders and begin greeting everyone in sight with a roaringly confident, "Hello there, Poppa," until there was no question as to whose empire they all occupied.

Angel also turned racing savant. He immersed himself in Thoroughbreds, both those he'd ridden and those he'd competed against. Whenever he ran at the front of the pack, he'd peek under first one shoulder and then the other to check out the action behind, filing away details as to how each animal managed the race. If he spotted a jock making the slimmest of mistakes, Angel would point it out to the trainer while the horses were still cooling, often landing the mount for himself the next time around.

Though many jockeys would be hard-pressed to recognize a horse they'd ridden two days earlier, Angel spent countless mornings studying workouts and evenings poring over grainy track films. He could spot a filly from the opposite end of the course and know by the bob of her shoulders that she was the one with the tendency to drift outward who'd beaten him by a length the week before last. Stories abounded. In the late 1980s, riding against a high-strung and nearly unbeatable sprinter named Groovy, Angel used to chirp and holler as soon as they approached the starting gate. He'd rile Groovy to no end, all the while soothing his own mount with a sleepy stroke of the hand. By the time the gates burst open, Groovy required an extra fraction of a second to gather himself. Angel would shoot forward and assume control of the race.

One summer near the tag end of his career, his war-torn body closer to fifty than forty, Angel went down in a thumping collision on the track at Saratoga in upstate New York. As the paramedics rushed up with stretchers, Angel—flat on his back and nearly immobile—demanded a look at that day's racing card. One of his rescuers unfolded a program from his back pocket and held it up in front of Cordero's eyes.

"Alright." Angel nodded, finally giving them the okay to lift him up and cart him away. But if he'd been on a live mount in the next race, he'd had every intention of rising up from the carnage, walking back to the paddock, and climbing aboard.

THOUGH ANGEL spent his career preparing for battle, he always remained remarkably free from one of race riding's most debilitating struggles—the struggle to stay slim. Perhaps the most striking aspect of a jockey's physique isn't the inches he stands but the absolute sparsity of his frame, a man's face and an athlete's grace on a child's body. Before and after every race, sometimes eight or ten times a day, jockeys step onto a giant standing scale to weigh in. A jockey's career stands or falls by that scale. A horse carrying an overweight rider loses a precious edge, like a track star forced to run the four hundred meters with a barbell in either hand. Each piece of equipment a rider dons—nylon pants and T-shirt, leather boots, hard hat, and protective vest made of high-density foam—is specially designed to weigh as little as possible. Jockeys can be fined for carrying too many extra pounds. The smallest fluctuation, one extra beer or two bites of dessert, might tip them right out of a race.

Angel's hummingbird metabolism meant he could eat anything he pleased. While most riders monitor their size to the quarter pound, he blithely bounced up and down that precious window of 108 to 114 pounds. He folded this God-given asset into his strategy, consuming huge snacks while others sipped diuretic teas, jogged miles wrapped in sweat-inducing plastic garbage bags, and spent hours in the jockey's "hotbox" sauna. One of Angel's main rivals, a muscular five-foot-five Panamanian jockey named Laffit Pincay, led a permanently starving existence to maintain his 115-pound racing weight. He tested a slew of bizarre diets, languishing on less than eight hundred calories a day and at one point subsisting for months on unsalted nuts and raw bran. A trainer who once accompanied Pincay on a cross-country flight marveled as the rider removed one nut from the snack packet of peanuts, split it in two, ate one half, and kept the other for the ride home.

The freedom to stuff himself provided Angel with both a physical and a psychological edge. Maintaining near-starvation weight takes its toll on an athlete, and riders often battle severe dehydration, muscle weakness, kidney stones, and heart palpitations. It's not uncommon for them to pass out in the paddock before even making it to the track. If they fall midrace, many jocks break not just wrists and collarbones, but more serious ribs, legs, and hips, due to bones grown brittle from continuous malnutrition. Like Naomi Campbell tormenting fellow supermodels by absorbing platters of french fries, Angel could arrive in the jock's room and regale his colleagues with details of his previous evening's meal: steak, rice and beans, two different vegetables, salad, bread, and fried bananas for dessert—more calories than Pincay could consume in a week.

Riders like Pincay who are constantly at war with weight often wind up decimating their futures. They take powerful diuretics like Lasix, a medication that prevents thin-blooded horses from spontaneously hemorrhaging during a race. Although racing officials have debated the safety of Lasix in Thoroughbreds for over a decade, jockeys, lured by the drug's diuretic properties, regularly down heavy doses and risk dangerous toxic buildups in their livers. Many riders suffer from anorexia or bulimia. They chew food, then spit it out before swallowing, or regularly "flip"—throw up after meals—spending their nonracing hours as gaunt and depleted as the twiggiest supermodels. Some jockey's quarters include special purging rooms furnished with oversized porcelain toilet bowls, chrome spray nozzles similar to handheld showerheads, and signs instructing "Regurgitators, Please . . . CLEAN AREA Before Leaving." Most racecourses have special on-site rehab programs, "recovery houses" for riders who come to rely on cocaine or speed to keep them at racing weight.

Charismatic's Triple Crown jockey, Chris Antley, spent his entire career plagued by forced hiatuses as he battled to control his weight. Antley, with his cherub's face and honeyed Carolina voice, first reached racing's big time in the late eighties. Like Angel, he had the lightning. He was the sort of jockey May-May would've put on her reading glasses to watch, just so she could study the wonders emanating from his hands. He could align his own mood flush to a Thoroughbred's—calming the horse's anxiety or adding electricity to its doziness with just a subtle jigging of the reins. He knew how to coax out every last dribble of effort and then some. He won races not just on long shots but on runners most people had stopped believing in altogether—horses like Charismatic, who went off at Derby odds of 33–1, and on little more than a wing and a prayer.

Once he touched earth again, Antley's gift took on another aspect. The flashes of brilliance were edged in doubt, and early on this tendency towards self-sabotage revealed itself via a string of addictions. He lacked Angel's ability to fight, that steel-rod resilience replaced by something fragile and searching. It was as if the gift came too easily, genius without the corresponding effort, so that he couldn't quite appreciate the height of the mountain he stood atop. In the early part of his career, Antley entered drug rehab programs six times. Six times he cleaned himself up and returned to riding. Through it all, the gift remained undiluted. It seemed to separate from the man, standing alongside to wait for his corporeal body to either recover itself or disintegrate.

Though he managed to ride through serious flings with cocaine and alcohol, it was an addiction to food itself in the mid-nineties that sent Antley spinning off the track and into severe depression. He spent months stuffing this hunger, his spare 115-pound frame swelling to 145. He retreated to his childhood bedroom in South Carolina and interacted with little more than a flickering television set. Though just in his early thirties, he could fathom no other life than the race riding he'd started when he was sixteen.

No matter what form their injuries, if they have any choice in the matter jockeys rarely stay down long. It was watching a horse race on that muted bedroom television that finally breathed life back into Antley's calling. Memories evolved into desire, and he convinced himself that any struggle would better the one he'd chosen. The next morning he embarked on a brutal diet and exercise regime. Devoting hours to the Stairmaster and jogging up to twenty-five miles a day, he began chasing his old racing weight and—perhaps even more challenging—his old racing mind-set. In February 1999, after eighteen months away, he returned to the track, having reattached himself to that engine of belief.

Jockeys who succumb to the pressures of bodily perfection are far from uncommon. Racing's accelerated lifestyle—glamour and enough cash to fund anything from crates of whiskey to bricks of cocaine—has left behind a domino line of fallen stars. Isaac Murphy's flourishing career collapsed in the 1880s amid crash diets and regular dips into the champagne bottle. After an 1887 race debacle in which he slid from the saddle and fell to a drunken heap in the center of the track, the racing paper *Spirit of the Times* trumpeted: "A popular idol shattered." Around the same time revered British jockey Mat Dawson, who each spring brought his weight down from 154 to 110 pounds with the help of a sootlike mixture rumored to contain gunpowder, shot himself at age twenty-nine, decimated by "wasting"-induced misery. Tod Sloan, the 1930s rider and dandy who became personal jockey to the Prince of Wales, eventually sacrificed his international stardom on the twin altars of alcohol and gambling. At the end of his luminous riding career, he dissipated into a parody of himself, stumbling through stints as a bookmaker and a vaudeville artist until he was eventually arrested for violating antigambling laws and barred from the track.

After his own slip from celebrity, Chris Antley, once a champion rider, had become an unknown quantity. In a business where each race alters a horse's net value, few trainers are willing to chance an unknown. Finally, an old friend and leading trainer, D. Wayne Lukas, tested Antley on several of his lesser horses. When he performed like the brilliant jockey he'd once been, Lukas gave him a Kentucky Derby mount aboard a distant long shot named Charismatic. The pair of underdogs took first place. In the winner's circle just after the race, Antley's tears spilled onto the blanket of roses covering his lap. Marble-blue eyes glittering but still the tiniest bit hard, he vowed he'd pulled his life permanently together.

"A miracle happened for me here today."

A month after Antley's dramatic ride in the Belmont, those demon pounds started creeping on again. He began resorting to his old fixes—water pills, flipping, early morning saunas—until one afternoon his legs trembled so badly he couldn't walk from the jockey's room to the track. He begged off the rest of his day's mounts, confronted a flurry of negative publicity, and the next morning got up early enough to run twelve miles along the beach. Come November, he staged yet another of his customary disappearances, claiming he needed to get control over his barely restrained weight and "regain his enthusiasm for racing." He attempted another brief comeback in March, but won only one race before slipping away one last time.

The racetrack acts as a magnet for lost souls. People cleave to the danger, and grow dependent upon living in the moment. They use the present to eclipse the future. Some don't survive. Close to a year after Chris Antley's final disappearance, the thirty-four-year-old jockey was found dead of a drug overdose in his million-dollar California home. His recent history bespoke tragedy from every angle—a methamphetamine possession collar a few months earlier; a black-dog depression; a separation from his new wife, who was eight months pregnant with their first child; and not a Thoroughbred in sight. Though initially police investigated the possibility of a drug-related murder, the toxicology report later revealed a less scandalous but perhaps more unsettling truth. Antley's system was steeped in drugs, including an antidepressant, a seizure-control medication, a straight amphetamine, and an amphetamine-based appetite-suppressant called Clobenzorex that jockeys acquire illegally via a Panamanian black market and often use to lose weight. The combination was enough to blindside any human heart.

For me, part of Chris Antley's brilliance as a jockey always lay in his apparent fearlessness on the track. He seemed to think nothing of gunning his mount into a sliverlike hole, or maneuvering recklessly close to the clipping heels of someone just ahead or beside or behind. It was as if the guardian angel preserving his natural gift had also promised him a kernel of immortality. Whatever fears descended upon him once his feet meet the ground were lifted, pushed aside by the ingredients of flight. His was another of racing's fairy stories—at times David slinging stones at a shadowy and ever-present Goliath, at times Icarus careening a little too close to the sun.

ANGEL CORDERO retired from race riding when he was nearly fifty, following a serious on-track spill in 1992 which left him with a broken elbow, three broken ribs, and a ruptured spleen. These days he splits his time between New York and Florida, working as a jockey's agent lining up mounts for a young Puerto Rican protégé named Johnny Velasquez. Any jockey bent on a serious career must immediately hook himself up with an agent. Agents operate with a single purpose—to hustle rides for their clients. They spend their time chasing down trainers to suggest their riders for upcoming races, and smoothing over miscommunications, mistakes, and bouts of sports-star temper. Some are solid everyday businessmen who thrive at being independent operators; others are racing's version of snake-oil salesmen, hawking a product in which they only partially believe. Agent-client relations are simultaneously tenuous and tight. When riders hit a slump, one of the first things they do is jump agents, hoping to break up whatever pattern has dragged them down. This can be devastating. Unlike in most other sports, jock's agents represent only one or two athletes at a time. Payment comes in the form of 25 percent skimmed straight off their rider's earnings.

Though he's shifted from generator of chaos to organizing principle, agenting seems a natural role for Angel, one requiring charisma, connections, and a certain degree of guile. He now does for another rider what he once did so expertly for himself—concoct a strategy, then angle in on someone else's terrain. Agents are political appointees, the track spin doctors, and Angel's wily charm is ideal for "dropping" a trainer's horse—pulling out because Johnny got a better offer for the same race—without erasing all hope of future business. He still keeps a hawk eye out for other riders' mistakes, only now it's Johnny he's quick to propose as a replacement. He still knows every Thoroughbred and jockey on the backstretch. Then there's the edge Angel alone can bestow—to book Velasquez is to garner a slice of the deity.

People kept telling me that meeting my childhood idol would be seriously risky; that if Angel didn't measure up it would ruin everything we once had together; that my dream bubble and his reality couldn't possible match up. I didn't listen. Instead, I actively hunted Angel down. Along the backstretch at Gulfstream Park in Florida, my hero and I finally met.

He still looks like the Angel I once tacked up on my walls— broad face, curly dark hair, and jet bead eyes that signal "Don't mess." He still made my heart flutter as it might have for Cary Grant or Sean Connery. We sat on the concrete steps outside the racing office, and as we talked, he kept one hand poised over a cell phone clipped to his belt loop. His sneakers had been long ago stained the sandy brown of track dirt, and a gold cross gleamed around his neck. Every few seconds he shot a glance over one of my shoulders, alert for any action bubbling up behind.

The phone rang before we'd even gotten started.

"What is it?" Angel yelped into the receiver. Then he launched into a jagged, half-comprehensible verbal tap dance with whoever was on the other end, almost forty years in the United States having done little to tame his Puerto Rican accent.

"The sixth on Wednesday but no can Thursday. We'll do the Stakes then switch the second on Sunday. Would I lie to you? Call me back in an hour."

Once he'd hung up, we exchanged some idle track gossip, then I asked him about the secret of his blazing success. He began tapping his foot, and ducked his head like an embarrassed kid.

"I just rode like everyone else did."

Growing up in the 1940s, he studied the Movietone reels of American races at the local cinema. He dreamed of becoming those riders, legends like Eddie Arcaro and Bill Shoemaker, just like any kid boxer dreams of becoming Muhammad Ali. When I pointed out that few people manage to attain this goal, he flashed back an impish grin. This grin is a chief component in his arsenal, a smile that might get anyone to believe anything at all.

"You just gotta be good at what you do, that's all." He hesitated for barely a second, foot still tapping away. "And don't get too full of yourself. Always let the horses call the shots."

His chest inflated like a rooster's as he told me that they're thinking of making a prime-time television movie about his life story. Then the phone rang, and I lost him to another back-and-forth rat-a-tat of Spanish, English, and racetrack.

Later, I asked why he'd become an agent. He laughed so hard his still wiry body couldn't quite contain itself, actually rose up off the ground.

"Shit, I don't know. You're done with riding. What else are you gonna do?"

Then a trainer sauntered past and he excused himself, trotting away to conduct more business.

"Call me whenever you want," he tossed over his shoulder as he went.

After he'd blazed off I had to pause to catch my breath. He and racehorses are still perfectly simpatico.

I've seen Angel plenty of times since then, always in the mornings, making his agent rounds with that same cock-of-the-walk strut that intimidated his paper-skinned rivals when he was a rider. He inevitably flashes me the center-of-the-world smile, and then a heartbeat later he's gone, finessing someone new. He still sports that aura of devil and genius riding on the same breath. And I still wish I could have seen him live, just once, exercise it aboard a Thoroughbred.

I asked him a few times how much he missed riding. He always just shook his head.

"I don't miss it at all. It's over. I'm too old. I can't get on those horses like I used to, so . . ." A shrug, a hop from one foot to the other, another disarming grin.

Then, one early afternoon down at Gulfstream, I spotted him slipping the wrong way through the turnstile half an hour before the start of the first race.

"You're leaving?"

"Sure. I never stick around here."

For Angel, life outside the races hasn't flown as smoothly as it did on the track. He's been married, divorced, then married again. Not quite a year after I first met him, his second wife, Marjorie, a fellow ex-jockey and sometime trainer, was killed in a hit-and-run accident just down the road from their Long Island house. They have three children—two daughters and a son named Angel III— who live with Angel at home. In the back half of the day, he visits the dog tracks, takes the kids to Disney World, or watches the races from his living-room TV. If he must stay at the track for the afternoon, he does so under duress. And he leaves the second the horses have crossed the finish.

"I can't get out the front gate fast enough," he admitted that afternoon.

"So you do miss it?"

"Sure. Why not? The competition is great. It's not like life." He held for two or three beats, the longest I'd ever seen him absolutely still. "It gives you a bad feeling to watch something you can't do anymore."

I thought of Chris Antley, and of the legions of riders, past and present, who'd submerged themselves in drugs or alcohol to fill the hours not spent on a Thoroughbred's back. I remembered watching that Longacres jockey careen down the stretch, conjuring a single being out of two, then imagined hitting such euphoria three, six, eight times a day. Ordinary life goes pretty flat in comparison. Angel's is still a demanding art, this figuring out how to carry the races around inside.

IN THE late 1980s, a few years after Angel came down off my walls and nothing rose up to take his place, a groundswell began at the racetrack that couldn't help reaching even me. Women were becoming jockeys.

From the start, horsewomen had done their damnedest to force their way onto the track. In Italy in the 1550s, a peasant girl named Virginia rode bareback in free-for-all *palio* races staged through city streets and became lauded as "the belle of Sienna." Lady jockeys surfaced in England in the late 1700s. One of the most popular, Mrs. Thornton, caught the attention of the racing papers by riding sidesaddle in "purple jacket and cap, nankeen skirt, purple shoes and embroidered stockings." She also beat Frank Buckle, one of the top riders of the era, by half a neck in a two-mile race at York.

Female jockeys took to the American turf around the same time, racing at an informal track set up in Brooklyn. They competed directly against male riders, most of whom operated on aggression, subduing their charges with a whip or a brutal yank at the reins. Fred Taral, one of the top jockeys of the late nineteenth century, slashed his horses so ruthlessly some had to be blindfolded before they would admit him back on board. Female riders, often smaller and less muscularly developed than their male counterparts, knew they could never hope to be strong enough to conquer a Thoroughbred's will. Instead, they focused upon a more subtle art of communication. They tended to be gentler, more sensitive, as focused on receiving signals as sending them, and their mounts responded. Those same women who'd started out as a novelty act proved unexpectedly serious competition. As soon as the sport began to organize itself, the ladies were quickly written out of the rules and into the stands, replaced by slaves and gentleman jockeys, including a young George Washington.

In 1847, members of New York society in Saratoga Springs were witness to an impromptu trotting race between women drivers when a bemused reporter watched a socialite named Mrs. Healy exercising her harness horse and bet no other woman could be found to stand her in a race. Another woman emerged from the crowd instantly, a noted horseman's wife named Mrs. Elijah Simmons, who met the challenge with her colt Elias. The first time around the track the two women drivers were accompanied by gentlemen chaperones, the male half of their audience convinced the "dear creatures" wouldn't be safe controlling such mammoth beasts all alone. In the break before the second lap, both women kicked out their male passengers. The *Spirit of the Times* newspaper reported the contest and its split-decision outcome as delicately as possible, referring to the women only as Mrs. H— and Mrs. S—, as if elaboration would irrevocably damage the readers' fragile sensibilities and the participants' even more fragile reputations.

That Saratoga trotting race generated a wave that May-May would climb aboard fifty years later, slapping her reins against Spesushi Island ponies and driving Countess Highland and Dr. Rhythm past scores of male pilots. But it took more than a century for the Mrs. Simmonses and Mrs. Healys of the world to make it to a Thoroughbred track. In the late sixties, after fighting through a web of antidiscrimination lawsuits, the first female jockeys finally overcame claims they were too frail, too precious, and too inexperienced to survive against the males. In 1969, a few months before men first walked across the moon, Diane Crump made a far tinier bit of history by riding a horse called Bridle 'N Bit to a tenth-place finish at Florida's Hialeah Park.

The advance spread slowly, water trickling through cracks in

the fortress walls. Women fought gender prohibitions as aggressively as Angel had the racial ones—turning face forward to rocks
pitched at their makeshift dressing rooms, nicknames like "honey
knees" and "sweet cheeks," and the industry's public prediction
that the trend of girl "jockettes" would fade as quickly as go-go
boots or the hula hoop. By 1973, the year Billie Jean King quashed
Bobby Riggs in their tennis "Battle of the Sexes" and *Roe v. Wade*
surfaced in the U.S. Supreme Court, only a few dozen women had
forged their way onto the track.

When I began nursing my earliest jockey dreams, I found
almost no female role models in high-profile races. It wasn't until
the mid-eighties, as I was entering high school, that the barricade
started to crumble. Women riders exited the fringes and entered
into the barns of leading trainers, Triple Crown races, and the front
pages of the *Racing Form*. May-May never stopped marveling at the
rise of names like Robin Smith, Patricia Cooksey, or Patti Barton-
Brown, reading them aloud each time they popped up in a major
race as if she'd unearthed another unexpected vein of gold. The
dividing line didn't by any means disappear. Most talented women
riders still had to choose between modest success at small tracks or
continually scraping for mounts in the more competitive circuits
like New York and southern California. A jockey's gifts are measured in numbers—dollars earned and percentage of races won or
lost. Only a very few women survived the statistical cut.

The queen of the mountain became Julie Krone, an ace horse-
woman who hit the competitive New York tracks in the late eighties like a stick of blond dynamite. In 1993, she became the first
woman to win the Belmont Stakes, aboard a colt she called Big
Daddy but everyone else knew as Colonial Affair. She was of
Angel's ilk—brilliant, cocky, and capable of inspiring racehorses
like a muse. On the way to the starting gate, as the male riders
adjusted their goggles and collected their concentration, she could
always be spotted patting and cooing to her mounts, massaging
their confidence as if it were a muscle before the pair of them burst
out into the fray. At the finish, win or lose, she would be petting
and stroking again, exchanges so automatic that you could believe

she loved horses more than people and imagine the horses had begun to believe it, too. Julie grabbed the national spotlight—*People, David Letterman,* the *New York Times.* When acquaintances heard I followed racing, hers was one of the few names they could draw forth. She was the jockey poster girl, the female rider I shared with the world.

There was another woman who rode like wildfire, not quite as splashily as Julie Krone, but still competitive enough to pass racing's documented wins-and-losses test. Donna Barton started riding professionally the year May-May died. The first time I heard about her I was sitting alongside the hospital bed in May-May's room, helping her to flip through a *Blood-Horse* magazine. May-May plucked Donna from a back-page article, reading her name aloud because Donna's mother had been a jockey, too.

"You should watch for her," she told me.

It was tiny, that exclusion of herself from the sentence, but when I took her hand to say good-bye, for once she was the first to let go. I left that day with no intention of following Donna's career. I certainly didn't want the end of May-May tangled up in the start of anything new.

In the next few years, Donna Barton disappeared from my radar as she bounced around small tracks in New England and the Midwest. Then, in the early nineties, just after I graduated from college, I spotted her name in a race at a Kentucky track. I was tempted to pretend I'd never seen it, aware that the likelihood of Donna rising to the top echelon of riders hovered at slim to nothing. Something, I suspect May-May, kept me fixed.

I was far from easy on Donna Barton in those next few seasons. Part of me hoped she would fail, that her porcelain prettiness and icy reserve would somehow translate into lack of skill. Donna refused to cooperate. She began riding for first-class trainers at Kentucky's trio of tracks, and finished second in a million-dollar Breeders' Cup race. Julie Krone may have taken on the role of national sweetheart, but it was Donna Barton who kept tugging me back toward the races.

Like Angel, Donna came to horse racing down the family line.

Her mother, Patti Barton-Brown, had been one of the pioneer female jockeys. Barton-Brown started riding professionally aboard rodeo broncs, running counter to a sedate suburban family who found horses so alien they made her strip off her riding clothes on the front porch before entering the house. She made the jump to Thoroughbreds in the mid-sixties and slowly worked her way up from morning exercise rider to afternoon professional. Three children and a few broken bones later, she was working local tracks from Pikes Peak, Colorado, to Waterford Park, West Virginia, searching out any trainer who would give her the chance to ride. Donna grew up hearing Barton-Brown creep out of bed at four every morning to hustle mounts for that afternoon. She stood along the rail and watched her mother roll off horses' backs and down under their hooves. Before she knew how to diagram sentences or do long division, Donna had unraveled what race riding was all about.

As a teenager, Donna worked exercising Thoroughbreds to earn money for college, but she'd always planned to abandon racing's gypsy lifestyle once she was on her own. Jockeydom seemed dull, a default path into the family business. Riding came naturally to her—a skill gleaned as soon as she could walk—and her mother had pressed home the message that life was meant to challenge. In Donna's case, rebellion meant becoming a lawyer. Then, when she was twenty-one, a friend convinced her to ride a single race, simply taste-testing a possible future. In two minutes around a Birmingham, Alabama, track, the gentle rock of an exercise gallop was transformed into heat and pace and strategy. Law school ended before it had started. Donna had uncorked a passion.

The path for women riders was still rocky, but Donna's earliest influences had conditioned her against doubt. Seeing what Barton-Brown had overcome, she simply knew—the way she knew crotchety colts might be nursed into virtuosos—that comments could be ignored and obstacles circumvented. In the mid-eighties, just as Donna's career started rumbling, a racetrack spill pitched her mother headfirst onto the track, causing serious, lifelong brain damage. Such an accident might have provided anyone else with an understandable escape clause. Donna nestled into the track even tighter. Her mother's accomplishments became armor, protection against owners who insisted girls were too weak to drive a race-horse home and male riders who hovered in the corners of the jockey's quarters whispering, "Let's get the girl."

Soon after I picked up Donna's career again, she became the second-leading female jockey in the country. She'd turned race-riding machine, racking up championship horses, high-caliber stakes races, and a fistful of new records at her home-base tracks.

Everything I'd aspired to as a child Donna Barton had gone and done.

I MET Donna at Churchill Downs, the day before Captain Steve's Kentucky Derby. We sat and talked at the back of the Paddock Pavilion, a windowless bettors' extravaganza featuring races tele-vised from around the country and a cold cuts and potato salad buf-fet. Waitresses kept filing past, shouldering 1:00 P.M. cocktail trays packed with mint juleps and Bloody Marys.

On first greeting, Donna comes across as gracious, polite, and china-doll lovely—none of them qualities you'd particularly look for in a jockey. She also retired from race riding in 1998, and now works as a television anchor for Churchill's in-house handicapping show.

"I looked like a guy when I was riding," she offers up quickly, making clear that the person sitting across from me in a peach-colored silk jacket is not the one I would have encountered two years before. "I wore jeans and no makeup and chopped off all my hair."

They were conditional sacrifices, part of making herself over in concession to the track. A few details of that alter ego seem part of her more permanent fabric—short, straw-colored hair and an ana-lytical way of addressing things. The rest she easily resurrects, lay-ing them out before me like an architect reconstructing a blueprint.

"I did everything that I could to get away from the feminine image," she explains, pausing to deliver a silky "No, thank you" to the waitress offering us drinks. "I acted tough and cool, and I never cried."

Everything became a test of mettle. The first time an injured horse collapsed under her, she made a point of gazing on icily even when the men around her turned their heads and covered their eyes.

"I learned right away to control my emotions," she continues, using her fingers to tick off each article in the female rider ensemble. "If I got upset or angry, I just held it in. Then I'd release it onto the track."

Physically, she was small and lithe with uncanny balance, her weight always perfectly collected over the horse's withers so that the animal could brace itself against her as it stretched across the track. She could gun a mount into the melee along with the most aggressive jocks, but she was also practiced in patience. She knew when to ease up and let the horse's instincts take over, maintaining communication with a simple tug on the mouth as a reminder that she was still there. Equine movement is a complex mechanism. To maintain forward momentum, a horse's mind and body engage in an elaborate loop of feedback and adjustment. In the case of a less-sensitive rider, a human's added, unpredictable weight knocking around up top can throw such inborn symmetry into irretrievable confusion. Donna matched her movements to her mounts like a shared internal metronome.

But natural ability wasn't enough. Donna lacked the strength of the male riders. Sometimes her feet slipped in the stirrups and her legs bowed and wobbled by the finish of each ride. While the men around her concentrated on paring down food to bare subsistence levels, Donna designed a high-protein diet that tricked her body into building muscle instead of fat. She studied the riders built lean and rangy as she was, then analyzed and adopted their particular strengths. She taught herself to wield a whip, maneuver along the rail, and shoot from the starting gate in the image of the profession's most lauded masters.

"I consciously developed a style that looked good," she admits. "Looking familiar to people, so they could recognize pieces of other jockeys, was almost as important as actually riding well. Everyone was watching me carefully. I couldn't afford to let them think they'd found any flaws."

Each mistake even insinuated, each afternoon skipped—usually to recover from injury, because a day off for pure pleasure verged on suicidal—could be measured in mounts permanently lost to other jockeys. Plenty of owners were still fence-sitting as to whether a woman could be strong enough to ride against the boys. They'd grab any excuse to drop Donna from their horses. Loyalty arises through a history together. For women and race riding, such a history didn't yet exist.

Perhaps courtesy of her mother, Donna read this complex equation from the start. She deliberately played the chameleon, all grace and fluidity on horseback but bold and brassy when the situation demanded. One of her first seasons at Churchill Downs, she won the opening race on opening day and, for that half hour until race number two, Donna became top rider of the meet. The next morning she tracked down D. Wayne Lukas, the tribal chief of trainers. She informed him that she had been leading rider, and he'd do well to hire her. She volunteered to work his horses in the mornings, even if he wouldn't guarantee her a mount on any of them come afternoon. Lukas didn't take her up on any of her offers right away, but Donna made sure he saw her at the track, working every single morning and every single afternoon. He noticed. Eventually, he tested her on a few young horses, including a colt named Hennessey, who would take her to the Breeders' Cup.

To succeed like Donna meant to succeed required a full commitment. It required pouring all corners of personal and professional self—not to mention four broken noses, six concussions, miscellaneous cracked vertebrae, busted ribs and collarbones—into the cause.

"For me, and I think for any woman, riding can't just be a job. It has to become who you are."

AFTER ELEVEN and a half years as a jockey—having finally earned enough hard-driven respect to equal any other jock in town—Donna did something that great riders simply don't do. She retired. When jockeys quit riding, it's usually because they've been irreparably injured, caved in to age and arthritis, or, most often, can no longer make weight. Donna exited at the top of her game. She left to marry a Kentucky-based trainer, and confined her mounts to exercising his horses in their morning workouts.

"It was the hardest choice I've ever made," she tells me, without hesitation. "But I realized there were other things I wanted in my life."

The track is lonely for female riders, certainly not conducive to a well-rounded existence. In a world twined tight by communities— the jocks, the trainers, the grooms, the exercise riders—Donna didn't fit anywhere. Maintaining a steel-rod exterior meant avoiding emotional relationships. Attachment made you look too much like a girl.

In the midst of her career upswing, Donna had caught the attention of a round-faced, hardworking southern horseman named Frankie Brothers. They dated for a while, but when things got serious, Donna ducked out with the excuse that she needed to focus on her career. Frankie didn't buy it, nor did he fade away. They would date a little, split a little. He asked Donna to marry him. She said absolutely not. A working jockey can't marry a working trainer, not without bowing to complicated conflict of interest rules that make it impossible to pursue a legitimate career. Still, Frankie didn't seem to get the message. He wasn't interested in Donna Barton, spectacular girl jockey. He wanted the person lodged behind the career.

May-May journeyed well into spinsterhood before she finally married in her mid-thirties. Her family had long written her off as a black sheep who would never return to anyone's fold. She was working as a nurse for the Kennicott Copper Company on Latouche Island off the Alaskan coast, one of only three dozen local women, including the occupants of a bordello in nearby McCarthy. My grandfather, a second-generation Irishman, had worked his way across Canada manning railroad telegraph offices and memorizing full volumes of Robert Burns. He and May-May met when he was named supply officer for Kennicott Hospital. Soon he was traveling the hundred miles down from the copper mines every other day to check on misplaced gauze bandages or deliver an extra bottle of iodine.

They began meeting most evenings outside the two-room hospital. He'd offer up a scraggly flower or a smuggled pair of cigarettes. Then they'd go to dinner at the single restaurant in town, a gaslit bar serving nothing but salmon steaks and whiskey. On weekends, they would row a dinghy out into the sound, May-May taking up the oars when my grandfather inevitably got lost. Less than a year later, on a business trip to Seattle, he bought an ill-cut diamond off a trading ship docked in the harbor and, upon returning to Kennicott, kneeled down in the sawdust covering the bar floor and proposed. It took six months for her mail-order wedding dress to arrive from Baltimore. They were married in the Latouche Island chapel in front of a congregation of miners with well-scrubbed fingernails and ill-fitting suits.

Marriage meant many things in the 1920s, even in trailblazer territory. It meant the end of glacier walks, pack trips, and bighorn sheep hunts accompanied by an unmarried male trail guide. It meant the arrival of my aunt and then my father, and a move down to the more civilized environs of Seattle. When I was a teenager, I tried to convince May-May she should resent having been forced to sacrifice her independence for something tame and shared. In return, she asked me which I liked better, galloping Grey Lady across the prairies or the two of us ankling slowly down a mountain slope toward the river opening up below.

"I like both," I told her.

"So did I."

Eventually, Donna realized that her feelings for Frankie weren't the sort that could be beaten out over a racetrack. Growing up mobile and adaptable, she had spent years polishing that skill of not needing other people, a survival tactic far preferable to missing them once they disappeared.

"I was so independent, so focused on taking care of myself, that I had no idea what to do when someone wanted to take care of me. I had no idea how to connect to another person. I had to learn how to be vulnerable."

As she learned, she found she didn't crave that physical outlet of the track quite so intensely. She'd fallen out of love with her job and in love with a person.

"It was frightening to ride," she admits. "And it was even more frightening to quit. But jockeys have to follow their instincts. Instinctually, I knew both of them were the right thing to do."

RACING FANS tend to keep a mental catalog of unforgettable jockeys and unforgettable horses. Occasionally, two such phenomena will even bump up against one another to form an unforgettable ride. I found my first of these a few months after that inaugural visit to Longacres, in a small stakes contest broadcast from Churchill Downs a few weeks after Alydar's Kentucky Derby.

The race favorite was a rangy gray filly, her jockey a faded champion who could still weave figure eights around younger riders. The pair broke from the gate relaxed and easy, tucked along the rail, and covered the first half of the race without expending an extra atom of effort. Coming around the far turn, the jockey still had his horse settled inside, perfectly poised to shoot through the smallest of openings. He'd found that absolute coupling, animal and rider rocking together as one. Then the horse in front of them wilted and began to drift outward. The space they'd been waiting for opened up along the rail. For the first time, I felt that exact instant in which the jockey had to open his reins or perhaps just touch the filly lightly on her neck, whatever they'd agreed upon to send forth the message to charge.

Then the instant was gone.

For some unfathomable reason, the jockey balked. He tightened his reins, sat back in the saddle, and let the space close. A moment later he was steering his mount to the uncongested outside edge of the track. In that shaving of a second, the harmony they'd shared dissolved like a genie stuffed back inside its lamp. The jockey tried to make up for it, slashing the air with his whip, but they were going at cross-purposes now. An immediate and unscalable wall had risen up between the two.

"Why did he *do* that?" I demanded, practically choking on eight-year-old indignation as they scraped across the finish line full lengths behind the leader.

"He's riding scared," May-May replied.

"What for?"

May-May filled in the details, a near fatal fall two years earlier, a cracked skull and a bruised heart, and months away from the track. A jockey who'd made it back but left invincibility behind and started skirting around the edges of a life he'd once taken straight to the heart.

I stood up, hands on hips. "I'll never be like that," I announced.

May-May smiled. "I hope you won't."

It's the only time I ever remember her telling me what not to do.

On the surface, jockeys come across as all bravado. They file into the paddock before a race clad in amusement park colors, kicking up dirt with their boots, spitting on the ground, flipping, slapping, spinning their whips. Whatever their attitude, they've donned it— slim and neat, taut and cocky, sauntering along unfazed or rushing in late with straps and energy awhirl. Fallibility has been temporarily shed.

"You just can't think about it," Angel told me, when I asked him about riding scared. "You do and your future is over." He mimed slitting his throat.

"You can't think about the fear," Donna echoed. "But you always know it exists."

Race riding is just that, a study in contrast: knowing it's possible to become mortal again, even as you're unfolding your wings.

Chapter Five

GENEROSITY:

Breaking onto the Backstretch

O n opening day of my second spring as a racing fan, a few
months after I'd turned nine years old, May-May and I
left the city and set out for Longacres in the muddy pink
half-light of dawn. We arrived at the track just as the sun emerged
from a thin layer of fog. The gates to the front parking lot were

cinched shut with a giant padlock. Instead, we followed a long slop-
ing road past the box seats and shuttered hot-dog stands to a clutch
of barns on the far side of the track. The guard nodded at us before
May-May had time to roll down her front window, lifting the one-
armed wooden gate to let us through. We were on the backstretch.

May-May had explained mornings at the racetrack long before I
ever witnessed one myself. Starting at dawn and often earlier,
horses stretched and circled, building muscles and refining talents
until they were ready to cut away at an afternoon track. Horses
working up to a race were breezed, given an easy run that could
billow their muscles without taxing their strength, then handed
over to hotwalkers whose feet traced endless figure eights in front
of the barns to cool their charges down. The backside of the track
was the domain of grooms who rose at four each morning to brush
and bathe and feed, and exercise riders who passed lifetimes negotiating that morning track. You only worked on the backstretch if
you went in purely for Thoroughbreds. By the time you landed
there, all exterior glitz had dissolved.

That morning at Longacres, there were horses everywhere,
walking dirt paths to and from the track, lined up outside
shedrows with steam rising off their backs. They came within feet
of us. I could see each flexed muscle carving grooves along their
coats, and sweat lathered against their necks like laundry suds.
Sunlight glanced off horses and riders so both looked newly lacquered. They were easily the most beautiful things I'd ever seen.

We only had to turn around and a whole second world
unfolded, the one of the racetrack itself, where those same Thoroughbreds wove in and out, forming jigsaw patterns over the
course. Some looked awesome, chiseled like boxers primed for the
ring. Others were fine-boned and agile, so lean there couldn't have
been a millimeter to spare for anything but locomotion. Along the
inside rail, animals smoked past at a breathtaking run. Farther
out, near the center of the track, they traveled a slow gallop, the
exercise riders curbing their reins so tightly the horses' necks
arched like shepherd's crooks and their hooves started to take
them sideways with energy unspent in pulsing ahead. Some ani-

mals had no one aboard them at all. They just danced at the end of a lead rope connecting them to another rider who galloped alongside. May-May kept me close to her the entire time, one hand clamped on my shoulder or her fingers laced tightly through mine.

Occasionally a series of yells would swell up among those circling the track: "Loose horse! Loose horse!" Heads would swivel to pin down the renegade careening solo across the track. The first time it happened on the opposite side of the oval. I had to squint to spot another rider pin the loose animal against a hedge and collect the dangling reins in his hand. But the second time, I saw the horse break even before the call. She had been standing still against the outside rail only a few yards down from us, her rider leaning lazily back in the saddle, when something—a scent in the wind, the crack of a branch—cut an invisible trip wire. She reared up onto her hind legs, dumping the rider into the bushes behind her as if shaking loose a fly. Then she twirled around and wheeled out through the entrance gap, loose reins fluttering behind her like ribbons.

May-May moved quickly for her eighty-eight years, yanking us both deep into the bushes behind us. But I moved faster. I slipped left when she went right and darted out onto the dirt path just as the filly came barreling off the track. For a second her head rolled in my direction, and she pulled up her front legs again, letting loose a high, bubbling whinny. Her eyes rolled white and she drew back her lips.

I'd read and reread those passages from *The Black Stallion* where the boy Alec stepped straight into the raging fury of the Black and subdued him with his own small hands. I'd spent hours imagining myself in that same situation, elaborate fantasies that involved winding my fingers through the stallion's mane and using sweet talk to soothe the savage beast. Now that the longed-for moment had arrived, I didn't even move. A stranger grabbed my arm, knocking me back toward the bushes, and I clutched at May-May's woolly cardigan. All trace of devil-riding courage fled.

The horse left us, turning outward and tearing a few yards toward the barns before her manic energy began to dissipate. She halted, quivering, in the middle of the path. A groom carrying a handful of carrots approached her, clucking and cooing, and she scuttled backward a few steps. He stood still, waiting as her breathing eased and the whites disappeared from the edges of her eyeballs. He tried a second time, still moving slow and easy, and a second time she skittered away. Again he waited, stone still, listening to her breath and seeming to match it to his own. On the third try, it was the horse who took the first twitching steps. This time, when the groom slid his hand forward, she took the offered carrot. She allowed him to run a gentle hand up her cheek, take hold of the bridle, and lead her home.

I was uncharacteristically silent for the rest of the morning. When we eventually pulled into the porticoed driveway of May-May's condominium building, she turned off the engine and looked in my direction.

"Did that horse scare you?"

I nodded. "I couldn't do anything."

"What did you want to do?"

I told her about Alec and *The Black Stallion,* how I'd planned to reveal unknown but prodigious horse-soothing talents, and how I'd let myself down in every possible way.

"You're forgetting something," she told me. "The horse."

"What about her?"

"It was all about her. Nothing to do with you."

I nodded again as if I understood, but I didn't quite. Not yet. It took several summers' worth of morning visits to fully absorb what May-May'd meant, how the moment I set foot on the backstretch Thoroughbreds eclipsed all else. Every step, thought, action led back to them. Backstretch people had a kind of romance different from my own, one rooted in divining and serving the horse's needs. The moment they lost that equine rhythm and got pumped a fraction too full of themselves, the horses called them back by wheeling into the air and breaking free.

IN 1944, during the final stages of World War II, Longacres racetrack had suffered a desperate shortage of backstretch labor. Grooms, riders, and hotwalkers had been drafted, and too many didn't return. Meanwhile, with a few exceptions—like California's Santa Anita Park, which served as a Japanese internment camp for the duration of the war—tracks flourished, buoyed by the same hunger for escapism that filled dance halls and movie houses. In January 1945, the Office of War Mobilization and Reconversion proclaimed too much gasoline and tire rubber were wasted in transporting racing fans to and from the source of their enjoyment and, for the next five months, all tracks went dark. But until then, backstretches all over the country scrambled to keep apace with the front side of the game.

Trainers from Longacres tacked up pleas for part-time workers at local stables and feed stores, hoping to lure the migrant workers headed east to pick raspberries and the spring apple crop. May-May read one of the hand-printed signs posted outside Countess Highland and Dr. Rhythm's barn. At 5:00 A.M. the following Saturday, she showed up for work. A number of the trainers knew her already, knew her prowess as a fine harness driver and her affinity for all aspects of the Thoroughbred. Even so, when it came to the workplace, the old ideas stuck. Ladies watched races from the stands, or perhaps owned a Thoroughbred or two. They never pulled on rubber boots and mucked out a stall. May-May waited for close to an hour as the smattering of workers lined up alongside her were claimed and led away. Finally a young trainer, who'd lost two assistants to the war effort, beckoned her over.

"What do you know about horses?" he asked. They spoke for several minutes, long enough for him to realize she probably knew more than he did, for him to bounce between need and propriety. Long enough for him to offer her a job.

For three months, May-May spent four mornings a week volunteering as a groom for the young trainer and his motley collection of horses. She picked dirt out of hooves, hoisted full hay nets into stalls, jammed a pitchfork into bales of straw bedding, then drove back to Seattle just as my father and his sister arrived home from school. The local ladies watched her come and go in her flannel shirt and manure-streaked jodhpurs. Not for the first time, May-May sent the neighborhood grapevine buzzing.

At the end of her first week at the track, my grandfather dug out the old hand-printed sign from Countess Highland's stall and hung it on their front door.

LADIES
KEEP OUT

Once again, the ladies all stayed clear.

RACING CAN be a study in geology, bits of the past constantly bubbling up through surface cracks to spill over into the present, lives intersecting and overlapping. I often visit the track now and find another piece of May-May, people who trigger some tiny echo of who she was and what she believed. Perhaps no one else would meet a wiry black groom named Clevie and see a fifty-five-year-old genteel southern spitfire. When I form a picture of May-May working the backside at Longacres, Clevie Raines is who I see.

Clevie has been grooming horses most of his sixty years. He was born in Georgia, raised in the Carolinas, but when he mentions his roots, he's talking about the track. I got to know him at Gulfstream Park in Florida, though he spends the summer and fall months in New York. For the past decade, he's been hooked up with a trainer named Frank Alexander, a long-term relationship as far as stable help goes. Before that, he got around.

Like the majority of backstretch labor, home for Clevie is a cramped, utilitarian room in one of the on-site barracks erected for grooms and exercise riders so they'll always be near. He falls asleep every night around 9:00, bathed in the television flicker of old movies, then wakes up at 3:30 and watches an *Untouchables* rerun over coffee and a cigarette. He's at the barn by 3:45, beginning his workday against a backdrop of shuffling hooves and heavy sighs. Most of the other grooms don't show up until around 4:15, but Clevie likes to arrive early.

"I don't care to be rushed," he explains when I join him one morning, already a few hours into his regular routine. He has the loose, agile build that seems a guaranteed offshoot of physical work with horses. That day, his own personal touches include a tidy mustache, a gold neck chain, and a neon-yellow T-shirt from the 1996 Atlanta Olympics.

"Some people just want to get things done as fast as they can and collect the money. Me, I take pride in my job."

I sit on a bale of hay just outside the stall door as Clevie begins cleaning around the petite, dark-bay filly inside, all the while singing, humming, talking under his breath. He begins by clipping her head collar to an eyehook fastened to the far wall.

"This is just so she won't go getting any funny ideas about escaping," he tells me, patting her on the shoulder. "Or about trying to kick me in the behind."

His routine is comfortable, purposely soothing since Thoroughbreds respond all too willingly to stress. He replaces the hay-flecked water in her plastic bucket, then picks up a pitchfork and begins tossing straw bedding out the door onto a torn canvas tarp. He spreads open a fresh bale, sifting it through his hands to separate the clumps, until the floor is evenly covered in a deep fluffy carpet. Then he mixes oats, bran, and carrots with vitamins and medicines in a red rubber tub, and rubs the filly's back as she consumes her breakfast. Some days he'll throw a slight variation into the routine, a pack of peppermint Lifesavers slipped onto her tongue one by one, or a sponge bath when it's a little too cold for a hose.

"Horses can get bored just like people do," he explains. "You need to spice things up for them. I treat my horses just like I would a lady. If she's happy, then so am I."

He shows me the different brushes he'll use for grooming, fingering them like old friends—the concentric rows of rubber teeth on the oval-shaped currycomb that pulls loose hairs from the undercoat, the burnt-orange rubber glove he rubs around the hard-to-reach spots like the top of the throat and the backs of the ears.

"Some people," he complains, popping an accusatory finger against the glove itself, "use this as a shortcut to wipe the whole horse. But there's no shortcut to getting this filly shining in bloom."

Clevie always opts for the currycomb, followed by a sturdy, hard-bristled brush. He demonstrates the smooth circular strokes in the air before laying the comb against her flank.

"Nobody appreciates technique anymore," he offers.

I would guess that the horses do.

CLEVIE'S RACETRACK career began when he was twenty-six, more by fluke than anything else. He showed up at the track looking for work as an exercise rider, because he was small and strong and liked to gamble. He rode for a few years, but the physical wear and tear showed up early, and the chance of crippling injury seemed too high. He had no glittering jockey ambitions; he simply wanted a space amid the competition and camaraderie of the backstretch. He'd been studying the electronics business, planning for an office job and a financially stable future, but he barely hesitated over the sacrifice. He'd heard the siren song of the racehorse.

He tends to three horses at a time, his charges always shifting due to injuries, old horses retiring, new blood shipping in.

"I've developed a reputation," he lets me know, kissing at the filly to get her to inch over in the stall. "No one around here wants to work with any difficult personalities. But me, I see it as kind of a challenge." He chuckles. "If things get slow, I just might take out an ad in the Yellow Pages. Got a nag who's mean and nasty? Call Clevie."

He knows the intimate geography of each of his charges, like knowing a lover or a child. He can trace the lick of white hair hidden behind one's ear, how another likes his hay net hung a bit lower for easy access, the individual patterns of night-eyes—small knobby calluses that distinguish each animal as distinctly as a fingerprint—on all of the twelve legs under his care. He spends more time with them than anyone else, arriving just as the animals are first shaking themselves awake then returning again at four for the late-afternoon feeding. He ices their legs and wipes their feet and clucks at their little idiosyncrasies. He's usually the first to spot an injury, the earliest clues etched in the way a horse stands, shifts, smells from one day to the next.

"If I see something's off, I just watch it. Then, if it's still there the next day, I'll watch it some more. Sometimes I'll say something, but mostly I wait for them to figure it out. People don't listen to what a groom thinks like they used to. They don't want to believe I know better than anyone else."

When one of his horses is running, Clevie will brush her until she glows, perhaps soak her hooves in ice water to take away any stiffness, and carefully wrap her rear legs in bandages to prevent burns from the coarse dirt of the track. Then he spruces up himself with a quick shave, pressed blue jeans, and a fresh button-up shirt. About half an hour before the race, he'll lead her over to the paddock, carrying a blanket for after the race and a brush for last-minute primping, all contained in a canvas tote bag printed with the legend of a local Florida bank. He'll watch the race from just outside the winner's circle, maybe sneaking off to the betting windows to put a little something down first. Once all the excitement has passed, he's on hand to spread the blanket over her on cool days or splash a hose across her back when it's warm, then guide her toward bath, dinner, and bed back at the barn.

The garnishes in Clevie's life are spare: evenings spent with a few hours of TV, three or four beers, and a good meal. He claims to be an expert cook and promises next time I come around he's going to whip us up a southern feast—smothered pork chops, lima beans and broccoli, risen biscuits, and corn bread done the Carolina way, with pats of butter melted inside. Grooms' salaries vary; the country's backstretches have yet to unionize, but pay usually settles in at around $300 a week. When he has a few extra bucks, Clevie might blow them on his one day off, taking a lady friend out for dinner and his second true love—dancing. He shows me a few moves, swiveling his hips around the back end of the stall. The filly gazes curiously over one shoulder for a few seconds, then decides it's nothing to be alarmed or particularly excited about and returns to staring at the wall.

"What do you think?" he asks, puffing a bit as he comes to a stop. "You don't see many sixty-year-olds so swift and light-footed as I am." He slaps his companion on the rear. "They keep you young, don't they? She's my magic formula."

He says he thinks he might retire in a year or two, maybe get married again or take a cruise someplace hot.

"Won't you miss it?" I ask.

"What's to miss? I've done my job. No one around here's ever gonna forget Clevie."

ONCE GROOMS like Clevie ran thick on the backstretch. He's a lingering piece of the old school, a time when a barn equaled a tiny community. In off-hours, a hotwalker might cut hair, an exercise rider sideline patching britches. In the nineteenth century, the "stable lads" who cared for the horses were true lads, apprentices twelve or thirteen years old. The trainer's obligation included three square meals, outfitting each boy with a full suit of clothes, and delivering them to church on Sunday morning.

Clevie's history at the track spans a couple of wives, ten children, and fourteen grandchildren. Years before anyone dreamed up in-office day care, he used to bring his kids to the barn in their strollers. But times change. Racing stables are more akin to conglomerates now, with employees appearing and disappearing over the course of a month or two, searching out higher wages and grander opportunities or simply fading away because the work proves too hard. Clevie likes to complain about the sad state of today's grooming population.

"All the good ones are dead and gone" is his most popular refrain. "This game used to depend on teamwork, but not any more. Now everyone's got greedy. They just want in and out, cheap and fast, and they don't give a damn about anything else. These days, you come in the back gate and you don't know what you're going to find."

Later that same morning, he shakes his head at a handful of

young grooms slinging feed into the stalls fifteen minutes early, then dodging off to watch the races.

"That's not how you run an outfit. Lord have mercy on these horses, that's all I have to say."

A few minutes later his affront melts into a hoot of laughter when the boss shows up and those same grooms scamper to hide their open cans of beer. One of them saunters up to Clevie and offers to help him drag a heap of soiled straw to the manure pile. They lurch in step toward the far end of the barn, discussing who's going to triumph in the following afternoon's featured race. Clevie's attention to what isn't fades, roped in again by everything that is.

AROUND NOON, when all three of his horses have been exercised, fed, bathed, and bandaged, Clevie sits down next to me on the hay bale to wait. For a few minutes, we say nothing at all. I'm reminded how I love this about racing, too—the soft spots and ebbs and silences, the way ripping intensity is always balanced by contemplation.

Clevie's a storyteller, pure South in speed and drawl. He begins reminiscing about the pedigrees of his past charges in the way some people can recite the Bible, weaving back names and generations as if they were his own kin. Illnesses and triumphs, race fractions, bloodlines and broken records all form a part of his verbal photo album. He also knows a few off-color yarns about Angel Cordero, which he gleefully passes on when I reveal Angel as my onetime icon. He then gets me to promise three times over that I won't repeat any of them.

"Cordero would ride anything," he says. "He didn't have an inch of the fear in him. That's all you've ever got to write down about him."

The last story we get to is about Clevie himself, about how just last spring he rode in the back end of a trailer all the way from New York to Ocala, Florida, with a colt who turned colicky forty-five minutes into the trip. For twenty-eight hours, he held the horse's head cradled in his arms, knowing that as soon as the animal lay down and tried to roll he could twist his intestines into a fatal knot. Clevie didn't expect extra pay for his care. There's no possibility of promotion or even a bonus day off to catch up on sleep. He just stayed awake all night, bobbing down the interstate, because Thoroughbreds are fragile. Three of them need Clevie to survive.

I don't know whether the backside of a racetrack creates such generosity in a person or simply teases it out, the same way it can tease speed out of a fresh new colt. But there's something about stepping down those open shedrows that makes you seem a little less important, so that mucking out stalls, holding colicky heads, or just stepping back into the bushes doesn't feel much like a sacrifice. Those horses have a way of filling you. Anything else becomes just pocket change.

DURING MY senior year of college, an acquaintance who wrote for the school paper invited me to visit the Santa Anita backstretch with her one morning. She was doing a story on offbeat local activities and wanted to include the races. We drove out early and parked in the near-empty lot alongside the track, a green-and-yellow fantasy palace set in the palm of the San Gabriel Mountains. It was sunny and only the slightest bit smoggy, so the brush-covered mountains were etched clear against the sky.

A publicity assistant met us at the front gate and led us to the lip of the track where trainers and jockeys had collected to trade opinions and information. Gamblers swarmed around them clutching heavily marked copies of the *Racing Form* and hoping for the gift of insider knowledge let slip. We leaned against the rails for a while and watched the horses work. I focused on the legs, churning and circling, beating out a tattoo I could almost separate from the physical presence of the Thoroughbreds themselves.

Eventually, my friend went off with the publicity assistant for a tour of the stable area. I stayed behind, hovering on the edges of the horse talk with my back to the dirt path leading from the barns to the track.

"Hey! Hey! Hey!"

He must have called three or four times before I realized he was talking to me. I turned and saw an exercise rider standing along-side a muscular chestnut colt who was still blowing and sweaty from his gallop around the track.

"Can you hold him?"

"I'm not . . ." I tried to find a simple phrase that could explain why at that point in time I didn't take hold of horses, especially Thoroughbreds. In the space before the words, he shoved the reins into my hand.

"He's an angel. No trouble. I'll be right back." He sprinted off toward the barns before I could object.

At first, I didn't even look at the horse, just at my hands. They were shaking ever so slightly, but enough for the colt to sense every ounce of discomfort quivering through my body, down the reins, and into his own. He stood still, gazing toward the track with a gentle curiosity that didn't seem to demand any sort of action, and waited for me to adjust. After a minute or two, he must have decided I wasn't quite as fragile as I'd first seemed, because he began to shake his head, challenging me to pay a bit more attention. I reached out to touch his neck, the way I'd seen other exercise riders do to calm horses dancing back and forth along the track. I started talking to him, inventing a little singsong melody, and the head-tossing slowed. I flattened my palm against the sweaty hair along his neck, still humming. Neither of us moved.

"He likes you." I jumped. The exercise rider had returned and stood at my shoulder. "You want to get on?"

I laughed. "I'm not a good enough rider for this one."

"You can to talk to him. That's all he needs." I shook my head, not quite sure whether he was kidding. I knew the open flow of give-and-take that had to go on between us should I climb aboard. Whatever his exercise rider might have believed, I certainly couldn't give that colt what he needed.

"Maybe next time," I said, handing back the reins.

He shrugged and lifted one foot, indicating he wanted me to

give him a leg up. I'd seen it done often enough in the paddock to know the proper movements, so I laced my fingers under his knee and lifted just as he jumped. He was so light I felt as if I'd simply cupped my hands under a current of air and sent it spiraling up.

Before they turned to walk away, I laid my hand against the colt's neck one more time. His weight leaned all the way into mine. It felt as if he didn't want me to go.

LIKE MOST backstretch work, riding horses in the mornings is unsung hard labor. Exercise riders arrive predawn and by ten o'clock one of them will have climbed aboard nearly every horse on the backside—walking, jogging, galloping constant circles to ensure that the star players stay fit for the demands of the afternoons. They're the same general shape as the jockeys who'll replace them on race day, but a bit younger, older, heavier, creakier, a bit more or less of something that's kept them off that afternoon track. They get no share in the tropical-colored decoration, or in the hundreds of thousands of dollars a top jockey can earn in a single year. What remains is the appetite for danger, and the link to, and love for, the racehorse.

Occasionally, a rider will evince enough skill and forward drive to rise up from among the rest. One morning in Florida last February, I scaled a wooden viewing tower on the backside and waited for Gulfstream Park's resident virtuoso to glide past in his green protective vest printed with vintage champagne bottles. I heard him before I saw him, tucked right underneath me along the outside edge of the track. He was babying along a filly who looked as though she wanted nothing more than to bolt back to the barn.

"Hey, hey princess," he trilled, massaging her neck as they stepped forward. "Hey, good-looking, what you got cooking?"

His name is Findley Bishop. Though he's known for his flashy style—strutting around in wraparound sunglasses with a cell phone latched to his hip and whips jammed into each back pocket—his true talent lies in the fact that he's a magic man. The craziest of horses get passed to Findley, those with tempers so frayed they can't even hold it together long enough to circle the track. Under his spell, time and again, such hopeless cases are fed in fragmented and come out the other side whole.

Twenty-five years ago, Findley came to the United States from Belize, where he'd worked as an exercise rider and then a jockey with dreams of becoming the next Angel Cordero. In the States, he started riding under contract for New Jersey track kingpin Jimmy Iselin, an arrangement orchestrated because Findley's aunt worked as Iselin's maid. He spent fifteen years race riding, but his weight was too high, his personal life too hectic for his gift with horses to translate into success. Ten years ago, he finally shed both ends of the seesaw and moved to Florida in the hopes of starting again.

Free from the pressures of performance, Findley resurrected what proved a genius for communicating with racehorses. Word spread among the trainers that if you had a difficult horse—one bent on dumping riders, bucking mid-gallop, spooking at shadows—Findley could break it of its sins. He charges extra for his services, climbing on twenty horses a day instead of the usual ten or twelve, and driving among the three Florida tracks—Gulfstream, Calder, and Hialeah—in a turquoise convertible littered with riding helmets, empty beer cans, and exercise saddles the size of table napkins.

Later that same morning at Gulfstream, he idled his car alongside me and I asked about the filly I'd seen him aboard earlier. He immediately pulled over onto a patch of dead grass and hopped out to fill me in.

"This horse is tiny, but she's got a heart big like a mountain," he gushed, taking a swig from a bottle of orange juice, then offering it to me. "She goes out on the track, and she gets all tense, makes this big ball of silliness inside of her. But Findley knows what to do."

Once grounded, Findley moves like an unbonded atom. The muscles of his arms are round and tight against his skin, his elbows thickly callused from rubbing against the withers of so many horses. He can't converse without physical accompaniment, fingers, hands, arms, knees all battling for something to say.

"She just wants love, the same as you or me. I can make it so she loves the track. She'll be like a child playing." He mimed a kid kicking a soccer ball. "Like she can't wait until tomorrow, and it's time to go out for more."

"What are you going to do with her?"

"You watch me." He checked the car clock, then plopped down on the sheepskin cover of his front seat, tossing the empty orange juice bottle onto the floor next to him. "Twenty-four hours. That's all I need."

The next morning I spotted him aboard the filly again. He rode with his body pitched full forward, his head next to her ears so he could keep mooching and flirting as they moved along. His knees were braced against her shoulders and his hands kept traveling between the reins and the soft hair along her neck, tiny lapping motions as if just tickling the notion of trust. Already I could see her starting to unwind, her gait less jerky, her neck not quite as sharply bowed. Ever so slowly, she was realizing how it was to be the center of somebody's world.

RACEHORSES, EVEN the sweet-tempered kind, are unpredictable. They're born with a flight mechanism that tells them to break wild at anything they can't immediately understand. Any exercise rider, any jockey, runs up against this sort of danger whenever he climbs atop a Thoroughbred. Beyond this is Findley. Sometimes Thoroughbreds arrive at a place from which even they can't figure out how to return. Their world goes dizzy with potential threats, and they kick and shy at every single one. They acquire habits that threaten to get them permanently disbarred— throwing stamping fits as they're loaded into the starting gate or "savaging," reaching over and sinking their teeth into a rival's hip or shoulder in the heat of a race. Sometimes such fragile temperament is their genetic stamp, a quality passed down the bloodline alongside quick acceleration or turned-in knees. Other times, one early incidence of rough treatment—a whip or a chain or the flat of a hand against the head—can embed a lifelong belief that humans shouldn't be trusted. Without warning, such horses can plunge into fences, back through hedges, and rear up so high they topple over backward. A rider is just that much more baggage to be shed in the panic.

In the early years of the sport, someone like Findley would have been driven out of town before winning permission to employ his ever so gentle touch on a racehorse. Early animal behaviorism was largely rooted in one principle only: To control a horse you must break its spirit. Greek charioteers used bridles armed with spiked cheekpieces, so that each pull on the reins drilled a pointed bit of metal into the outside edge of a horse's mouth. In the thirteenth century B.C. Egyptian horses were steered via thick leather bands roped around the ends of their noses. Since horses can't breath through their mouths, the sensitive tissue between their nostrils was then sliced open to allow for a more comfortable passage of air. In Elizabethan England, trainers would tie a spiked ball below a horse's abdomen and link it to a cord the rider could pull upon, yanking the blades up into the horse's belly as soon as it misbehaved. For more extreme cases, a stable boy would stand behind the horse holding a pole with a tomcat tied to one end, belly up, teeth and claws exposed. As soon as the horse displayed any independent spirit, the cat was thrust between its back legs and allowed to savage at will.

By the 1800s, techniques for taming any willful edges had grown less painful but possibly even crueler. Racehorses were kept in line with grueling exercise gallops, covering up to four miles each day over hard ground. They worked clad in heavy wool rugs designed to sweat out any excess weight or energy. As soon as they stood still again, the sweat was cleaned off with long metal scrapers and fresh blankets and hoods applied. The horses lived in windowless stables, kept roasting hot by steadily stoked woodstoves, and their drinking water was strictly limited. Lest any of them still feel feisty, they received daily "purging" concoctions of herbal diuretics. By the time they reached the racetracks, they were gaunt as scarecrows and drained of any energy beyond that required to advance in a straight line. If they tried, they received a steady whip to the flanks, thighs, and testicles.

Findley's belief that a horse will learn more readily out of faith than fear is relatively recent, a by-product of horse whisperers like Monty Roberts and a growing understanding of animal psychology. These gentle roots don't trace back to the racetrack, but to early cowboys who used to tame wild horses by studying their natural rhythms, then re-creating them back at the barn. Such range riders operated with the barest of resources, and they couldn't afford to give up on a creature just because it came in a difficult package. Instead, they searched out a shared vision or soothing note that could turn whatever had shattered back into a whole. Some of the horses Findley rides become superstars, winning races like the Hong Kong Cup and the Kentucky Derby. For most, victory just means learning how to relish the run.

Findley's personal style is far from understated. On the rare occasions he finds himself aboard a well-behaved horse, he's wont to begin trick riding—dipping out of the saddle at a dead run to touch his foot to the ground, or standing balanced like a waterskier atop a galloping back. Once when he was charged with accompanying a particularly nervous runner all the way into the paddock before a race, he did so clad in a spotless white satin tuxedo. Such grandstanding isn't always best for business. Trainers have been known to recoil from his tendency to claim full credit for any horse he helps turn around, or from his loose-lips policy of broadcasting the idiosyncrasies of all his mounts.

"I don't work for people, I work with them," Findley regularly informs me. "They need me. No one else in the world can do what I do. Every day, I'm making racing history."

Once he phoned me up in New York just after midnight and announced:

"Everyone here says, 'Findley is the mailman.' Ask me why."

"Why?"

"Because I *always* deliver." Then he hung up.

Such talk is too heavy gilding, swelling his gifts to cartoon levels.

It can require peeling back a layer or two of hotshot to find the underpinning of sacrifice that links all those on the backstretch. But it's there. In order to make space for his horses, Findley has shoved aside everything else.

His offtrack life is filled with all the accoutrements of burning empty time. He watches the races in the afternoons, wearing a sports coat and a gold tie, drinking screwdrivers from plastic cups, and betting on the horses he rides in the mornings no matter what their afternoon odds. The one time I ate dinner with him, it was sandwiches of sliced turkey, white bread, and mayonnaise shoved into his mouth while standing over the kitchen sink. His Florida condominium was all white walls and mirrors, littered with racing memorabilia and a bar stocked with every sweet, undrinkable liqueur imaginable. The television played race recaps in the background. His girlfriend was watching a movie on the other TV upstairs.

"I've never kicked a woman out," Findley explained between mouthfuls of sandwich. "But none of them stick around for more than a few years. Eventually they realize I've got another lover. My horses will always comes first. This is my life."

I asked him if he ever got scared maneuvering aboard such delicate construction. I'd watched his impeccable touch and sense of command often enough to believe his prowess stemmed from absolute confidence. I expected him to tell me what all the jockeys say, that he never even thinks about the fear. Instead, he bent his head forward until we were just a few inches apart.

"Sometimes I can't sleep for fear of the animal I'm going to get on tomorrow," he whispered. "I know what he can do to me. Sometimes a horse is just angry at the world and no one, not even Findley, can bring him home again."

"Then why don't you quit?"

He looked at me as if I were crazy. Backstretch workers aren't known for their eloquence. Words are a secondary form of communication, something resorted to on those rare occasions when touch and intuition will not do. But Findley's answer might speak for any number of them.

"Because this love of the horse is the only true thing I've ever had."

I WAS fifteen years old before I saw my first horse break down on the track. I knew injury existed, that any one section of the dainty architecture of a Thoroughbred's leg—cannon bones, pasterns, kneecaps, hocks, stifles—could burst in the middle of the race and send a horse crashing down. Even those huge hearts themselves had been known to give out mid-stride. I knew that there were less forgivable acts involved as well. Horses were pushed to run when they were unfit, exhausted, popped full of barely legal medications to convince muscles to do something they ordinarily could not do. I'd heard the arguments that horse racing was cruel, sending inno-cent animals into an artificial environment to pour out their hearts for profit. I simply hadn't listened.

Whenever I went to Longacres in those pre–driver's license days, my father would play chauffeur, dropping me off near the grandstand gate at noon and returning to pick me up around five. During those solitary weekend afternoons, I somehow developed a talent for reading the horses. I don't know exactly how the ability evolved, certainly not from study or theorizing. I would just look at how a runner's face rose toward the air, its shoulder muscles twitched, its eyes rolled back or settled forward and alert, and know whether it felt ready to run. I was far from infallible, but if I'd been a bettor that year, I would have finished deep in the black. Two interlocking pieces—one me, one racehorse—seemed to have found each other and clicked.

One drizzly Saturday, before the second-to-last race on the card, I stood hunched in my turquoise rain slicker watching a handful of horses trek around the paddock. They were a workmanlike bunch, typical currency for late-season, just-average races, standing obedi-ently like ducks in a line. As I paced the length of the fence, they bowed their heads against the weather and paid no attention to anything else at all. There was one exception, a filly black as ink and so skinny her ribs showed beneath the saddlecloth. Her legs were too long for her body and you could see the outline of each muscle rising from knee to shoulder. She tugged hard against her lead shank, pulling toward me and the paddock rail. Each time her head broke loose, it felt like she'd released a tiny lick of flame into the air. Her eyes looked focused, thoughts collected. If I'd had $100, I would have bet it all. The odds were generous. She'd run only twice the year before and both times sloppily. She hadn't been on the track for six months, but in that gap of time something seminal had happened. I watched her trot across the track toward the starting gate, chin cocked and tail flowing. I simply knew she would come first across the wire.

It was a sprint race, just five furlongs. My filly broke at the front of the pack and stayed there, gliding along like a gift and leaving all the other horses strung out behind. Then, as she swung around the turn and came to the head of the lane, something happened. Something too tiny to spot—one heel clipping another, a glitch in the track, or maybe nothing at all—and she dropped to her knees right there in the middle of the homestretch. The jockey bounced off her back, forming a tight ball as he hit the ground and rolled free. Somehow all the other horses kept going, parting like water around a rock. My filly froze on her twin kneecaps, as if in prayer, as if she knew what would happen when she tried to stand again and was putting it off as long as possible. Finally, she rose on three strong, steady legs. She tried a step on the fourth, and rocked back in surprise. The hoof wouldn't meet the ground. Instead, it dangled from her shin with the skin and flesh broken away and the end of a bone jutting out, snapped clean in half.

Since I couldn't bear to keep looking at her, I turned toward the people around me. They were all doing the same, swiveling their necks, shaking their heads, imprinting something they wished they could erase. I glanced back toward the track. The jockey was up and walking, and the grooms who'd been waiting near the finish line had ducked under the rail to join him. The filly took a stumbling step or two, as if expecting her other leg to reappear. Then she stopped moving entirely. Someone grabbed her reins and began patting her neck. She didn't look panicked, only bewildered. And maybe a little bit betrayed.

"She's a goner," mumbled an old man next to me. Then he made the sign of the cross, and though I hadn't been inside a church since sixth grade, I crossed myself, too.

The equine ambulance drove onto the track. The vet and one of the grooms locked their hands around the filly's rear, half lifting and half pushing her into the trailer. As the van drove away, the grooms peeled off to care for their own horses until only one was left kicking at the dirt with the scuffed toe of his boot, as if digging deep enough might uncover what had happened there. After a few minutes, he, too, drifted off, and it was just track and drizzle and sky. The odds went up for the next round of horses, and the cycle started again as if it had never stopped. I skipped the final race and waited leaning against a cement post in the parking lot until it was time to go home.

I usually called May-May as soon as I got back from the track, but that evening I kept putting it off. Finally, our phone rang just after nine.

"It's your grandmother."

I picked up the receiver. For a moment, I considered not telling her what I'd seen, but as soon as I opened my mouth, the words had launched off my tongue. Just as quickly, tears formed underneath until I was speaking and gulping and had to repeat the grisliest details two and three times until May-May understood. I went on about how unfair it was, how it never would have happened if we hadn't pushed that horse onto a racetrack and forced her to run. How I couldn't possibly go on loving racing if all it did was destroy what it created.

I waited for May-May to deliver answers or advice, but she didn't do either. All she said was that there was something true in all those things. I'd need to find my peace with it in whatever way I could.

"How?"

"I don't know."

It's taken me years to fashion such a peace, and it's still only a rough patchwork that will never be quite free of holes. I've drawn what I can from the purpose horses like that filly carry with them into the paddock, from the whiff of anticipation telling me that they want, maybe even need, to run. I've drawn from humans who spend lifetimes making sure legs and hearts break as seldom as possible. And I've cleared some space for compromise. That filly forced me to ask questions, and as yet, I haven't found any answers. What I have found is tolerance. Staying with the racetrack means slipping away from black or white and residing in varying shades of gray.

It isn't about the nature of the track. It's about the nature of love.

THIS PAST May, I was at Belmont Park one morning, standing with my back to the track and my elbows on the rail, watching the horses file back toward the barns. They pranced along sideways, well-lathered and still frisky, sloshing in their own speed. An older man stepped up beside me, holding on to a little girl in crooked pigtails and cowboy boots. She was maybe four or five, her face still baby plump. There was what looked like strawberry jam smeared down the front of her shirt.

"There he is, there he is, there he is," she chanted just loud enough for me to hear. She kept pulling at the man's hand, and he would let her lean until she was about to topple, then wordlessly pull her upright again.

I said hi, and he said hi back, the girl glancing briefly in my direction then focusing all her attention back on the parade of horses. The man and I started talking. He told me how he'd worked for twenty years as an exercise rider in Maryland, and how he'd quit the previous spring, because when he woke in the morning, it took him five minutes to uncurl his back. Now he helped out a friend, a small-time trainer at Laurel Park who usually had ten horses in his barn but sometimes as many as twelve. He and his granddaughter had come up for the weekend, because they had a horse running on Saturday, and his friend couldn't be there to saddle him up.

"So we're taking a little vacation," he explained. When I asked

him what sights they planned to see, he said the barns, the clubhouse restaurant, and the training track across the way.

A solitary bay colt came off the track and his rider guided him
into the grass behind us. The girl's chant picked up volume, and
her grandfather nodded.

"There he is."

She was still pulling, gunning directly for the horse. Her grandfather swung her up on his hip and let her stroke the colt's nose. The
horse skittered sideways a few feet, then settled again as the small
hand patted his forehead and cheeks. Her grandfather set her down
and crouched low to the ground, probing ankles and knees. I'd
stopped watching the horse, captured now by the child as she obe-
diently backed away from the animal, then struggled with the urge
to touch him once again. When her grandfather reached the left
rear leg, the latch sprang and she shot straight toward the horse's
lightning-quick back feet.

"Wait," I piped up, too slow to do anything more. Her grandfather heard me, or saw her, and seized her by the shirttail, diverting
her a few feet short of the goal. I saw a quiver of uncertainty travel
up the colt's hind legs, but he only shifted an inch or two.

"This way," the man instructed, and once again took her by the
hand.

I've known since I was that little girl's age about maneuvering
around the dangerous back end of a horse. There are two advisable
paths. I expected him to lead her along the most common, making
a wide arc to the rear, well out of range of any hooves flashing
through the air. That was respecting the horse, negotiating his circle of space instead of just sticking to your own. It meant being
aware of what the horse needed and how you fit into the spectrum.
It meant stepping away.

The man surprised me by taking the second route instead.
Hanging on to his granddaughter's hand, he lay an open palm on
the colt's rear hip, pausing a moment to allow him to register their
presence. Then he slid as close as possible around the horse's back
legs, enfolding both haunches in his body like a cloak, so that there
was no room for the horse to raise a tentative foot and strike out.

The little girl followed, her cheek brushing against the long, coarse tail hairs, the three of them forming a kind of embrace.

"This way he's comfortable," the man explained as they came around the other side. "He hasn't lost us. He knows just where we are."

Part 3:

THE STRETCH RUN

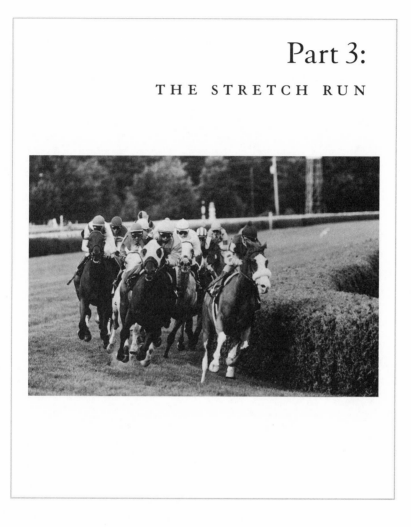

Chapter Six

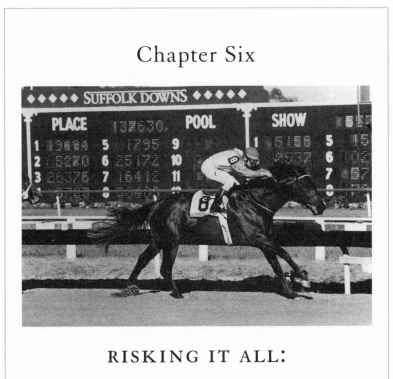

RISKING IT ALL:

The Art of Gambling

They say true gamblers have to be born that way. If so, then I most definitely qualify. Since childhood, I've never been known for doing anything in a small way.

I learned to bet the spring I was in fifth grade, with May-May as my own private bookie. Bankrolled an initial $20, I was free to spend it on all three Triple Crown races in any combinations I fancied. I could place the full twenty on my Derby favorite to win, spread it in $2 pops over ten different horses, or hang on to my bounty until the Belmont in the hopes that some of the more serious competition would drop out along the way. May-May's own betting philosophy was simple: Always value experience over profit.

I began by consulting the *Racing Form* charts, planning to wield all that printed data like a miner's pick to pry loose the best horse in each race. I came up against a paralyzing obstacle right away. It was impossible to choose. One colt stood out because he'd won his past three races by more than two lengths; another because he always won at the mile-and-an-eighth distance of the Derby; a third because his father had won two Triple Crown races nine years before. Did I pick because of strong morning workouts, a month-long refresher break, or a trainer who'd won the Derby the previous year?

I started tentatively, laying $5 on my chosen colt to win. He wound up running mid-pack, far behind a filly named Genuine Risk, the first filly to win the Derby since Regret in 1915. Looking back at the charts, it seemed obvious I should have bet her, so I did the next time around, putting $5 on her to win the Preakness. She came in second to a horse named Codex with Angel Cordero aboard. How could I not have backed Angel? Betting according to the *Racing Form* seemed to do me about as much good as consulting a crystal ball.

Come the Belmont, I had $10 left. Without even glancing at the charts, I spent it all on an unspectacular bay colt named Temperence Hill, just because his odds were so high it seemed nobody else had cared. The track was sloppy, the field erratic, and, in one of those crazy kinks of racing luck, Temperence Hill won by two lengths. He paid $53.40 to the dollar, which made me $500 richer than I'd been just two and a half minutes before. That was all it took.

In the next few years, I became a betting fiend.

Gambling with May-May was first-class. She'd spent years putting money down with East Coast bookies, and our home-operated casino proved far closer to Damon Runyon's Broadway than a track mutuel window. She'd mastered the slangy patois that accompanied each wager: phrases like odds-on, late scratch, daily double, and morning line. Even better, she could still resurrect lingo from the thirties and forties, gangster slang cut with her languid southern accent, sounding like polished marbles rolling off her tongue. "Fuzzies" were race favorites, "chalk-players" the ones who bet fuzzies, and "leviathans" the gamblers who bet heavily on any action at all. "Shills" and "touts" sidled up to the leviathans and, for a fee, handed out hot picks on which long shots and fuzzies to favor. "Boat races" were fixed races, and the "stable push" was the inside dope about whether a boat might be in the works. "Markers" meant bets made on credit, and "desperadoes" meant gamblers who disappeared before making good on their markers. May-May's very best patter had drifted from across the Atlantic, Cockney backslang—"ruof" for 4–1, "net" for 10–1, and "cockles," rhyming slang from "cock and hen," again read 10–1. I couldn't bet fast enough to crawl up inside of it all.

There was only one rule I stuck to religiously: Always bet to win. To urge a horse to come in second or third seemed to run counter to our entire relationship. Otherwise, I shed the charts, seized Temperence Hill, and dove straight into irresponsibility. If I wanted to wager a trixie on the three longest shots in the race or parlay my Derby winnings directly into the Preakness, no one forced me to do otherwise. The sole repercussion was that I lost, race after race, year after year. Aside from that first $500 windfall, I never once emerged from the Belmont with so much as 50¢ in my pocket. Often I blew the whole amount on the Derby, then watched the next two races as I'd always watched them, a poor but passionate fan. I probably had the knowledge to bet more cleanly and prudently had I been so inclined, to weigh options and to try to generate some reasonable rate of return. Instead, I grew addicted to having something seriously on the line.

Such a straight shot of adrenaline couldn't sustain itself. I kept placing riskier and riskier bets, elaborate combinations involving nets and cockles and every horse that went off at anything higher than 20–1, searching out that same charge I'd first found with $10 on a casual chance. Finally, three years after May-May'd launched our in-home gambling concern, I decided to shut it down. I was broke, and I was bored. When you compared betting to what went on in the mind and hands of an Angel Cordero, not to mention the stride of a Genuine Risk, it didn't seem particularly risky at all.

In truth, figuring odds and prophesying winners made racing feel tame. I didn't want to solve all the mysteries of the Thoroughbred, to erase the thrum of possibility contained in the simple fact of racehorses across a track. It seemed far too great a sacrifice for the mere pleasure of placing a bet.

RACETRACKS LIVE and die by just how far their players are willing to risk it. In the United States, the earliest gamblers were more akin to crusaders, battling to burst puritan seams that had stitched the country together from its inception. Beginning in 1802, racing fought on-again, off-again legal battles with clean-living advocates who published pamphlets headlined "Horseracing and Christian Duties and Principles Incompatible." With pulpit-thumpers applying steady pressure, tracks from New England to California opened, shut down, and opened up again as state legislatures tussled over the basic human right to put $10 on the two horse to win. Reformers never quite managed to knock the sport down. People kept circling back to an underlying urge to tilt bottles and let loose a rain of champagne.

American racing first took hold in the South, where plantation owners tossed slaves aboard imported Thoroughbreds, then tossed money, tobacco crops, and twenty-six-room mansions at each other in the hopes their horse would come first across the wire. But it was New York City, straining under a mid-nineteenth-century surge of immigrants, that gave birth to the popular track. There heavy bettors like Pittsburgh Phil and John "Bet-a-Million" Gates turned local heroes; tipsters and gangsters acquired an aura of seedy romance; and senators and business tycoons formed the core clientele for thriving gambling dens. Small racecourses opened and folded all around the city. Then, in 1863, an Irish immigrant named John Morrissey decided to risk everything he had on the spark of an idea, a track in the upstate spa town of Saratoga Springs.

Morrissey was a legend long before he entered the racing world. He came to New York through Ellis Island as an infant and grew up in the upstate town of Troy, working as a steamboat hand and bordello bouncer before reaching the big city. He signed on at New York's "Nativist" Americus Club as an immigrant runner—an errand boy sent to round up fresh immigrants, register them to vote, then direct them toward anti-immigrant candidates who had their very worst interests at heart. In his early twenties, Morrissey temporarily abandoned a political career for the illegal arena of bare-knuckle boxing. At twenty-two, he went thirty-six rounds with veteran fighter Yankee Sullivan and finished the less battered and bloody of the two. The victory earned him the title "Boxing Champion of the World." Morrissey had grander plans.

By the early 1860s, Morrissey had opened a handful of gambling houses, most in Manhattan but one in the resort town of Saratoga Springs. Saratoga was the favored escape of city society in search of dancing, drinking, and gathering around the roulette wheels. Around the same time, new antigambling legislation passed featuring a legal loophole designed specially for horse racing. Thoroughbred tracks could stay open under the auspices of "improving the breed." Morrissey flirted with the idea of backing a racetrack in Saratoga, just as he flirted with Tammany Hall politics, society bigwigs like Cornelius Vanderbilt, and statesmen including Abraham Lincoln. Then came the Civil War. With the South buried in gunfire, the country's racing public had to find itself a new home. Morrissey knew when to move quickly. He gathered a handful of wealthy investors, and in August 1863, less than a month after the Rebels surrendered to General Grant in Vicksburg, he opened a racetrack in Saratoga Springs.

It was clear from the start that Morrissey's creation filled a communal need. Spectators—that pocket of society not party to the fighting or subject to the draft—flocked to Saratoga by railcar, buggy, and horseback. Gambling, technically illegal at the track, took place in the basement cardrooms of local hotels instead. A month later, when Lincoln declared a national holiday dedicated to church worship and "humiliation and prayer," fans flooded the races and rid themselves of nearly $4,000 in admission fees alone. Though high society happily funneled their incomes into Morrissey's creation, they weren't prepared to give an immigrant bootstrapper any credit for his vision. To tie a noted gambling impresario to the sport was simply too scandalous. Officially, credit for Saratoga's stratospheric success went to William Travers and John Hunter. They were casual investors, but they were gentlemen.

Unfazed, Morrissey went on to serve as the country's first joint gambling kingpin and U.S. senator. He spent two terms in office, during which his most noted accomplishments included an offer to step into a boxing ring with any man in the House and his failure to show up the February afternoon his compatriots impeached President Andrew Jackson. Government service proved exceptional only in how slowly it could move. It ran against Morrissey's gambling nature to stay in one place too long. Having been ousted from Tammany Hall for espousing democratic reform, he didn't bother trying for a third term.

Morrissey continued to parade around Saratoga clad in white flannel suits and a diamond stickpin. He lost most of his fortune in the stock market panic of 1869, then amassed a second one by opening Saratoga's first three-story brick casino modeled after those in Baden-Baden, contributing a percentage of his earnings to the upkeep of local schools and churches. The *New York Times* labeled his establishment "the finest hell on earth." Henry James, on holiday from Europe, called it democratic and vulgar. All the while, Morrissey's racetrack continued to thrive.

MORRISEY'S SARATOGA venture spawned one entirely unexpected phenomenon, the rise of the female gambler. In the sport's early days, women had only bartered behind the scenes, letting fans, silk gloves, jewelry, and cigarette cases ride on the backs of their favorite runners. By the 1890s, amid the gambling houses flowering upstate, women began openly to cast their lots. Several Saratoga hotels featured all-night poker games exclusive to female players and dealers, with special bars in which the clientele could partake of breakfast or evening cocktails between rounds of cards.

The track fashioned its own women's betting circle upstairs, and connected it to the men's ring by private telephone line just a decade after Alexander Graham Bell's invention debuted.

In 1894, *New York World* tabloid reporter Nellie Bly visited Saratoga and was shocked by women and children traipsing about in silk dresses and gold-embroidered parasols, shamelessly pitching coins after their chosen mounts. In a series of articles headlined "Wild Vortex of Gambling and Betting by Men, Women & Children," she sought to raise public outrage about the loose living that flourished at the track. She also revealed that Saratoga's twin betting rings were far from separate but equal. Women gamblers received 40–1 odds on extreme long shots, while downstairs men were promised $200 for every dollar they wagered on the exact same horse.

By the time May-May started frequenting the track, women everywhere were gambling more freely. They paid boys dressed in long frock coats and buttons reading "I Bet for Commissions" to place their money with the bookmakers downstairs. But the bookies themselves were still off-limits for the more tender half of the population. Upon arriving at Pimlico, May-May surveyed the action swirling around such bowler-hatted characters chalking odds on slate boards, digging for gossip, and swiveling binoculars to check out the competition. It seemed obvious the betting ring was the place to be.

While other young ladies shared tea in the stands, she took to arriving at the track on the arm of a gentleman escort, then instantly abandoning him for the crush of undesirables downstairs. Through sheer persistence, May-May eventually became a regular with the Baltimore bookies, roaming the packed, smoky betting ring in search of whoever was offering top odds. At first, only the most eccentric of the lot would accept her money: an ex-vaudeville actor known to pad his patter with a little slide-and-shuffle, or the mathematics professor who factored mud density and barometric pressure into his predictions. Eventually, word spread that she knew her horses, was willing to back them healthily, and never asked for money down on credit. Before long, she'd acquired a string of admirers who would conceal her behind a wall of long-legged bar stools whenever track security passed through.

May-May folded this inside line directly into her betting tactics. She befriended the "tic-tac" men who stood on wooden crates along the rim of the ring, telegraphing a catcher's kind of code over the tops of the bettors' heads to keep bookies in touch with the odds their competitors listed. Studying their hands whipping across their bodies, tugging on earlobes, patting heads and chins and wrists, May-May gradually got to know the odds by their tic-tac signs. A tap on the shoulders meant a horse had gone to 9–4, on the wrist 5–4, fingers fanning the forearm 11–8. Thumbs pointed straight up meant a bookie had just accepted a heavy bet. Eventually May-May convinced one of the tic-tacs to start tipping her off a few seconds in advance of the thumbs-up sign. Then she'd scramble to get her money down before, like an electric current jumping bulb to bulb, odds began to shorten all around the ring.

"MAKING BOOK" on the races began in England at the start of the nineteenth century, when entrepreneurs invented the idea of offering odds on every horse in the race instead of just for or against a single runner. Initially, nobility scoffed at fishmongers' and butchers' sons trying to squirm their way onto the royal track, but the allure of the game proved strong. Soon lords and dukes were steering their carriages through the common folk to toss down sacks bulging with coins. Originally, the bookies gathered in any makeshift locale—taverns and cock-fighting pits and, at Epsom Downs, around a recently retired gibbet—but eventually circular rooms known as rings were incorporated into the tracks themselves. By the 1820s, the scoundrels had been welcomed inside the palace to ply their trade.

Bookies didn't cross the Atlantic until 1866, when the first betting shop opened in Philadelphia, but once they had arrived, they blossomed unlike anything overseas. Bookmaking functioned like fertilizer to America's self-made spirit, swelling off the tracks and into the towns. By the turn of the century, New York City—where organized crime dwelt alongside immigrants eager to jump from

small-timer to big shot—had turned into the focal point of the profession. It also became one of gambling's most legendary battle-
grounds, the site of a bookie war so full-blown it culminated in the
shutdown of the entire sport.

In 1906, the bulk of New York City bookmaking took place in
downtown poolrooms, the race results traveling along telegraph
lines from tracks in Brooklyn and Queens. In most cases, such
arrangements slid along smooth as imported whiskey—the track
owners simply bought a share in the gambling halls. A key benefi-
ciary in such an arrangements was Western Union, which gleaned
much of its $5 million yearly profit from the wires connecting pool-
rooms to tracks. One of the few people not happy with the setup
was recently elected Governor Charles Hughes, who'd committed
himself to staunching the political corruption emanating from
another of Western Union's major backers, Tammany Hall. Hughes
began a full-scale campaign to outlaw corruption, including those
same downtown gambling dens that thrived off the tracks.

The Gravesend racetrack in Brooklyn was one of the few operations run independently of Tammany Hall. Started in the 1880s by
Phil and Michael Dwyer, Irish immigrants who'd made a small
fortune in the meat-packing industry, Gravesend survived by
charging bookies a flat fee for their services. As the growing popularity of city betting drained Gravesend of customers, the Dwyers
took a bold step. In 1906, they quadrupled the fee they charged offtrack bookmakers. When the bookies refused to pay, the Dwyers
cut their telegraph lines, also cutting all profits for Western Union.
The telegraph company retaliated at once. Backed by major gambling concerns, they bought a dilapidated hotel adjacent to Gravesend. They hired runners to infiltrate the track, then dash next
door with the latest results to be telegraphed to the city. Upon
learning of this on-site invasion, the Dwyers took the next logical
step. They locked the track gates.

It was an open declaration of war.

The 1906 racing season heralded a fierce territorial battle
between the Dwyer brothers and Western Union. Screwball high-
jinks worthy of the Marx Brothers ensued. The Dwyers hired 130

Pinkerton detectives to patrol the grounds for any suspicious patrons, and their security force came up against all variety of creative onslaughts. Western Union runners donned the colors of the horses in each race, then staged mock finishes in the paddock within sight of the hotel tower next door. A woman opening and closing her umbrella to entertain a baby sent Morse code messages about the latest winners. Another was arrested at the gates with a dozen carrier pigeons sewn into her dress. When the track closed for the summer, Western Union erected a sixty-five-foot tower atop the hotel that provided an open view of the finish. Within days, the Dwyers erected a fence to block their sight lines. A can-you-top-us game of higher tower, higher fence followed until the twin structures teetered precariously whenever a wind whipped through Brooklyn.

The escalating warfare drained track and gaming parlors of revenue and raised the ire of journalists and patrons. Meanwhile, Governor Hughes got to work surreptitiously stitching together a commission of lawyers and politicos to back a piece of legislation called the Hart-Agnew Bill, outlawing gambling of all sorts. The bill passed in 1910 thanks to a single vote cast by a Republican senator so ill he had to be carried up the Capitol steps.

The Dwyer brothers no longer needed to fret about Western Union, or vice versa. Hughes and his commission had sent the racetrack tumbling to its knees.

CHARLES EVANS Hughes scored his victory, but not even governmental legislation was capable of holding the gambling rackets down for long. High-profile horsemen, such as the Whitneys and the Vanderbilts, had political clout of their own. New York racing came alive again in 1913 with the legalization of "oral wagering." Bookies and gangsters continued to operate on the fringes of the racetrack, where they were permitted to accept bets but not solicit them. As Damon Runyon described it: "It is against the law, of course, to make book on horse races in New York state, so gentlemanly gentlemen stand around in convenient spots and permit you to hand them slips of paper on which you might note your theory of

a race. You pay off, or collect, as the case may be, the next day."
Then, in 1919, the federal government handed such gentlemanly
gentlemen a gift that would allow them to crush their reform-
touting enemies like a cigar under a wing-tipped heel. They voted
in Prohibition.

Those in the racing business evinced no moral dilemmas about
profiting from the Eighteenth Amendment. A clutch of entrepre-
neurial New Yorkers began running an underground liquor railroad between Canada and Saratoga Springs. When customs officials
finally halted one of the suspiciously frequent railcars full of Thoroughbreds, they uncovered a case of Spanish wine and eight quarts
plus sixteen pints of home-brewed whiskey wedged between the
passengers' legs. But Prohibition's greatest impact came from low-
rent, slightly unscrupulous gamblers who began investing in rum-
running and speakeasies. Fortunes sprouted overnight that
couldn't be reported to the law. Where better than the races to win
and lose hundreds of thousands of dollars at a pop?

For those who couldn't make it to the track, a fresh round of
gambling parlors, illegal as the cocktails they served, arose in empty
basements and hidden bedrooms up and down Broadway. Local
police struggled to keep apace with this offtrack graft, but their
competition proved wily. When city bookmakers found themselves
too closely monitored, they sent their wives and daughters to do the
collecting. A few lady bookies even opened operations of their own.
Mobile gambling dens invaded churches and funeral parlors, so
that police tended to barge in on impromptu christenings and
funerals instead of the anticipated numbers game.

Some of the heaviest hitters in town moved into the bookmaking racket. Arnold Rothstein, the kingpin rumored to have insti-
gated the 1919 Chicago World Series fix, invested in New York
gambling dens and pumped most of the money he earned back into
the track in the form of enormous wagers. The use of beards—
anonymous racegoers whom known gamblers hired to infuse betting circles en masse—had come into fashion a decade earlier. The
job was a popular one, filled by the likes of retired bank robber
Frank James and William Allan Pinkerton, the founder of the

Pinkerton Detective Agency. On July 4, 1921, Rothstein employed a slew of such front men, from Park Avenue bankers to a small-time hustler named Morris the Boob, to lay down money on a long shot called Sidereal at New York's Aqueduct racetrack. Sidereal, owned by Rothstein but run under a buddy's name, provided the sort of untraceable setup at which racketeers excelled. The horse had run three races that spring and finished poorly, probably aided by a jockey pulling back a little too hard on the reins. Since his last race, Sidereal had been secretly training at a private track and Rothstein knew the horse was razor-sharp, tiers above his July 4 company. He borrowed from every wealthy acquaintance he could summon up.

Rothstein's winnings that afternoon topped out at $800,000, an amount only eclipsed a few years later when Al Capone lost a million dollars in a similar venture. Track officials grew so suspicious of Rothstein's regular betting coups they banned him from the New York tracks on all but weekends and holidays. Which was why the cynical gangster suddenly warmed to celebrating Good Friday, Mother's Day, and Rosh Hashanah.

When Prohibition was repealed in 1933, Rothstein and its other investors scrambled for new sources of income. Mobsters like Lucky Luciano and Meyer Lansky set up in the bookmaking business, skimming cash off the Depression-era disenfranchised who placed money on horses and prayed for miracles in return. Even as Franklin Roosevelt gave horse racing the stamp of legitimacy via a publicity jaunt to Saratoga in an open-roofed sedan, offtrack bookmaking turned serious business. Employees showed up for work in three-piece suits, silk ties, and snap-brim fedoras. They hired an on-track staff to time races and transmit results downtown via multiple telephone lines. Most large-scale operations were in collusion with grooms, jockeys, and trainers to "secure" results in a given race by sending a horse to the post tranquilized or by pulling a Sidereal-style fix. Corruption escalated, and with it came a dangerous dose of hubris.

The era of the New York bookies crashed in 1939, a decade after the stock market. The culprit was pari-mutuel wagering. Pari-mutuels (mutual bets) dated back to the 1870s when a French *par-fumier* named Pierre Oller, unhappy with the odds he received from French bookmakers, devised a system through which his clients could bet among themselves, then divide up the profits. Soon the Paris tracks adopted his invention, taking a percentage of each betting dollar directly from the patrons instead of a flat fee from independents operating their own stands. The odds on each horse were dictated solely by how much money the public had bet on it, not by bookmaker opinion. Oller's idea evolved into Total-isators, elaborate adding machines that recalculated the odds each time a patron bet. The machines spread to England and as far as Australia, where the tote and on-track bookmakers found a way to coexist peacefully. By the time the mutuels reached the United States, racing officials were neck-deep in organized crime and all too eager to rid themselves of the old ways. They excised the book-makers with a clean surgical slice.

The ends of the bookies on American tracks signaled the onset of a more general sort of demise. What remained was still gam-bling, but under the auspices of the pari-mutuels it turned suspi-ciously tame and secure. What social reformers had demanded more than a century earlier the sport itself had finally granted. The freewheeling American racetrack gave way to that well-cushioned middle ground known as control.

AFTER MY gambling stint with May-May, I doubted something as straightforward as the pari-mutuels would ever seem a tempta-tion. But if you spend enough time around the races—absorbing tips, formulating opinions, and wishing you could take some fur-ther part in what's swelling up around you—you will eventually reach into your pocket.

The first time I ever bet at the track, I won.

It was the spring after I returned from St. Timothy's. May-May was ninety-six and for the most part condominium-bound, so that Saturday I ventured out to Longacres alone. My father dropped me off, and as he pulled away, I just stood in the parking lot. I could smell the familiar mix of damp hay and hot dogs, hear stray conversations sprinkled with speed horses, class-drops, and "I'm telling you, he can't lose." I must have waited there for a full five minutes just retooling my senses, welcoming myself home.

Sun poked through gray, bottom-heavy clouds and, with the sort of willpower sun possesses only in Seattle, held back the rain. When I made my way to the paddock, each horse looked carved and glossy as if expressly delivered to prove those Arabian show horses at St. Timothy's were nothing more than dumpy, distant cousins. I watched the first race before even bothering to buy a program and flip to the entries for the second. Listed halfway down the page was a filly called May's Regal Girl.

It had to be a sign.

I called May-May on a pay phone and began reading the filly's history into the receiver. She was a maiden, had raced three times and never finished better than fourth. She'd been bumped and jostled, and one brief description read "shows no inclination to run." Her breeding was unspectacular. Her morning line odds were 12–1.

I finished with a deflated sigh. "I guess she doesn't have a prayer."

"Look at her in the paddock," May-May told me. "If she looks alright, bet her. Ten dollars. To win."

By the time I reached the paddock, May's Regal Girl was circling along with the competition. She looked as unremarkable as her record, small and a bit potbellied. Her ears swiveled forward, and there was no hint of the nervous sweat covering a few animals trodding along behind her. She looked solid, but no miracle worker. She didn't look as if she'd break my heart by stumbling to her knees in the final furlong. She just looked like an ordinary, lovely racehorse.

The odds slipped down to 10–1 then popped up again to 12–1. Her jockey floated onto her back, and she didn't object. I checked out the favorite, long and gray and rangy. She looked keyed up, which made her fallible. I couldn't decide. All the horses looked tight and full of potential. Nothing about May's Regal Girl but her name spoke to me at all. I wanted to call May-May again, but there wasn't time. I snaked my way toward the betting windows and hoped that in those hundred yards I would accrue some sort of wisdom.

Instead, I found a white-haired woman leaning on a cane, unfolding dollar bills from a black leather pocketbook, a *Racing Form* tucked under her arm. I couldn't bet myself, not until I was eighteen, so I walked up to her and asked if she would place a bet for my grandmother. Ten dollars on May's Regal Girl to win. Suddenly, I felt quite convinced. Not that May's Regal Girl would win, only that I should bet on her. I'd come to the track because I'd missed the presence of chance, and here it was in spades.

The woman glanced at the tote board.

"Are you sure?"

I nodded, and she took my money, returning a minute later with a slip of white paper that looked like a grocery store receipt. I wasn't sure what to do with it. If I put it in my jacket pocket it might fall out again. Clutched in my hand, it would turn crumpled and sweaty. Finally, I settled on the front pocket of my jeans. I slid it in flat to my thigh and kept checking every few seconds to make sure it was still there.

It wasn't a beautiful race. The horses broke sloppily, the favorite getting squeezed toward the rear of the pack and May's Regal Girl choosing to skirt the fray entirely and run wide toward the center. She swept through the first turn still far, far outside, covering yards of ground the others had bypassed. While they jockeyed for position, she sailed along on her own, as if choosing to disassociate herself from the entire racing process. Her rider tapped at her right flank with the whip, trying to get her to move inward, but she ignored all messages from the outside world. As she poured out of the turn, I began to feel a tickle of hope for May's Regal Girl. She was an independent thinker. She had ground to make up, several lengths on a pair of speed horses who'd vied for the lead the entire race. The gray favorite had recovered from her early shuffle and now hovered strong just a bit off the lead.

What happened next was that thing every racing fan can only

pray for. May's Regal Girl and I got lucky. The two front-running horses, having battled for more than half a mile, grew tired. The favorite, bottled up behind them, had to slow and move around them before she found clear space to run. Traffic jams galore occurred along the rail, while May's Regal Girl kept skimming pleasantly down the outside. She wasn't the best horse in the race. Perhaps she would never win again—she hardly possessed the competitive spirit. But for her, for us, everything lined up perfectly that afternoon.

May's Regal Girl finished in front by a nose. The tote board flashed photo finish, but I knew she'd taken it. I'd won over $100, but that seemed an afterthought. I didn't even cash the ticket until the tail end of the day, spending all afternoon touching the tip of white paper poking out of my pants pocket like a talisman, a symbol of I didn't even know what. May's Regal Girl shouldn't have won but did. Odds got defied all the time, carved into the stride of a mild-mannered chestnut filly, arbitrary and delicious.

The following day, I fanned out my winnings to show May-May—five twenties, a stack of singles, and a small heap of change. I described the race and the white-haired lady at the window and how May's Regal Girl had ambled back toward the winner's circle as if she didn't even realize the race was hers.

"I felt like I created her," I told May-May.

She didn't tell me that I hadn't.

I kept that $100 for a long time, sealed in a blue envelope in my bottom dresser drawer beneath old swimsuits and pajamas and the field hockey uniform I'd worn at St. Timothy's. I moved bedrooms, then we moved houses. Somewhere along the line the envelope disappeared. I don't know that I was so surprised. It was money earned from the uncertainty principle, mine for only as long as luck, and the racetrack, allowed.

NOT QUITE a year after May's Regal Girl, I came home from school one April Wednesday and found my father in his basement office slumped in a black leather chair. When he saw me, his eyes crinkled up at the corners as if he were about to smile. Then a single tear slipped out and rolled off toward his ear. It was the first time I'd ever seen him cry.

I knew May-May had died.

Death was more orderly than I'd expected. I went to a funeral at Epiphany Chapel and a reception in our living room where people ate Brie in puff pastry and our cats went into hiding under the back deck. Then it was over, and I was cleaning up wineglasses and crumpled napkins and carrying out the trash. I kept waiting for fate to step in the way it had with May's Regal Girl, to hand me some sort of sign or direction, but nothing happened at all. The way it was—the luck, the odds, the power of creation—just dissolved as quietly as an aspirin in a glass of water. A few weeks later, I packed up my plastic horses. I took the picture of May-May and me at her ninetieth birthday out of its blue plastic frame and dropped it into the trash. I no longer lived in that world.

In the coming months, I had to make a decision about racing. I had to find some way to remodel that childish infatuation so it suited my new code of disengagement. I found my answer in those hollow-eyed horseplayers I'd seen at Longacres. They were the bettors who never stepped into the daylight to examine a runner, who watched the races on closed-circuit televisions and had a marked-up *Racing Form* permanently affixed to one arm. Their universe appeared perfectly self-contained, a consciousness that hadn't parlayed itself into circumspection. I'd seen such players lose thousands of dollars and not seem to register the fact of loss. It seemed an enviable quality. My freshman year in college, I decided to teach myself to handicap.

The word *handicap* originated at the racetrack, drawn from an old horse-bartering game in which buyer and seller negotiated by opening and closing hands inside the bowl of a cap. In track parlance, it referred to races in which horses carried greater or lesser amounts of weight—handicaps—in accordance with their ability. In the ideal handicap race, one in which the scales had been perfectly balanced, every horse would cross the finish line at the same time. Eventually the word earned an *-er* and evolved to describe the track official hired to assess each runner's ability and to assign weights. It also came to signify those bettors who manipulated the same information—a horse's past performance record, its speed, its rate of improvement or decline—to make assessments of their own. A horse's handicap is the number of pounds under which it must travel, usually between 111 and 126, a condensed measure of the advantages and disadvantages it carries. A human handicapper is one who analyzes such advantages and disadvantages and spins them into profit.

I began my handicapping career by shifting my weight. My connection altered from Thoroughbred flesh to those charts in the center section of the *Racing Form,* racehorses packaged into elements I could control, instead of elements that controlled me. By the spring of my freshman year, with two first-class southern California racetracks within driving distance of campus, I had developed a careful formula for detachment.

I bought the *Form* the day before I went to the track and spread it out across the tan linoleum floor of my dorm room. I always worked at night, sometimes until two or three in the morning, always alone. Horse by horse, I went through the charts, reading each hieroglyph and abbreviation, looking at facts and attempting to divine the future. I analyzed how each race would play out, a paper chase in which I threw away those long shots like May's Regal Girl who had no chance in print. I compared times and speeds, jockeys and trainers, and studied the shorthand histories of each runner, looking for weak links that might lend one animal an edge over the rest. I tagged horses who'd been bumped or squeezed the last time out and still finished strongly, who'd run a solid race against sterling competition and now were slipping back in class, or who'd acquired new equipment like shadow rolls or blinkers designed to bestow focus and nurse out extra speed. I identified my picks the way a true handicapper did, by number not by name, and chose winners from my dorm room without ever looking at a horse. I could spend an hour over a single race, stacking up pluses and minuses, daring fate to have an opinion I couldn't foil.

My track of choice was Santa Anita, which ran two meets a year, one in the fall and another in the spring. I'd find a seat behind one

of the consoles in the fluorescent-lit basement, home to all hard-
core handicappers not willing to shell out $20 for a space in the
Turf Club upstairs. I'd arrange my red markers and ballpoint pens,
open my dissected *Form,* and begin reassessing my previous night's
assessments. Sometimes I didn't even bother watching the races
live, but just raised my head to the TV monitors bolted to the ceiling, noted down winners and losers, and bent again to my task.

The horseplayers who gathered in the Santa Anita basement
were stained, bent, shrunken, and scarred, a quirked-up medley
worthy of Fellini. But they were human, and humans form communities. Eventually—by sheer fact of being there every Wednesday and the occasional weekend—I became a part of theirs.
Legitimacy was granted via physical presence, nothing more or
less. After a few weeks, people began to clear their sheaves of
papers to make room for me, bum a few quarters for a cup of coffee, or offer me sticks of cinnamon gum.

At one point, I noticed a man, in his late thirties or perhaps his
early fifties, regularly adopting the seat next to mine. He was small,
blue-pale and jittery, with a cigarette permanently parked between
his third and fourth fingers, though more smoke seemed to spiral
off through the air than into his lungs. His daily uniform consisted
of sweatpants and yellowing T-shirts from all variety of professional sports teams, swapped each time I saw him with a brazen
lack of loyalty. All afternoon he drank sweet black coffee and ate
peanut M&M's, one at a time, by the jumbo-packful.

After a few days of brushing elbows, he began offering me
advice on the horses I'd circled. No social graces mucked up the
lines of communication. I'd just flip the page, he'd open his little
round mouth like a fish, and out would bubble a single phrase:

"No chance."

"No prayer."

"No dice."

"Nope."

Finally, I asked him whether he had a better suggestion. Which
he did. As he began dissecting the choices I was about to make and
the reasons I was about to make them, I realized that in those few

days of glancing over my left arm he'd completely deciphered my cryptic version of marking-up code. He was, in fact, taking an interest in me. I would have freeze-framed things right there, except for one small matter. He was almost always right. I began, cautiously, to ask him how he came to his conclusions. The answers, though gems of deductive logic, were rarely brief. One day he reached his hand across the plastic wood paneling and announced:

"Albert."

"Nan." A clammy handshake.

"So do you want to learn how to gamble?" With the clear connotation that as yet I'd learned nothing at all.

The only possible answer was yes.

Albert was a professional horseplayer, the first I'd ever met. In his twenties, he'd been a film studio whiz kid, the sort who'd catapulted from coffee-fetching assistant to vice president in a breathtaking couple of years. There were still bits of that lacquered past stitched into his slumpishness: a cigarette lighter from Tiffany's, the perfect arc of his palm smoothing back his hair, a habit of passing on wisdom in the form of clichés.

"You've got to have ice in your veins, kid."

"Learn how to go with your gut."

Or his favorite: "Watch and learn, kid. Watch and learn."

Prior to his cinematic leanings, Albert had been a country kid growing up across the street from a rural Oklahoma track and hanging out on the backstretch all summer long. When he was eleven, he read his first handicapping primer, ripped apart most of the theories it swore by, and began to formulate a wagering system of his own. He could outbet the handicapper from the local paper long before he was legally allowed to bet, and earned his college tuition selling his own handwritten tip sheets in front of the track. He accrued an encyclopedic knowledge of racehorses, stats and times, pedigrees and payoffs, like those baseball savants who can reel off the entire 1932 World Series lineup, then deliver it backward and upside down. Eventually, he moved on to the even more dazzling arena of show business, but the glamour of the racetrack stuck.

In his early thirties, curdled on Italian suits, marbled office suites, and starlets who couldn't remember his name, Albert—who still made it to the track every single Sunday even if it meant forty-eight sleepless hours—decided to sacrifice ambition for obsession. He cashed in his Hollywood nest egg, walked off the studio lot and into playing the horses full-time. Ten years later, racing had become his kin, cartography, and component parts. He bet close to a quarter-million dollars a year, most of it on the track but occasionally, when the tote odds had dropped too low to please him, via car phone with a floating casino off the Cayman Islands. He had no family, no hobbies, no pets, just a one-room apartment strategically located halfway between Santa Anita and Hollywood Park. Come summer, when racing shifted to Del Mar near San Diego, he rented a room just a few yards from the beach, though he claimed he was too busy betting to ever don a swimsuit and get in the ocean. Some years he made hundreds of thousands of dollars, some years he made nothing at all. He always called himself a gambler, not a handicapper.

"Might as well tell it like it is."

THE WEDNESDAY of our formal introduction, Albert commenced a mix of math, science, and philosophy that was to become my horseplaying education. We started with an arena in which I was serenely comfortable: analyzing the facts. As far as I knew, the facts were what I'd already been analyzing on my dorm room floor. Facts for Albert entered a whole other time zone. He carried two scuffed brown leather briefcases back and forth to the track every day just to transport all the knowledge he hadn't room for in his jam-packed brain. Inside the cases were stacks upon stacks of index cards, cross-referenced, color-coded with Magic Markers, and grouped together with red rubber bands. They contained the extended histories of every horse, jockey, and trainer at work in California—their patterns, strategies, records, and flaws.

Albert's cards told him which trainers excelled with two-year-olds, fillies, turf runners, and two-year-old fillies on turf. They charted each animal's pedigree, whether its grandparents, parents, brothers, and sisters won in six-furlong sprints or mile-and-a-sixteenth routes, dirt races or grass, tracks graded sloppy, good, or fast. He arrived at Santa Anita just after five every morning to watch how the horses moved and to time their workouts with his own multidial stopwatch, not trusting the official clockers hired by the track. Each evening he went home, mixed himself a single martini—another artifact of his movie days—recorded his newly accumulated information on more index cards, then transferred it to the next day's *Racing Form*. He owned copies of the *Form* dating back twelve years, stacked in mold-resistant plastic tubs lining a storage locker somewhere in the depths of Burbank.

From the facts about horses and trainers and jockeys, we moved on to facts about the races themselves. Albert could vet the physical track as thoroughly as he did the creatures who poured across it. His mind whirred, like fingers flying over the beads of an abacus, calculating variables and combinations. He registered each subtle track bias that developed over the course of the day: whether the moisture, depth, and lay of the dirt favored speed horses or closers or those who sat just off the pace; whether sprinters ran better breaking from the rail or closers were winning on the turf. In any given minute, he knew whether those runners starting in post position one or three or seven had won four races or two races or no races at all.

He could watch a race the way a grade school teacher eyed a classroom, with one eye on the star pupil, another on the steady plodder, and a third on the kid getting into trouble in the back row. We'd stand together on the balcony of the second-floor grandstand, Albert with binoculars pressed to his eyeballs and a finger of ash from his unsmoked cigarette dangling over the rail. I'd follow the progress of one horse or maybe two, the favorite and the colt returning for his second start after a serious injury whose trainer excelled at bringing horses back off an injury and who Albert thought might be ready for a big win. Between races, Albert over-

flowed with information, arcane and essential, but once the starting
bell sounded he went completely silent. He'd watch the track without moving, save an owl-like swivel of his neck as the horses traveled around the oval. When the last straggler had passed the finish,
he'd lower his glasses and ask:

"What did you think of the seven horse?"

The seven? The seven hadn't been in the race. As far as I could
recall, the seven had started near the back of the pack and stayed
there all the way around. I'd glance up at the results on the tote
board and notice he had in fact eked up to finish fourth. But even
so . . .

"He got a nightmare of a trip. He clipped heels with the four
horse coming out of the gate and got trapped against the rail all the
way into the far turn. Then that idiot of a jockey took him four
wide into the stretch. Still found enough run to pick off six horses.
That's a runner."

Then we'd jog off toward the television monitors to watch multiple replays, first from the side, then head-on. I got split verifica-
tion of what Albert had noted, and he studied the one or two horses
who hadn't received his concentrated focus a few minutes before.
I'd write the seven's name down in the steno pad I'd taken to carrying around with me, and watch for him the next time around.
Minus the nightmare trip and the idiot jockey, the colt would
inevitably prove he had something. Albert's seemed a God-given
gift, like playing piano by ear or a photographic memory, that ability to watch seven or eight races while everyone else was only
watching one.

Just as I began to think I understood the general curve of Albert's
system—information, information, information—he started tossing in the occasional dose of something wacky.

"Flexible, flexible, gotta stay flexible," he'd mutter under his
breath whenever I accused him of breaking what was supposed to
be a cardinal rule, betting on a three-year-old carrying high weight
versus older company or against the only speed horse in the race.
One afternoon, as we stood along the crook of railing where the
paddock broke off and angled toward the track, Albert informed

me that despite the hours he spent on index cards the paddock was the hinge on which the entire handicapping process truly swung. Sure we were checking the horses for the usual signs of ill-health— nervous sweats or bandage-wrapped legs or just a general aura of the wan or neurotic (unless they always looked wan or neurotic, and Albert, or his cards, could tell us if they did)—but he wasn't just after physical details. He was alert for a vision.

Once a month or so, Albert explained, a horse came through the paddock who'd been kissed by providence. Some luminous, on-the-muscle, toe-walking creature would strut sideways round the parade circle as if Mercury had pasted wings onto his feet just that morning. He could be the 2–5 favorite, he could be the slimmest chance on the board, but when he arrived everything Albert had so meticulously calculated went out the window and onto that hunch horse. He pointed out such a vision to me once, a dark-bay filly with an average racing history. Though I thought she looked polished and alive, the charmed dusting apparently hovering about her didn't reach me. Not this time. I didn't know whether to be relieved or alarmed that I'd lost the gift of divination. When Albert asked me if I saw "it," I told him that I did. The filly pulled away and won by six lengths.

The more I got to know Albert, the clearer it became that gambling wasn't simply his hobby, his career, or even his passion. It was his life philosophy. A gambler's style, he insisted, had to fit his or her personality. Some were clear-cut fact-and-figure people with no imagination. They'd bet California races from Las Vegas or just some darkened corner of the Santa Anita basement, moving animals around a theoretical track like a general with a stick pointer plotting battles from the Pentagon. Albert was more of an on-the-scene man. He favored the personal approach, aiming to burrow into a horse's brain, and those index cards weren't just crammed with data on wins and losses. They provided extensive insights about Thoroughbred character—skittishness or a taste for cool weather or a long-standing grudge against a jockey who'd once been too liberal with his whip.

"You can't forget that horses are people, too."

Albert's briefcases also contained the latest treatises on animal psychology, and his betting choices were rife with behavioral theory. His basic thesis was that horses always reverted to the primal urge for fight or flight. If a horse was the sole front-runner in a race, he'd spring loose and fly, a stress-free wire-to-wire victory. If two front-running horses went at it neck and neck—even running at the exact same pace as that single horse had—that was a fight, and each would wither under the emotional pressure of trying to hold the other one off. Physically, the output in both races was identical. It was the mental tacking that proved tantamount.

Albert carefully monitored horses moving up and down in class. A horse with a brief history of eighth- and ninth-place finishes against high-quality competition was destined to blossom against lesser company, eager to establish his self-worth once again. That was fight. But a horse who'd been running too long in company too exalted would lose his confidence entirely. Even if he took the lead at some point in the race, he would gladly hand it over. Flight. He'd established his place in the herd, and that place was not coming in first.

In general, Albert steered clear of horses who didn't win, even if they'd finished second five of the last six times out. A perennial runner-up lacked the necessary goods. He was by nature a follower, not a fighter, and, no matter how skilled his jockey or trainer or how weak the rest of the field, nature usually won out.

There were other basic rules of nature to be followed:

Never bet on anyone—horse, trainer, jockey— who's in a slump.

Always give the benefit, a large sweeping benefit, of the doubt to anybody in the midst of a streak.

Destiny is forever at play at the track.

ONCE ALBERT had educated me in the dizzying number of factors that went into handicapping a race, we moved on to how to bet them. Once again simple rules, like bet to win, gave way to a more complicated overall strategy. Bets could be divided into two categories: straight bets—win, place, or show—and exotics—things like exactas, trifectas, daily doubles, pick threes, and pick sixes.

With the exotics, it was all about determining the angle of diminishing returns. If you'd narrowed down the probable winners to three or four, exactas or trifectas were the way to go. You could lay a minimum of $2 on a straight trifecta—horse A to finish first, horse B second, horse C third—or, for a bit more money, you could box them so that one ticket covered A, B, and C finishing first, second, and third in any combination.

Albert regularly bet daily doubles (picking the winners of two consecutive races) and pick threes (three races in a row), but he wasn't a fan of the pick six. The payoffs could wander into the six figures, but they only matched the odds. He figured winning on a single pick-six ticket was on a par with the likelihood of Ronald Reagan's embracing Communism. Occasionally, if he felt one or two races could be narrowed down to a single horse, he'd roll a pick around that sure thing. He'd position his chosen horse as the anchor for numerous combinations involving runners from the other races, creating a series of twenty or thirty or fifty pick-six tickets. He'd won the pick six only once, down in Del Mar the year after he'd dumped show business. The payoff had been $96,000. Albert said it was fate rewarding him for choosing the honorable path in life.

At some point, Albert's idea of teaching me how I should play the horses shifted into an illustration of how he played them. As an independent being with an independent life, there was no way I could re-create even a sliver of his all-consuming system. Albert's was a seventh-wonder-caliber business venture. Despite the fact that my funds consisted of money I'd earned scooping ice cream the previous summer, I absorbed any number of monologues concerning the horseplayer's version of sound financial investment.

Albert's goal wasn't merely to figure out who would win each race. The common fan did that, and did it far more effectively than Albert. They wagered simply—win, place, show—on horses with visibly strong records. They bet low-risk, sentimental choices. Albert had calculated his winning ratio at around 20 percent (Albert calculated just about everything). The general public weighed in at 33 percent. But Albert wasn't just looking to be right.

He was looking for value, for overlooked and forgotten horses and for patterns other people didn't spot. A winner who went off at odds of 2–1 didn't make Albert any money. One who defied common faith to the tune of 12–1, that was a worthwhile investment.

Full-time handicapping demanded that you be ruthless. If a horse was in a decline—no matter how brilliant it used to be— "drop it like a hot potato." This was no place for sentimental affection. There was, however, a place for restraint. Of the nine races usually run a day, Albert only bet four or five of them. Only when all his informational input produced a horse with a definite edge, and only when that edge wasn't so obvious as to be heavily backed by the racing public. He never wagered on the last race, because it was purposely designed to be indecipherable, a stew of bottom-level runners pitched together for those gamblers with less self-control than Albert who couldn't resist a final grab at deliverance. It was one last-chance chance to earn back their dignity. Management took full advantage of the fact that they would've emptied their pockets on a line of monkeys running backward down the stretch.

AFTER A few months, my purely informational relationship with Albert began to do what relationships do when plied with time and substance. It grew complex. I was clearly his protégé, but, just as clearly, he didn't want me to turn out anything like him.

"You deserve a better life, kid," he repeated constantly.

I told him he didn't need to worry. Our aspirations were far from the same.

Albert was so immersed in playing the horses that it dyed his skin and slopped into his eyeballs, affecting the very way he thought and moved. Gambling wove a net all around him, one too narrow to catch anything else. It gave him an aura of loneliness, a grudging acceptance of a future in which no one else would have time or space for his obsession. Racehorses did what they did— arched and swerved, defied capture and defined captivation—and Albert's existence could be slimmed down to a shadow dancing away behind it all. His relationship with the track contained all the renunciation of a religious conversion. The relationship I'd crafted consisted of something else entirely. The numbers, the figuring, the angles only provided me with what dirt gives to an ant—raw material for occupation.

Albert cottoned to our differences. He was always telling me in a teasing way that I bet too conservatively. I had to learn to play fast and loose, to have a little fun and develop a flair. I was still a handicapper, but he was going to make me a gambler "or die trying." Then, one afternoon just before school broke for the summer, he sat me down on a slatted wooden bench near the paddock and delivered what for him was an extremely condensed and focused speech. I don't remember the exact words, but it ran along the lines that he didn't understand me. I had "it"—the instincts, the touch, the gut knowledge. I understood the horses. I'd parsed every piece of the gambling puzzle. So why did I keep putting it together wrong?

"It's like"—and this part I remember quite clearly—"you don't want to enjoy it. It's like you're afraid of the whole damn track."

He asked if I had any idea what the hell he was talking about, and I didn't have an answer. Except, of course, that what he said was true.

I left Albert and Santa Anita that afternoon, and I never went back. I told myself it was because playing the horses required too much work for too little reward, that I would never achieve Albert's expert status so there was no use in trying. The truth was, with that afternoon speech Albert had waltzed his emotional carnival into the very thing I'd been avoiding. He'd tapped into that space which had gone hollow as soon as I let go of the track.

I didn't return to Santa Anita again until I was thirty. The track had switched ownership, traded up for a more brightly hued spit-and-polish, but the windowless basement room had barely changed. It still smelled of cigarettes and old plastic, looked fluorescent, and felt comfortingly stale. I paced the aisles between the dented metal chairs looking for twin briefcases, an Astros T-shirt, or peanut M&M's. Albert wasn't around.

I hadn't really expected to find him. A decade was a long time for a horseplayer not to do any drifting. I'd just wanted to tell him, in case by some chance he was still there, that I'd finally figured out what he was talking about.

There's handicapping—dangers bypassed, roads predetermined, life conducted via a series of systems. And there's taking a gamble.

For me, they can never be one and the same.

Chapter Seven

UNCONDITIONAL LOVE:

The Anatomy of a Racing Fan

Thère is a way we meet, the racetrack and I, like lovers
always joining up on the same park bench. We can be in
California, New York, Florida, Kentucky. The seduction doesn't change.

I come through the turnstile and buy a program, but don't open it right away. I step outside with still-unexplored promise gripped in my hand. Then I head toward the top of the stretch. That end zone of grass or cement is usually empty. It's not considered desirable viewing, just a plot of ground a breath away from the horses as they flank the turn but full furlongs from the finish. For me, it's an essential part of the transition, like those buoyancy tanks that gradually accustom astronauts to a world without gravity. It gives me time with the races before I ever cross over into the track.

It wasn't until years after I'd outgrown my jockey dreams that I finally admitted my life at the races would not be my life. At first, I couldn't shake the idea that my career should tie me inextricably to racehorses, that we had a history together I was meant to honor. The trouble was that no job seemed right. I wanted racing on my own terms, and working around the track—for the racing commission, the racing papers, or even in a trainer's barn—would require experiencing it on someone else's. It wasn't until my sophomore year of high school, just returned from St. Timothy's and braced against the Longacres paddock fence Saturday after Saturday, that I realized my ache for high-pitched involvement had faded. I was in the midst of a satisfying, healthy relationship. Perhaps my future at the racetrack needed to stretch no further than being a fan.

The hardest part was telling May-May. I kept spooling back to a day six years before when I'd perched on one of her wrought-iron patio chairs and struggled to explain why I'd quit riding lessons at the local stable. I'd admitted that trotting ponies in tight little circles made me feel as if millions of spiders were crawling up my legs, that if we didn't break into a gallop in the next second, both the pony and I would explode. May-May had laughed and told me that the racetrack and I were destined to be together. How was I supposed to let destiny down?

I allowed months to drift by without saying anything, just growing quieter and quieter about my designs for the future. I'd always been a big planner and an even bigger dreamer, so it didn't take May-May all that long to discern something off-kilter. Once she'd pinned me, there was no point to wriggling. So I confessed.

"I don't want to work at the track after all. I think I just want to stay a fan."

I was convinced I was a quitter. I'd made a momentous, disastrous, and—worst of all—cowardly choice. May-May just eyed me over her reading glasses.

"Of course you're going to be a fan. What better thing to be?"

It hadn't occurred to me until right then that a fan was exactly what May-May had been for almost eighty years.

When I left her condominium that afternoon, May-May slipped me a secret, something she'd been saving, perhaps for signs of a less fierce, more focused granddaughter. She said the next time I visited Longacres, I should watch a race from the top of the stretch. I did.

The races and I have been meeting up there ever since.

There's no complex wizardry to the top of the stretch, none of the art required in piecing together a perfect trifecta or spying a winner in the paddock. It's just Thoroughbreds free and clear. The empty track spreads out like an unspoiled page. Then the horses break from the gate, a band of color rippling forth as if gliding across water. As the runners shimmy down the backside, something inside me shakes itself awake. Sometimes it starts from my chest and moves outward, sometimes in my toes traveling up. The horses angle into the bend, and the jockeys spread their reins, "throwing crosses," an invitation to the animals beneath who click into some slingshot gear even longer and looser than the one before. I empty my brain, because distraction now would mean missing the crucial part. Coming around the far turn, and the transfer of the spark.

The horses peel out in front of me, and it happens. The rail separating us disappears. I merge with those dirt-flecked chests reaching and churning, thrusting forward and falling back. Our strides sweep sicklelike over the dirt, humming, pumping, gathering up the track, then spitting it away. For an instant, I become the races. Then they're gone. Backsides disappearing toward the finish, a smear of heat left on my imagination. And I'm ready for a day at the track.

That's it. That's the secret. No bugle calls or blankets of roses, just one moment whittled down to unadulterated racehorse. The far turn is my own honeybee, knee-walking brand of intoxication. A hand-tailored version of unconditional love.

I'M FAR from the first person ever to love racing to distraction. The sport has been casting its spell for generations, following close on the heels of colonization in Europe, India, Africa, and the Americas. And it's made people do all sorts of crazy things.

In England in the early 1800s, racing grew so popular that tracks sprouted deep in the countryside. London fans demanded instant news of the results and officials responded. They began transporting information via capsules clipped to the feet of carrier pigeons or tucked into the collars of specially trained dogs who took to the dangerous rural roads solo. Such creatures cornered the sports-reporting route until the telegraph arrived in the 1860s.

In nineteenth-century Russia, a Tartar man who wished to marry would challenge his intended to a horse race, to be run before a gathering of the entire town. If the man won, the two were automatically wedded. Should the woman prove faster, victory earned her the power to choose. Still farther east, in Mongolia, longhaired mountain ponies competed in a yearly derby run over thirty miles of rough steppe. The jockeys were the most light-weight young boys capable of lasting the distance and they rode bareback, rolling their cotton trousers high up their thighs to better clutch the pony's ribs. In one hand, they wielded a long whip, and in the other rawhide reins attached to a bridle with a silver disk fixed to the pony's forehead. The winner received a lifetime of "honourable idleness," financed by the Bogdo, the royal patron of the race. Nineteenth-century West Africa boasted a slew of annual race festivals, scattered throughout the Kingdom of Borgoo. Jockeys, carrying elaborately carved spears and clad in turbans and red leather boots, rode Arabians decked in charms, bells, and multicolored tassels. The surrounding festivities swelled with acrobats, Muhammadan priests, and naked virgin girls wearing strings of beads and flowers woven through their hair.

As popular tracks continued their spread, such mass entertainment proved a powerful antidote to hardship. In England, the Newmarket racetrack remained in operation throughout both world wars despite grain shortages, grazing land plowed up for airstrips, and track buildings requisitioned as military outposts. When the German army invaded Poland at the start of World War II, they expressly ordered racetracks left open in hopes that gambling losses would demoralize the population. Every weekend, the Polish citizenry slid past panzer tanks and bayoneted Third Reich soldiers to wager a few scavenged coins on the horses. In occupied France, Hitler's government kept the races running even after both major tracks outside Paris were hit by Allied bombs in 1943. They also confiscated all Jewish-owned breeding stock, loading premier stallions onto railcars headed back to Germany. Any lesser creatures were expropriated and destroyed.

In contemporary Beirut, where the track once served as a playground for Middle Eastern sheiks and princes, races are still run every Sunday afternoon. Horses stretch past pocked stone walls and bombed-out buildings, around a five-furlong track called the Palace of Peace.

AMERICAN RACING fans boast their own daredevil history, beginning in the seventeenth century, when neighboring towns would pair their fastest horses against one another in match races. Intervillage rivalries rose up, and the contests regularly erupted into brawls flamed by local politics. With the onset of formal racetracks, fans still clung to that yen for participation. Many would gallop their own horses alongside the rail to watch—and occasionally interfere with—the action taking place on the track. In Washington, D.C., major race days were the equivalent of national holidays, with even Congress shutting down since so few of its members bothered to show up for debate. A bit farther north, in New York City, a handful of fashionable men's clubs surfaced that were devoted solely to racing. Gentlemen of property and sophistication had become gentlemen of the track.

In the 1860s, August Belmont—National Democratic Party chairman, New York head of the Rothschild banking operation,

and financial brain behind the city's soon-to-be-erected subway system—was so entranced by horse racing that he sponsored a stable
and then a leading stakes race run in his name. His closest competi-
tor, Leonard Jerome, juggled stints as a lawyer, publisher, financier,
and patron of the arts, though his most famous role would come
years later when his daughter married Lord Randolph Churchill
and gave birth to a son called Winston. In 1865, Jerome one-upped
Belmont by erecting an entire racecourse dedicated to himself.
Jerome Park, rising out of a dilapidated family estate in the Bronx,
was modeled upon the most glamorous European tracks and
included a ballroom, trap-shooting enclosure, skating rink, and polo
field. It would be forty years before Belmont's son, August II, lev-
eled the field by convincing the Westchester Racing Club to chris-
ten its luxurious new five-hundred-acre racecourse Belmont Park
in honor of his father.

By the time May-May reached the track just after the turn of the
century, such moneyed enthusiasts had transformed the sport into a
full-blown society venture, one of the few forms of decadence sanctioned by the upper crust. The country at the time was plunged
hip-deep in innovation. The Wright brothers had just invented the
airplane, intellectuals like Freud and Einstein were unleashing
their theories, and Thomas Edison, fiddling with the concept of
mobile light and images, had given birth to the first moving pictures. May-May read about such advances in purloined newspapers
she hid under bits of embroidered linen meant to form the beginnings of her trousseau. At seventeen, a reluctant debutante just
sprung from finishing school, she was ripe to shed her grandfather
and his archaic southern ways. Her lifeline to the modern world
was her brother, four years older and newly graduated from
Princeton. Growing up, Robert had taught May-May to play poker,
wield a shotgun, and ride with legs split over a hunt saddle. One
afternoon that summer, he offered to escort her to the track.

May-May agreed to the races because of her love for horses, and
because it was something, anything, as yet unexplored. But she
knew nothing of the sport's internal mechanisms. Proper young
ladies at the turn of the century were guarded like maximum-

security offenders from such indelicate pursuits. She expected Thoroughbreds, long-lined and classy, providing a fresh backdrop for the same social maneuvering she knew from concerts and dinner parties and any other event where the "right" people gathered. Instead, from the first point of contact, the Pimlico racetrack erupted.

May-May entered Pimlico at Robert's side and, for a race or two, stuck by him in the clubhouse. She absorbed the casual etiquette of greeting and gambling—money spilling from pockets, horses discussed, dismissed, or deified. It was an alluring crowd, ever so slightly dissipated, one unconcerned with earnestness or suffocation. But, glancing over the edge of the boxes toward the ground floor, May-May observed something even more novel going on down below. In the center of the betting ring, bankers stood bargaining with bookies. Robert's jim-dandy friends came dashing back upstairs bearing hot tips from stable hands and thirteen-year-old jockeys. Life was brushing elbows with life.

Mid-afternoon, Robert finally noticed May-May's attention fixed elsewhere.

"Do you want to go down?" He asked. When she nodded, he flipped her some loose coins and instructed her on how to place a bet.

"If anyone gives you trouble, don't tell them you belong to me."

With Robert's money pressed in her palm, May-May headed downstairs, past the sign reading "Gentlemen Only," and straight into the ring. She kept moving until a wash of suspenders and bowler hats had swallowed up the silk brocade of her dress. No one grabbed an elbow to turn her away. She tried four bookies before she finally found one, parked on the fringes of the action, willing to take her bet. Five dollars on the five horse to win.

Instead of returning to the boxes, May-May kept walking until she reached the far side of the circle, then followed the rail all the way round to the track. The horses were filing out for the next race and each one skittered past her, so close she could read each twitch and tremble. A dozen plumes of dust rose behind them, leaving her wreathed in grit. It was as if, after seventeen years perched on a cliff overlooking the ocean, someone had finally shown her how to unlace her boots and jump in.

May-May would spend the next decade and a half at the races—tramping through backstretch mud, mixing with the riffraff along the rail, finding a direction, coming of age. The track saw her through nursing college, a broken engagement with a doctor whose widowed mother disapproved of her penchant for gambling, and a new taste for old cowboy stories about driving cattle from Texas to Dodge City along the Chisholm Trail. Her heroes shifted from ponies to pioneers—British explorer Gertrude Bell trekking across Arabia and Mesopotamia, and the cowgirl "Little Jo" Monaghan who in 1867 had disguised herself as a man and journeyed to Montana to work herding sheep and busting broncs in a Wild West show.

Eventually, May-May's appetite for what the races could offer outgrew even the races themselves. The track had shifted her internal compass, flipping it due west. When she boarded the Union Pacific Railroad for New Mexico in 1920, she left behind her fledgling trousseau and instructions for Robert to forward any racing news by mail.

EVEN FROM the far edges of civilized country, May-May had no intention of losing the horses. Often months after the fact, she pored over any imported racing prose she could get her hands on. Most track reporters were unimpressive, stodgy old gamblers or novice journalists with little knowledge of the game. But in the early 1920s, shortly after she'd moved to Alaska, May-May happened upon a distinctive voice edging its way into popularity. He was a New York sportswriter who covered a bit of boxing, a bit of baseball, and a great deal of the track. May-May read a few of his columns and ordered Robert to stamp and send more, prompting a monthly delivery of thick parchment envelopes. This beat reporter intrigued her with his gift for language and ability to slip seamlessly from fan to critic to social commentator. Beneath his cool-guy prose, she found shared strains of a romantic, a man swept away by the racetrack and all its unorthodox splendor. He was a published poet, a Kansas-born Colorado boy, and a veteran of the Spanish-American War. His name was Damon Runyon.

May-May became a lifelong fan of Runyon's, roped in by those same tough-soft qualities that had drawn her to racehorses and the Wild West. She had a cracked hardcover collection of his stories, which we started reading together when I was only old enough to laugh at the wild language. Over the years, the more complicated underpinnings of the man began to soak through as well. Damon Runyon ran deep on contradictions—a soft-spoken, thin-cheeked aesthete who stocked his bedroom with shotguns and left his wife and two children for a teenage Mexican chorus girl. He wore wire-rimmed glasses, hand-tailored suits, and loads of shiny costume jewelry, and mixed with the likes of Al Capone, Bugsy Siegel, Pancho Villa, and Benito Mussolini. He spent an hour dressing each morning, matching suit to tie to snap-brim hat, drank forty cups of coffee a day, and smoked a cigarette with each one. He was a bit sad, a bit wild, a bit wistful. And Damon Runyon was most certainly in love. He'd toss around cynical phrases about hard-luck horseplayers and fixed races until you believed he'd grown as jaded as the hoodlums surrounding him. Then he'd start a column as he did in 1930 when a 100–1 shot called Jim Dandy won the Travers Stakes at Saratoga.

"You only dream the thing that happened here this afternoon."

Runyon started out as a newspaper man for the simplest of reasons: because his father had been one, too. Alfred Runyon worked as a reporter and typesetter for the *Manhattan Independent* in Manhattan, Kansas. He would write his articles as he set them, using a composing stick to pluck each individual letter from its box and arrange it upside down and backward inside a wooden frame. Then he'd crank them in tight, slap on some ink, and wheel his column down the hall to the handpress. Alfred's career was small-time, and his favored leisure activity came sealed in a whiskey bottle. As soon as possible, son Damon moved on. He signed up as a reporter at the *Colorado Springs Gazette,* then followed a journalist buddy to the real Manhattan in 1911. Almost at once, he snagged a job on William Randolph Hearst's *New York American,* his territory split between covering sports and downtown murder trials. He was thirty-one years old and already a married man, but the *New York American* is where Damon Runyon was born.

Fortunately for Runyon, the sports beat and the crime beat turned out to be perfectly simpatico. He could show up at the criminal court and ten minutes later know who was a lock for the next day's stakes race or prizefight. He'd landed in Manhattan just in time for Times Square's gangsterland debut, and Broadway packed more color into one square of cement than existed in the entire state of Kansas. Runyon befriended petty hustlers and horseplayers with tags like Bat Masterson, Big Frenchy DeMange, Sugar Plum Yude-lowitz, and Pussy McGuire, whose racket was stealing cats and selling them to rich old ladies. His love of legitimate games like baseball and football gradually gave way to more unpredictable ventures: a racetrack hewn by Prohibition, Arnold Rothstein, and the time-honored tradition of the fix. Though he didn't drink or tote a sawed-off shotgun, he took to other gangster pastimes—playing all-night crap games in cheap motel rooms, and zinging $100 bills to a bookie operating out of a doorway on Forty-ninth Street and Seventh Avenue—and he took notes every inch of the way. In his columns, he advised wagering on favorites, the sort of wing-footed *über* athletes who won races by walloping margins; but when he bet, he put his money on hopeless 30–1 long shots just as I did when I was thirteen.

Runyon excelled at popping open the seam separating the criminal element from the decent folk. He wasn't beneath taking the Catholic cardinal to a championship fight or above swiping a few dollars from a depression-era "Milk for Babies" fund when he needed cash to put on a horse. Once he got to know the separate strata of New York society, the breakdown seemed perfectly clear. Thieves were the honest crooks. Business tycoons and newspaper magnates were the dishonest ones, who also committed the far worse sin of being boring. Runyon eschewed the high life for the low, stepping inside gangsterland without editorial comment. To those who criticized his moral detachment, he always responded: "When you start asking questions, people are liable to think you are perhaps looking for answers." A potentially ticklish situation in Runyon's slice of the world.

Runyon's columns, combinations of poetry and machine-gun reportage, brought the track to national attention. He developed followers from the White House to the back room of Lindy's All-Night Delicatessen on Fiftieth and Broadway, and his short-story collections sold more than a million copies. He knew how to write like a Thoroughbred ran; musically, passionately, carving angles, slits, and valleys. He knew how to take people to the races.

AS RUNYON'S popularity spread, another relationship was developing, one which would further bind the sport to its growing legion of American fans. By the late twenties, newspapers began padding their race coverage with photos of cinema darlings like Mary Pickford and Eddie Cantor hobnobbing at the track. The country was in the midst of a full-scale movie mania. It seemed only natural that these two glamour worlds collide.

Hollywood glitterati proved born gamblers, enamored of the high life in any form it might take. Big-time performers like Jimmy Durante and Al Jolson quickly turned big-time bettors, with bookies regularly directed to their agents' offices to collect on overdue debts. A racehorse became an accessory as essential as a fur coat or a vacation home, and Thoroughbred owner rosters swelled with luminaries such as Fred Astaire, Betty Grable, and Judy Garland, who ran a string of horses under the name Rainbow Stables. Oriental Park in Havana—which until Castro's revolution in 1959 ushered in races, dance bands, and a grandstand casino all winter long—poured cocktails for the likes of Rita Hayworth, Nat King Cole, and Errol Flynn. For a time, the legendary siren Lana Turner linked herself with an equally notorious racetrack casanova, a South American trainer named Horatio Luro, and the two steamed up gossip mills by regularly slipping off for very long weekends in Argentina and Brazil.

The racetrack also became Hollywood's vice of choice. Rumors rose about a sanitarium in the desert where film stars a bit too loose at the betting windows could retrieve their resolve with a monthlong rest cure. In Los Angeles, enough money flowed from the big screen in the mid-thirties to float two premier tracks, Hollywood Park and Santa Anita. In 1937, when local businessmen decided to build a third temple at the resort town of Del Mar, Bing Crosby, a Santa Anita cofounder, became one of the track's leading investors. Newsreel footage of Crosby kissing the cheek of every woman to walk through the gates on Del Mar's opening day unspooled in movie houses across the country. Racing had arrived.

The track maintained its stylish status admirably in the coming decades, thriving through the fifties, sixties, and into the seventies before the combination of legalized gambling and flashier, wealthier organized sports like football and basketball began to push it off the pleasure map. By the time I joined up with the track in 1977, the idea of a day at the races had slipped from chic to passé. Unlike following the NFL, which merely meant turning on the television any fall Sunday afternoon, being a racing fan required effort. As the two of us matured together, I discovered how to find the sport when I needed it, digging up tracks and fans in whichever city I happened to land. But when I wanted to pretend the races had never existed, I discovered that could be pretty easy to do, too.

IN MY late twenties, I abandoned thoughts of a career in the movie industry and moved from Los Angeles to Manhattan in an effort to start my life anew. Instead, I began executing my usual dance between an uninspired job and uninspired relationship, spending hours with movies or museums or just walking the streets. After six months, I was already lonely, and desperately unhappy. I wasn't following the races at all.

That fall, when I visited Seattle, my mother suggested a day riding horses up through the shale cliffs and spiked greenery of eastern Washington. Though I hadn't been on a horse in several years, and though all my internal checkpoint voices warned "Get off and stay off," I agreed to go. The whole day—the smell of hay and worn leather, the muscles shifting beneath my thighs, the wind-whistle through the grass—felt ominous. Near the end of the afternoon, as we swayed up a dappled hillside back toward the barn, a wasp

zeroed in on my palomino's backside. He lit into a round of bucking and rearing that should have knocked me like a rag doll to the
ground. But while my mind juggled with what to do, my body
instantly remembered. I melted right into the small of that horse's
back, tucking my legs up around his belly and hugging into his
jerky rhythm. We danced and flew, strung together tight as two
beads, and I felt like a rocket readying for liftoff. I felt nine years
old and longing to stay aloft forever, bucking and wheeling in the
wheat grass. By the time he'd rocked it all out, we'd swapped places.
He had gone completely soft. I was left breathless and shaking.

"You can ride like the devil," the ranch wrangler told me.

I nodded. I'd given myself away. Riding those bumps felt natural, requiring none of the effort it took to negotiate the flatness of
my everyday world. The shape I was living was all wrong.

That palomino rattled me, but not quite hard enough that I was
willing to move. Back in New York, I spent the coming months
parked in the kind of apathy that crawls out from depression and
consumes everything around it. On the outside I still appeared
highly functional, and I managed to convince myself I could hold
off derailment permanently. Then, one night that spring, just a few
months after my twenty-eighth birthday, I got some unnerving
physical evidence of my imminent demise.

As I lay down to go to sleep, I felt my heart thumping. I was just
lying there, but it felt as if I was struggling up a mountain. I turned
on the lamp next to my bed, and checked my pulse against the second hand on the alarm clock. Perfectly normal. When I lay down
again, there it was again slapping away at my chest, not faster, just
harder, as if straining to find enough blood to keep me afloat. I lay
awake until 4:30, watching *I Love Lucy* and *Bewitched* and wondering whether I should go to the emergency room.

The next day was undiluted spring. Manhattan bulged with distractions, and even if I still felt groggy, it was easy to believe the
previous night had been some darkness-inspired nightmare, surely
not as bad as I imagined. Except that it happened again. Then the
days began to feel fuzzy, too, as if I were listing sideways into the
city. Finally I went to a doctor. She quizzed me inside out and

upside down. She ran an EKG—normal—and drew blood. The medical diagnosis was dehydration. She told me to drink Gatorade, then gave me a prescription for sleeping pills. I was too frightened to fill it, afraid of falling asleep and never waking up again.

After another week or so, the Gatorade, or my monumental willpower, stepped in and for the most part stemmed the pulsating. But from time to time, my heart would flare again. That month felt like one endless stretch of failing to fall asleep, lying between the sheets and listening to distant dog yelps, my hands folded over a heart where nothing would coalesce anymore. April ended. May began. The first Saturday, Derby Day, I walked into a Radio Shack and heard the beginning strains of "My Old Kentucky Home." Everything that had been so perilously held together finally fell apart. Those floodgates lodged inside me opened and, quite simply, the ability to fall in love flowed back. The first thing I did was cry for hours. The second thing I did was go to the races.

When I wobbled back onto the track after that Radio Shack Derby, I headed straight for the top of the stretch. I'd been gone for ten years, far too long for any lover with even slightly fickle tendencies to stick it out. The races, God bless them, were still there. I walked to the rail at the far end of Belmont Park and, ever so slowly, let that forward pulse fill me again. I didn't check the odds or visit the paddock, didn't buy a program, an ice cream, a bottle of water. I barely moved. Each horse who flew around that corner with legs spread long or tucked tight to his belly seemed to be flinging himself off a mountain.

By the end of the day, I'd shifted into some foggy demilitarized zone between nothing and something. I hadn't instantly recovered the reckless, devil-riding child as I'd hoped I might. Instead, what gripped me hardest that first afternoon, and each afternoon to follow, was the sense of being embraced. In an instant, I was forgiven ten years' worth of disloyalty, doubts, contradictions, and complications.

The racetrack took me back as if I'd never been gone.

RETURNING TO the races as an adult, I longed to pick up the romance exactly where I'd found it for the first time twenty years before. I wasn't interested in a newly defined grown-up relationship, one where knowledge balanced out discovery, intensity fell in with serenity. I wanted nothing less than the gut-busting, rule-flaunting seven-year-old me.

Then, one weekend at Belmont, I noticed a teenage boy circling the same path I was, from paddock to track, track to paddock, carrying a camera equipped with a zoom lens so large it took both arms to raise it to his eye. He was tall and skinny, his pretty freckled face at odds with the long string-bean body. He'd dressed as plainly as possible, in a striped polo shirt, grubby oversize sneakers and pants you couldn't recall the second you turned around. If anyone caught his eye, he ducked his head. I guessed he'd already steeled himself for a lifetime of not fitting in.

I saw him again and again on successive Saturdays, mentioned him to a few people in passing, and finally found someone who knew him and could introduce us. His name was Brandon and he was fourteen, a budding track photographer. In appearance he was fragile, caught in a limbo between child and adult selves. His teeth stuck out at funny angles and when he lifted his arm to steady that massive zoom you could count his ribs through the cloth of his shirt. But the first time I asked him about horses, it was like I'd blown a gust of wind up into a flag. The fidgeting stopped, replaced by a long, informed treatise on his current favorite, a bay colt named Lemon Drop Kid, the one who'd beat Charismatic in the Belmont the spring before.

"I've been watching him since last summer," he explained, detailing the exact moment Lemon Drop Kid first caught his camera-tuned eye and just what he'd need to accomplish come fall to be elected Horse of the Year. The details kept pouring out, so that I believed he could never quite be satiated. Lemon Drop Kid could run in every race, every day, at every track in the world and Brandon still wouldn't have enough of him.

"He's the best horse in America. When he wants to run, no one can beat him. Anywhere. Most of them won't even try."

"Have fun today," I told him when I finally let him go so he'd have time to prepare his cameras for Lemon Drop Kid's race.

He was already on his feet. "I will as long as Lemon Drop wins."

As he shambled off, a familiar twang traveled through me. Brandon was just now falling in love.

In the coming months, the two of us forged a lopsided friendship, one in which I asked him about his cameras, his pictures, his Lemon Drop Kid, and he never asked me anything at all. He was at the track almost every weekend, his mother driving him the two hours down from their house upstate in Millbrook. He would smile and wave when I saw him, but he always let me be the first to signal. Sometimes he talked eagerly, stuttering and stumbling, filling me in on a trip planned for Kentucky and new designs for his racing website, and later sending follow-up e-mails rife with exclamation points. Other days, he'd squirm as if just talking meant undergoing some quiet torture. Those afternoons I quickly let him go.

There were plenty of days in which we never spoke at all. I would just watch him wander alone into the winner's circle or along the edge of the track, his awkward, hesitant gait always managing to land him right in the face of the jockey, the horse, or the neck-and-neck fight to the wire. His aunt was a photographer by hobby, and she'd taught him what he knew of lenses and camera angles. He stored his pictures, thousands of them, in shoeboxes in his bedroom. When we first met, I asked him if he had a darkroom he could use at home or in school. He shook his head and looked a little embarrassed.

"I just drop them off at Walgreen's. For a drugstore, they do an okay job."

When I was a sophomore in high school, a year older than Brandon, I'd briefly taken to photography via an art class taught by an ex-county sheriff in the dank basement of the science building. I'd researched the history of race photography, how in the 1870s university founder Leland Stanford hired Eadweard Muybridge, a British photographer, to solve the mystery over whether a galloping horse ever lifts all four hooves off the ground at once. Muybridge set up twenty-four mahogany cameras, a contraption he called a Zoopraxoscope, to capture a runner in each phase of motion. His results would finally prove the racehorse's propensity for flight. Soon afterward, he figured out how to string a trip wire across the finish so the first horse across triggered a flashbulb attached to the rail. The printed image, just vertical lines against a white background, provided racing's first ever photo finish. All that sophomore spring I'd toted my brand-new and at times inexplicable Canon 35 mm to the track. I learned to capture horses midgait, with all four limbs skimming the dirt or tucked up under them in Muybridge's kangaroo hop. For a while, I'd even lost the uncertainty of adolescence in the certain science of movement, of cranks and gears and flywheels operating beneath the skin of it all.

Watching Brandon, I realized my whole life could be charted that way, twin time lines with one taking place at the racetrack and one in the world at large. If I cut open our relationship, I might read my life etched into the layers, like counting age from the rings of a tree. Swinging back to the core, to Brandon itchy-footed and just discovering, would be impossible. It felt grown-up, this admission that history matters, that I'm defined by what I've known, loved, and even lost. Racing and I have come too far to drop everything and begin the game again from scratch. There will be no more starting over. Only moving on.

ONCE UPON a time, when I fantasized about the races, I inevitably featured myself in the driver's seat—winning the Kentucky Derby aboard Alydar, beating Angel by a nose in the Belmont Stakes, taking all three Triple Crown races wire to wire. That, too, has changed. The hunger I need to fill has shifted to something a little more expansive. When I come to the races, I come to leave everything else behind. I want to shed responsibility, and melt into pleasure. Of course, I'm still curious about how those two speed-frenzied minutes would feel, about dirt-glazed goggles and thighs wobbling as I roll out of the saddle. But I've made room for another fantasy as well: a day at the races that includes me as just a fan.

My dream day would unfold at the French track Longchamp, a course so lush and a crowd so tuned it's known as heaven for horses. Every race there is run on grass, soft and forgiving. Exotic elements would add to the mystique—unknown trainers and jockeys, races run clockwise instead of counter, a racing lingo I only partially speak and understand. On my chosen afternoon, every horse would have a name like Regret or Alydar, something salty-sweet and sexy that takes up space on the tongue. I would spread out a blanket on the grass, bring Bing cherries, sugar cookies, and lots of champagne. I would bring friends, but the kind of friends who know when to drift away, so before that race late in the day, perhaps seven or eight on a nine-race card, I would stand alone along the paddock fence. And I'd spot that one horse, carrying his neck bowed and haunches taut, rippling like an electric current with wanting and needing to run. At some point he would glance over at me. He would be a colt, slight, long-legged, and temperamental, a bay with notes of red in his coat, a black mane and tail, and no markings except a dusting of white on his forehead. The two of us would merge.

The odds would be long, maybe 18–1, and I would bet a fistful of francs not caring if I lost, but knowing that I could not. I'd walk to the top of the stretch, the grass slipping in through the slats of my sandals, and I'd be alone there, too, resting my elbows on the white painted rail as the horses loaded into the gate. My colt would cock his head my direction and hook my gaze just long enough to cement our unspoken alliance. Then the bell would ring, and the runners would spring free. I don't need dreaming for the rest. It would happen just as it always does.

That's the fantasy. But in dropping away from the races and coming back again, even fantasy has taken a different sort of hold. It's still lovely, but it's only frosting. There is something deeper, a louder, crisper hum, emanating from real life. It's the whole package—the give-and-take of time and space, tolerance, loyalty, and humor. More than anything, it's just being there.

For every rendezvous with Captain Steve, for every May's Regal Girl or first-time visit to the Kentucky Derby, there have been hundreds of less spectacular moments, moments notable only because I was present. There have been humdrum races, lost bets, horses gimping across the wire. There have been sunburns and melted ice-cream cones, cups of bitter coffee, and coats clutched around my chest. There have been days when May-May hovered so close that I could've sworn I felt her shoulder brush against my own, and days when she was only the gauziest memory, and I felt completely and alarmingly alone.

The races and I each exist in tacit agreement about what the other is meant to supply. The track brings spontaneity, excess, an honesty of emotion. I bring a promise not to assume or plan or judge. We both stay primed to possibility. I can look into the future and see how we might continue in this way forever, thriving not on the peaks but on the potential for them.

Surely this is what it means to be in love.

Chapter Eight

FORMING A VALUE SYSTEM:

Hustles, Fixes, and the Drug Controversy

Innocence doesn't survive long at the track. I can trace the fatal crack in mine to the winter I turned nine years old. One evening as our family was sitting down to dinner, the network news made space between the gas crisis and test-tube babies for a horse-racing story. At first, I only paid flickering attention since the coverage seemed more to do with courtrooms and men in wide-lapel suits than Thoroughbreds. Then the announcer began a list of names I knew to be jockeys. Famous jockeys. And

last on the list came the most famous jockey of all, my rebel sweetheart, Angel Cordero.

A picture of Angel popped up on-screen, the same grinning
black-and-white photo I'd torn from *Sports Illustrated* and tacked
up on my bulletin board. Then the allotted minute of coverage
ended and the anchor shifted over to the weather report. I had no
clue what had befallen my hero. For the next three nights, I turned
on the television at exactly 6:30, displaying a first-ever interest in
world affairs. Angel made no encore appearances.

May-May had been following Angel's fortunes as well, and
when I saw her that Saturday afternoon, she solved the mystery
with a stack of newspaper articles set on her coffee table. All of
them featured headshots of Angel. All of them bore lead-ins like
"The Fix Is In" or "Racing's Big Scandal." We spent a long, slow
hour reading aloud. Some of the words were new, some details still
steeped in shadow, but we managed to shake loose a handful of
unbreakable facts:

*Following a five-year investigation, the FBI had infiltrated a giant
race-fixing scheme masterminded by a mobster from Atlantic City
named Anthony Ciulla.*

*Ciulla had confessed to bribing a string of jockeys, paying them as
much as $8,000 apiece to pull back on their mounts as other horses,
high-paying long shots, stumbled to victory.*

*Those jockeys had gilded reputations and famous names like Braulio
Baeza, Eddie Belmonte—and Angel Cordero.*

*Of all the jockeys, Ciulla claimed Angel was the most skilled and the
most costly.*

*A New York trainer stood up in a courtroom and swore Angel pulled
horses for money. Angel stood up and swore that his heart was clean.*

No one had any proof that Angel had done anything at all.

I'd already learned a few things about jockeys. I knew some
could be "convinced" to carry two-pronged electric batteries that
would deliver an almighty zap to a lazy horse as he loped down
the stretch. Others might be bribed to let a front-runner linger at
the back of the pack or force a closer to spend himself on the
lead. In 1900, the Prince of Wales's jockey, Tod Sloan, riding at

Cambridgeshire in England, had regularly paid off all the other riders in a race to let him win handsomely. The year May-May visited Churchill Downs for Regret's Derby, the crowd had been abuzz with the story of a Virginia jockey who, running through a heavy blanket of fog, had pulled his mount to one side of the track for a breather, then rejoined the pack on their second lap around.

I'd learned a few things about Angel as well. I knew he could be honey-tongued, but also reckless and nasty. I knew racehorses shaped his vision of the universe, the same way colors shaped a painter's or musical notes that of a pianist, and he didn't much concern himself with anything else. I knew he thrived on danger—the hotter things were, the happier he was.

The details of the Ciulla scandal erupted impressively in the next few months, dots connecting to form a mobster tale worthy of Martin Scorsese. Since 1972, six years before the investigation broke, Ciulla had been bribing jockeys from San Francisco to New Jersey's Garden State Raceway, rigging results at thirty-nine tracks and several hundred races. He employed a staff of runners and middlemen so extensive that it cost him $6,000 a week just to keep them in motel rooms, food, and booze. Ciulla had learned to play the horses from his father, a Boston fish merchant, who would pass him hot dogs through the fence behind the local Suffolk Downs grandstand because children, deemed too easily corruptible, were forbidden to enter. By the time he was nineteen, Ciulla was slipping tranquilizers to horses and bribing jockeys at state fairs in nearby Great Barrington and Berkshire Downs. Four years later, he engineered a Boston fix that took mob-affiliated bookmakers for close to three grand.

Such gall could have earned Ciulla a quick trip to the bottom of Boston Harbor, but the local gangsters were intrigued by his upstart savvy. They slapped Ciulla with a $50,000 fine, and demanded in on his next fix. Soon Ciulla's racing knowledge had him wriggled in tight to the big time, a New York bookie and prominent member of the Genovese crime family known as Fat Tony Salerno. By the time the FBI first caught on to him in 1973, the twenty-nine-year-old Ciulla had helped mastermind betting coups at nearly every track north of the Mason-Dixon line. Once, during a family vacation upstate, he even stopped long enough to skim a few bucks off a Podunk bush track called Pocono Downs. His most lucrative territory was always the prime cut of New York racing, Aqueduct and Belmont Park. The reigning monarch of that empire, the man with his finger dictating the pulse, was Angel Cordero.

Ciulla relied upon a thorough infiltration of the local jockey colony in order to execute his schemes. He would bribe multiple riders in a single race, preferably those aboard the favorites, so he could narrow the field of possible winners to only four or five "live" horses. Through Fat Tony's connections in Las Vegas hotels—the Tropicana, the Riviera, the Dunes—he would bet those live horses in various high-priced exacta and trifecta combinations, the payoffs often hitting hundreds of thousands of dollars. Ciulla preferred using the jockeys themselves as intermediaries, in New York relying upon a local rider named Con Errico to fine-tune all his double deals. Errico and Ciulla would meet up in a hotel room where Ciulla handed over a list of horses he wanted held in the coming week. Errico would contact the riders in question, pinning them down on the backstretch, over cups of coffee at a nearby diner, or even in some secluded corner of the jockey's changing room. The two would haggle over the amount of the bribe, then Errico would reconvene with Ciulla to cinch up the final strands of the deal.

The FBI finally caught up with Ciulla courtesy of one of those jockey messenger boys, an Atlantic City rider named Peter Fantini. After Jersey racing officials caught Fantini pulling a horse so hard the pair nearly toppled over backward, they called in the local police. Following a little gentle pressure, Fantini agreed to help entrap Ciulla. He wore a wire to their next meeting in Ciulla's twin penthouse suites at Atlantic City's Flamingo Hotel. Ciulla delivered the goods and then some, even offering Fantini a lesson on how best to hold a horse. As soon as they'd palmed the tape, the police issued a warrant for Ciulla's arrest. He scarpered to northern California, where he idled for a few months, then couldn't resist phoning an old consort to ship in a few horses and rig up a race. He was on the move again, headed for Philadelphia, when ten FBI agents grabbed him reading a *Racing Form* in a lounge at the San Francisco airport. Fearing he'd never survive the convoluted mob politics that ruled federal prisons, Ciulla agreed to turn state's evidence and begin life anew under the witness protection plan.

As soon as Ciulla had brokered his freedom deal, the stories started rolling forth. He had dirt on everybody from mob-franchised bookmakers to a small-time New York jockey named Mike Hole who refused to accept a bribe and later turned up asphyxiated in a car pulled off a Long Island roadway. But Ciulla's most grandiose boasts centered around his dealings with one tiny man, Angel Cordero. According to Ciulla, Angel was as hot-tempered and demanding as a Thoroughbred, insisting upon private consultations with Ciulla himself and requiring up to $6,000 to rig a single race. He lavished all kinds of praise on Angel's gift for fixing. Other top jocks went limp down the final stretch, but not Angel. He would "bend a horse in half" to secure a spot near the rear of the pack. He was the Houdini of pulling horses, slashing and pumping his whip with one hand while the other, almost imperceptibly, clamped the reins back in a jaw-breaking grip. Angel, and all the top jockeys implicated along with him, denied any link to Ciulla, insisting their six-figure incomes left no reason to consort with a wholesale race-rigger. Ciulla countered with a loud laugh. Jockeys, with their ego-fed appetites for fast cars and spoonfuls of cocaine, could always use an influx of tax-free cash in hand.

Ciulla's patter was convincing. So were Angel's effusive denials. I couldn't decide whether Angel was fully guilty, just a little bit, or not guilty at all, and I didn't know how to feel about him if he were any of the three. He was still Angel, still wildfire, and no matter what he'd done I didn't want to lose him. I told May-May I had no idea what I was supposed to think.

"You can think anything you want to," she replied.

I didn't think I wanted to think anything at all.

"Sometimes," she finally offered, "it's best to just throw out a race."

Throwing out races happens all the time at the track. Horses can run erratically, shift temperament or outlook for no apparent reason, and cast one disastrously flat performance into the midst of a glorious forward charge. When you look at a horse's overall record and decide whether or not briefly to align your future with its own, you are allowed to toss away such races: assume an off day or a misplaced hoof and just pretend it never occurred. Everyone is allowed a mistake or two, however blazing, as long as he eventually returns to form.

That evening I went home and ripped up all the articles on Anthony Ciulla. I assumed that Angel would do the same. Post-scandal, he returned to his raucous, brilliant, humdinging self, and I rode that lightning he created for fifteen more years.

There were never any official judgments about Angel's relationship to Ciulla, no further proof he'd tucked those reins up in his fists and mooched "slow down" instead of "speed up" into his horses' ears. Nor did I ever come to my own decision as to whether he'd temporarily fallen apart at the seams. Years later, when I met Angel down in Florida, I was too intimidated by rumors of his machine-gun temper to raise the specter of Ciulla. When I asked him about the toughest part of being a jockey, it was clear the past hadn't faded terribly far.

"The hardest thing I've learned is that you can't trust anybody," he answered. "Riding races, all you have is your reputation. Accusing a man of holding a horse is like calling a woman a whore. Around here, someone will do it in a second if it means he doesn't have to take the blame."

All I know now is the same thing I've always known: myth or mortal, Angel made my heart rip. Ordinary rules didn't suit either one of us.

It's proved more than enough to carry us through.

ONE OF the earliest accounts of American colonial justice included a 1665 York County resident confined to the stocks for fixing a horse race. In 1760, a justice of the peace from Charleston, South Carolina, suffered a public lashing after being found guilty of bribing a jockey. The racetrack and dirty dealing share a time-honored bond.

By the late nineteenth century, racing in America was so profitable and so corrupt that numerous tracks fell victim to protection rackets, tithing to local politicians, police, and gangsters in order to stay afloat. Such graft led a number of states to ban racing entirely, only repealing their efforts when a core of influential New York society gentlemen decided to vouch for the honor of the sport. But racing expanded far too rapidly for such honor to keep a foothold. By the 1930s, racketeers grown giddy on bootlegging profits had taken to tailoring the outcome of any race they pleased. Bullets rang across Oriental Park in Havana until officials withdrew unpopular decisions. Depression-era hustlers churned out counterfeit $100 bills that showed Ben Franklin winking at his dupes.

In 1931, May-May had already moved from Alaska down to Seattle. Longacres had yet to be built, Washington State still victim to those antigambling laws, and her only access to the track came from outdated racing papers a fellow devotee held for her at his newsstand. That year she decided upon a pilgrimage to visit Robert back east. In Maryland, historically liberal when it came to notions of pleasure, racetracks still abounded. The two of them planned a monthlong holiday spent on all the local courses, including a bucolic country track called Havre de Grace. There, they wound up colliding with one of the cleverest confidence men of the era, an Irish-born ringer artist by the name of Paddie Barrie.

Running ringers had long been a popular racetrack game, secretly replacing a slow horse with a fast one and then betting on the outcome. While still living in Baltimore, May-May had even spotted a few ringers herself—singling out some plodder with a chest too massive or head suspiciously elegant for his uninspired pedigree, following such instincts to the betting ring, and earning a bit of cash for her insights. But Paddie Barrie ranked far above such casual crookedness. He'd turned the ordinary dodge into his own personal art form.

Paddie came to the United States from England in the early twenties after Scotland Yard nearly nabbed him for buying cheap horses, dunking them in reddish brown henna dyes, then selling the altered animals back to their original owners for twice the price. Once he'd made his way to the States, slipping in illegally over the Canadian border, he immediately took up his old ways. He perfected a waterproof dye made of heroin, cola nut extract, and strychnine, used a full palette of reds, browns, and golds to transform expensive horses into cheap ones, then bet heavily on his masterpieces. As his experience grew, so did his dexterity. Soon he was employing a fine-bristled brush to add white stockings to his horses' legs, stars to their foreheads, and blazes running the length of their noses. In 1931, curious to test his talents on a more refined audience, he bought a fresh pair of racehorses and set out for Havre de Grace.

Havre de Grace was one of Maryland's poshest official racetracks. The day Paddie chose to unveil his latest canvas, the guest of honor was no less than the governor of the state. As May-May perused the horses in the paddock that afternoon, her eyes slid right over Shem, a dark chestnut colt with two white legs and an unimpressive racing record, listed at odds of 52–1. Eventually, she decided to bet on the favorite, Byzantine, who was fit and fractious and looked the classiest horse in the race.

May-May watched the finish from the rail, as surprised as everyone else when the unassuming Shem erupted across the wire four lengths ahead of the field. As the other bettors filtered off toward the paddock, May-May lingered to watch the grooms lead their charges off the track. She'd been impressed by Shem's unbuttoned stride, the stamp of a horse whose natural impulses ran to rhythm and speed, not one struggling to find himself the way Shem's record indicated. Closer inspection revealed clues that had eluded her earlier: sleek skull bones, high haunches, and the well-aligned legs of a runner. Watching Shem disappear toward the barn, his tall, sweet backside swaying like a camel's, she knew she'd fallen victim to a ringer. On the way home she offered Robert another casual side bet, $50 that Shem would one day prove considerably more horse than he seemed.

A few weeks after she'd returned to Seattle, May-May received a fat envelope from Robert in the mail. She broke open the seal and out tumbled a few folded banknotes, a stack of newspaper clippings, and a sheet of notepaper printed with a single sentence:

You win again.

Those articles provided a primer in the consummate skill of Paddie Barrie.

Through a small-time gangster Paddie hired to place his clandestine bets, Havre de Grace's security had stumbled upon the true identity of Shem. He was a high-priced runner called Aknahthon, a dark bay gelding with a white blaze down his nose (though Paddie's most recent efforts had turned him light-colored and stripeless). His breeding and race record made him worth ten times the real Shem. By the time detectives reached Paddie's barn on the Havre de Grace backstretch, he and Shem-Aknahthon had gone up like smoke. Paddie and his connections raked in close to a million dollars on the scheme.

May-May always had a soft spot for antiheroes, anyone not inclined to accept boundaries until they'd tested them themselves. She and my grandfather, another Irishman with a bent for improvisation, continued to follow Paddie's career as he led the Pinkertons in a dance for the next three years. In 1934, detectives decided to tail a dishy young blond who'd paired with Paddie in the past. She led them straight to their prey, seated behind the wheel of a horse van with a cigarette dangling from his mouth and his latest painted protégé nibbling at a bale of hay in the back. When the Department of Labor deported Paddie a few months later, my grandparents unwrapped two Waterford crystal goblets and toasted him with a belt of Irish whiskey.

Ringers abounded everywhere, people posing as what they were not. Paddie had damaged little more than pocketbooks, and he'd staked out his ground with style.

AS I grew older, I tried to hold on to that antihero identity May-May had supplied with tales like Paddie's, but the borders separating rules from values seemed murkier all the time. I couldn't always tell when I'd drifted away from what I wanted and toward what I thought I should want. Often, I caught myself midstep—a flush leaking into my cheeks even as I slouched down the middle school hallways moaning over having to visit my grandmother. Sometimes it was May-May who caught me, and there was no emptier feeling than knowing I'd let her down.

May-May set high store by dignity, preserving her own and allowing others to hold onto theirs. Such self-possession was one of the things she most admired about racehorses, the notch of reserve cut into their passion. Thoroughbreds stood a step or two apart from what was expected of them, displaying a whiff of arrogance because to be under the rod left them not entirely whole. You could train, strengthen, coax, and coddle, but come race day they would still do exactly as they pleased. One of the few times I ever saw May-May truly angry was over an up-and-coming trainer who erected his reputation on sapping that dignity away. He bought expensive young horses and then ran them unmercifully, as soon and as often as possible, a test of mettle to reveal just how much brittle legs and high-strung spirits could stand. He operated like those high school football coaches who build "character" by pushing their players to the line, treating Thoroughbreds like sixteen-year-old thugs with biceps and constitutions of iron.

Racehorses are fighters, and the heartiest animals did blossom in spite of, perhaps even because of, the rigors he put them through. May-May also noted what most people skipped over, those less-robust creatures who wilted and dropped away. Two-year-old horses are still growing, and his stable was plagued by injuries from unformed joints that buckled beneath the early strain. Saddest of all were those gentler souls who simply lost heart under such grinding, their hotfoot prances slipping through the hourglass and disappearing for good. Public memory faded quickly as empty stalls filled with new prodigies, but May-May refused to let go. She hated that line of broken spirits. And she wasn't a woman even remotely prone to hate.

At the time, I only half agreed with her clear-cut condemnation, secretly doubting success at the racetrack could derive from anything too cruel. One spring, I even decided I would back one of this trainer's horses to win the Kentucky Derby. The colt I selected was gorgeous, a showman in the tradition of Alydar with an iffy temper and a long, flaxen tail. He'd been a two-year-old wonder, winning more races than most of his Derby rivals had even entered. He ran like a tiger and his trainer, however questionable his tactics, had certainly proven capable of turning out brilliant specimens before. It seemed to me that he, like most trainers, just excelled with a certain type of horse. It was a question of toughness, and I had no doubt my colt was steel-plated. I nervously announced my Derby pick to May-May.

"Are you sure?" she asked. I nodded and studied her face for the slightest hint of pride at my bravado. I found nothing there at all.

In the weeks leading up to the Derby, it became trickier and trickier to buoy my initial faith. I perused magazine articles that tipped my horse as a hot pick and his trainer as an even hotter one. I found a sidebar offering postage-stamp photos of some of those earlier disappointments and guiltily studied each pricked ear and once-sassy tilt to the chin. I tinkered endlessly with May-May's views and my own looser interpretations about what might be considered humane. I was the one who kept coming up short.

That Derby horse caught me like quicksand. I didn't want to keep cutting against what May-May believed. I also didn't want to admit I'd been wrong. By the first Saturday in May, I secretly hoped my divine colt would just fade to unimpressive in the final stretch so that I might forget he ever existed. It was the most miserable Derby I'd ever spent. I know we must have sipped port and eaten Aplets & Cotlets, but all I can remember is sitting silently beside May-May on that rosewood sofa, feeling like a rock had taken up residence on my chest. When my horse labored through the race minus even an inkling of his former pizzazz, I felt nothing but relief. I was confident he would come streaking back in his next race or perhaps the race after, proof positive of what I'd always known to be true. Thoroughbreds could transcend it all.

My Derby colt didn't return. He ran a few more races that summer, all of them unspectacular, then broke his ankle in a morning workout, had it pieced together with screws and wires, and was permanently retired. Even his career at stud proved lackluster, as if he'd expended his full lifetime's worth of energy in his first three years. Ours was a short, unremarkable partnership, but he's stuck with me as surely as Alydar has—a reminder that despite their monumental power, racehorses are sensitive creatures. Much as they like to hold themselves separate, they are dependent on people in a transparent and trusting way in which we will never be dependent on them. It's one of their miracles that Thoroughbreds will press forward no matter what, run until legs or spirits crack right underneath them. It's up to humans, a line in the domestication contract, to read the more subtle messages and abide.

I TURNED twenty in 1990, but my first love had been a younger man. That fall Alydar was only fifteen. He'd retired from racing as a three-year-old and gone to stud at Calumet Farm, the Shangri-la of Kentucky horse farms where he'd been born and raised. I hadn't been at all surprised when his virile racing charisma transferred easily to the breeding shed. He proved a stellar stallion, his babies winning races all over the globe.

That September, I left for England to spend my junior year at a London university. So it was at a newsstand on Oxford Street, leafing through a British racing paper, that I stumbled across a photo bearing the simple caption: "Alydar Dies."

I knifed through the article for details, my mind processing lickety-

split, my heart not processing at all. I read how Alydar had shattered his hind leg with a single kick so mighty it broke through the
heavy oak door of his barn; how a night watchman had found him
standing stunned and silent in his stall; how, after surgery failed to
save him, he'd been buried alongside his mother in the bluegrass
graveyard holding all of Calumet's past stars. When I'd finished
reading, I slipped the newspaper neatly back into its bin and
stepped out onto the street. People whipped past me just as they
had ten minutes earlier, poking my shoulders with their umbrellas
and crunching my toes, but I felt as if the world had tipped right
off its axis. Alydar resided too closely to May-May and Kentucky
Derbies. His death shook something at my core.

I started returning to that Oxford Street newsstand every
evening, scanning the racing papers for further news. For several
weeks I found no stories at all and only some pervasive need for
closure kept me going back day after day. Then in Kentucky,
where Alydar's death had stirred up a wasp's nest of implications,
something cracked. Accusations began to pour forth, blanketing
Calumet's once pristine pastures. The tale left few redeeming values in its wake.

Decades earlier, at the height of the glamour days surrounding
World War II, Calumet Farm had defined racing. It was founded
in 1924 on 407 acres of limestone-studded bluegrass, the pet project
of William Monroe Wright, the Chicago entrepreneur behind the
Calumet Baking Powder can. Wright set out to breed Kentucky
trotting horses and succeeded valiantly, applying his Yankee
doggedness to the sleepy pace of the old South. But trotting races
were small-time game. Upon inheriting the estate in 1933,
Wright's son Warren studied the yearly losses incurred by his
father's hobby. Then he surveyed the ring of wealthy Thoroughbred farms encircling his own. He decided Calumet was due for a
change in identity.

In just months, Warren redrafted Calumet Farm to form a business venture as full-bodied as the Chicago factory that had made
his father. He embarked on a crash course in Thoroughbred horse

racing, expanding the farm by more than a thousand acres and
using his baking powder fortune to buy into the most valuable
bloodlines in the world. He ripped down his father's modest operation and replaced it with cupolaed barns, a private training track,
and miles of whitewashed fencing. Oblivious to his growing reputation for eccentricity, Warren concocted special vitamin supplements to create super-colts and fillies, hired private detectives to
check out each of his jockeys, and jotted down notebooks full of
horse wisdom skimmed off everyone from grooms to breeding
tycoons. A method slowly emerged from his madness. In 1941,
Warren's near obsession bore a wild-eyed colt named Whirlaway,
who tore around the track like a loose bullet and won the Triple
Crown.

The forties were one of racing's high times, a hunger for
wartime diversion driving crowds to the track and a giddy post-
fighting wave of consumption keeping them there. Calumet's blue-
and-devil's-red racing colors dominated the decade. By the time
Warren Wright died nine years later, the farm had earned a second
Triple Crown, a handful of Kentucky Derbies, and an aura of
immortality. Wright exited the sport the way few people do, a man
who'd fulfilled all his dreams. The grandson of a Chicago mill-
worker, he'd crafted a Thoroughbred empire to outclass the Aga
Khan's in England and the Baron de Rothschild's in France.

Warren left behind a twenty-three-page will stipulating his
desires for Calumet's future, a bramblework of trusts meant to
ensure the farm would become a family heirloom handed down
from generation to generation. Though his widow, Lucille,
intended to maintain Calumet's high standards, she remarried soon
after Warren's death, falling for a movie producer and Hollywood
gadfly named Gene Markey. Markey was Warren Wright's polar
opposite, a notorious Casanova whose previous wives had included
Myrna Loy and Hedy Lamarr. He promptly rid the farm of all
traces of Warren's dour business sense and transformed it into a
dizzying social cotillion. His guiding philosophies turned life into
one long, linked series of good times. He threw lavish weekend

parties with guests like John Wayne and Douglas Fairbanks Jr., composed limericks and love poems, and brewed homemade bourbon under the label "Old Commodore."

Markey's arrival sprinkled a bit more tinsel onto Calumet's glittering reputation, but it also marked the start of the farm's decline. Warren and Lucille's son, Warren Jr., was a budding hermit devoted to operating two-way radios and building model trains. He displayed no interest in taking part in Calumet's future. Throughout the sixties and early seventies, as the Markeys jetted off to Baden-Baden and the Ritz Hotel in Paris, Calumet's list of champions steadily dwindled. It wasn't until Lucille was so enfeebled she had to watch the races from a car driven up to the track rail that the old glory briefly fluttered to life again. In 1978, Alydar claimed his place on the tail end of William Monroe Wright's legacy.

ALYDAR RETIRED from racing at the end of his Triple Crown season. Shortly afterward, Lucille and her son both passed away. On the edge of the deal-crazy decade of the eighties, Calumet's old-world power shifted into the hands of someone modern-day and hungry, Warren Jr.'s son-in-law J. T. Lundy. Lundy, the son of a sharecropper, had coveted the Lexington horse-country wealth since he was a child. He carefully calculated his meeting and marriage to Warren Jr.'s daughter, Cindy, when she was still in high school. He knew the intricacies of her inheritance the way a breeder could recite lines of a pedigree. He wanted money, barnfuls of it, and he went after it with none of the flair of a Paddie Barrie.

Within months of Lundy's 1982 takeover, the rural idyll of Calumet—whitewashed buildings with devil's red trim, close-clipped fields, buckets hand-stenciled with each horse's name—dissolved and up rose swimming pools, tennis courts, and bright orange pickup trucks that clashed with the cool green Kentucky landscape. That spring, Lundy hosted a huge outdoor gala at the farm, not in honor of the upcoming Kentucky Derby, but to publicize the Indianapolis 500. Calumet would debut as a sponsor, its name splashed across one of A. J. Foyt's fleet of "coyote orange" racecars. Lundy spent lavishly on new barns and graded pastures, twenty-foot-tall iron gates, and a fully equipped veterinary clinic. In his mind, the farm was only tangentially a breeding operation. Much more valuable was its potential as launching pad into the wheeling and dealing of the moneyed elite.

In *Wild Ride,* a 1994 book on the demise of Calumet, *Wall Street Journal* reporter Ann Hagedorn Auerbach took four hundred pages to untangle the insane purging and splurging that accompanied Lundy's desire to inhale the fast lane. He tossed out the Calumet old guard and amassed his own retinue of advisers and good buddies, men united by wealth, greed, and somewhat shady pasts. With their help he began stowing away personal cash and setting up ghost companies in Kentucky, North Carolina, and Marathon Island in Key West, just a hop-skip from the Caribbean. He installed a paper shredder in the farm office and acquired a taste for hushed 3:00 A.M. phone calls.

In the early eighties, a tide of Wall Street wealth, spurred by newly formed equine divisions at companies like Prudential and Merrill Lynch, wandered into the bluegrass. Most were clueless about the Thoroughbred business, just groping for any potentially profit-turning hot commodity. Lundy and his crowd took full advantage of such naïveté by putting together record-setting deals, spending $25 million to import an unproven British stallion called Secreto. No one seemed bothered by paragraphs of labyrinthine fine print tacked onto the contracts, commissions, shares, and future breeding rights reserved for not for Calumet the corporation, but for J. T. Lundy the individual.

It didn't take Lundy long to realize his fantasyland would require heavier financing than he could squeeze from the Calumet treasure chest. In 1983, he took out his first loan, a collateral-free $13.2 million from the Second National Bank of Kentucky. Soon the debts, too, had spread like an oil slick. He took out loans to pay off other loans, tapping banks from Houston to Washington, D.C., for more than $100 million. His circle of business associates broadened to include a banker named Frank Chihak who had fled his position as president of the Texas Bank of Commerce under suspicion of fraud and racketeering, and Dan Lasater, founder of the Ponderosa Steak House chain, who was indicted on cocaine-related charges in 1986. Perhaps most troubling of all were Lundy's regular doings with New York businessman Robert Libutti and small-time Florida horse trainer Louis Gurino, both of whom would later reveal bosom ties to mob kingpin John Gotti.

Of all his prize acquisitions, it was Alydar, already producing a line of exquisite progeny, who became Lundy's diamond asset. With his first few crops of foals on the track and winning races, Alydar commanded stud fees as high as $350,000 from each new mare who came to be bred. To mine the maximum stallion dollar, Lundy concocted a setup, a version of which ten years later would become common practice. Instead of breeding Alydar for the usual February to July season, then allowing him six months of rest while the local ladies were out of heat, Lundy arranged to fill the off time by importing mares from the Southern Hemisphere, where the breeding season was reversed. This way Alydar could cover close to a hundred mares a year instead of the typical fifty or sixty. Whenever Lundy needed a quick influx of cash, he would simply presell Alydar's breeding rights. He could peddle a lifetime share, one that entitled its owner to send a mare to Alydar every year until the stallion died, for as much as $2.5 million.

By the late eighties, Alydar also carried more than $36 million in insurance, the bulk of it supplied by Lloyd's of London. Insuring racehorses was risky business, the opportunity for fraud extensive. Horses often died under suspicious circumstances, suffocating in barn fires or ingesting toxic plants that crept into an untended pasture. It was nearly impossible to prove more sinister forces at work. In the early 1990s a figure known as "the Sandman" would make a career of traveling the Thoroughbred and show horse circuits as an arranger of "accidents," delivering an injection or an iron bar to the ankle of any animal who carried an insurance policy far exceeding its worth. Even kidnapping was a legitimate danger. In 1983, Shergar, a $13 million Irish-bred horse owned by the Aga Khan, was kidnapped and disappeared into the Tipperary countryside. Calumet had received as yet idle threats, words cut from magazines demanding $500,000 or "your prize horses will be shot." Thoroughbreds were chancy properties all around, and the few insurers willing to play charged massive premiums. Alydar's coverage cost Lundy more than a million dollars a year.

At some point, Lundy's greed was bound to exceed even Alydar's capacity for brilliance. By the fall of 1990, he'd driven Calumet to the cusp of complete financial collapse. He'd presold nearly all of Alydar's breeding shares—lavishing the money on private jets and houses in Vail, Key West, and the Virgin Islands—so that his jackpot stallion brought in a mere million cash dollars a year, barely enough to cover the interest on Calumet's tiniest loans. Lundy's year-round overbreeding had created a glut of Alydar foals on the market, and as a result the prices for such babies were plummeting. His stud fee, already reduced from $350,000 to $100,000, would soon be doing the same. The nine banks Lundy had borrowed from were pressing for payment, holding the farm and all its horses, Alydar included, as collateral. On top of all this, Lundy had been delinquent in paying off Alydar's insurance premiums, and Lloyd's had hinted they were on the verge of canceling the coverage. Alydar's advancing age would soon begin to compromise his libido. There were already rumors that Lundy's twelve-month breeding merry-go-round had left the stallion less than zealous about his work.

One night in mid-November, Calumet's watchman, Alton Stone, made an unscheduled visit to the stallion barn located just behind the farm offices. He heard a faint moan and followed the noise to Alydar, standing in his stall white-eyed and sweating. Fearing a serious case of colic, Stone fetched a lead shank and opened the door. Only then did he spot blood speckling the straw under the horse's belly. He stared at Alydar, who stared back and then slowly drew his right rear leg up beneath him. The bottom half was dangling by just tendons, a quill of broken bone jutting through the skin.

Stone signaled an SOS over his radio, and in minutes a team of farm veterinarians had assembled. They sedated Alydar before his frozen state of shock could melt into panic, loaded him onto an ambulance, and traveled a crablike mile down the road to Calumet's on-site animal hospital. While the farm staff waited outside, swapping whispered theories about how the stallion might have gone to pieces in the middle of the night, one of Kentucky's most vaunted equine surgeons, Dr. Larry Bramlege, took nearly three hours to operate. He sliced open the skin covering Alydar's leg, screwed a steel plate into the split section of bone, and inserted four long metal pins that jutted out inches into the open air. Then he encased the whole thing in a stiff fiberglass cast.

The rescue operation was declared a success. Using a giant canvas sling, they hoisted Alydar back onto his feet and carried him to his stall. For a moment, he seemed simpatico to his new lumbering self, but then something—perhaps just the inexplicable awkwardness of his own body—frightened him. He made one of those hopping side steps that used to carry him around his paddock, pitching his weight onto the hip of his injured leg and expecting the rest of his body to follow. Instead, he stumbled into the weight of the cast. The femur bone in his right thigh snapped like a broom straw. Twelve hundred pounds jerked gracelessly forward and crashed to the ground.

Lundy was summoned immediately, and it was he who gave the nod to the only option left. Placing a steadying hand against Alydar's shoulder, the veterinarian injected a syringe full of barbiturates. They took two minutes to travel through his jugular vein into his heart.

By that afternoon, the stallion barn had been scrubbed clean of all sign of Alydar's night visit. Calumet issued a series of press releases stating he'd broken his leg kicking loose the eight-inch-thick, solid-oak door of his stall. Twenty-four hours later, he was buried in the farm graveyard. The insurance adjuster sent by Lloyd's waited several days to begin asking questions, but once on the move he had the claim boxed, wrapped, and settled after only a month of investigation. It was a world-record payoff, the largest and fastest in equine history.

No reporters wrote the words directly, but they danced so close that I had no problem deciphering their meaning. It was easy to believe Alydar's mysterious, cloaked-in-darkness accident had involved something more, a ringer scheme entirely bald and bereft of artistry. A few months later, $3.6 million in insurance money notwithstanding, Calumet declared bankruptcy and the entire enterprise caved in. I knew that racing was changing, turning less and less a sport and more and more an industry, but until then the damage had seemed subtle. Watching Calumet disintegrate was like watching the round smooth surface of a wrecking ball take out a supporting wall.

AS A child, I viewed the track as paradise: horses faster than the wind, jockeys weightless as angels, and only a few faint traces of original sin. When I returned to racing as an adult—no longer a handicapper or a reluctant tabskeeper, but a romantic once again—I was quickly reminded of what the likes of Anthony Ciulla and J. T. Lundy should have forever branded into my senses. Human fingerprints are everywhere. And they can leave behind a mess.

My reeducation came by way of the backstretch one morning, standing alongside an old man with a cigar and a porkpie hat as a bony, ginger-colored horse jogged by. I winced at his stiff jerky stride, the way he cocked his head and neck to the left as if wanting to free an entire quadrant of his body from the pressure of hooves against dirt. He looked like one of those old basketball players struggling to keep going on knees and ankles too thoroughly sacked for sport.

"I think he should have stayed in the stall," I remarked.

"That horse is running the day after tomorrow," the man told me. I obviously looked surprised. "Don't worry. They'll give him something to take the pain away."

A sinking curiosity brought me back to the track two days later. I looked up the horse's name in the program and found an old gelding with a checkerboard history. He'd won twice the year before, but any panache had faded in his last few starts. Now he was participating at the lowest possible level of competition, race number nine of nine on a lackluster Thursday afternoon card. I watched him warm up on the track, expecting some watered-down version of that uneven hindquarter bump. As he jogged past me, it was clear his earlier ailments had all too magically disappeared.

By this time, I had seen plenty of horses break down, and I knew what to steel myself against. It usually wasn't dramatic, just a horse jogging slowly across the finish line when he was supposed to be surging full throttle and a grinding in my stomach for a picture gone intrinsically wrong. The equine ambulance would wheel up, and vet and groom load the limping horse aboard. Maybe, if it was an important race, the next day's *Racing Form* would list his surgery status or the simple phrase "later euthanized." More often, I found out nothing at all.

Horses often splinter midrace because of bad luck—a chance misstep or an undetected genetic flaw. Sometimes human hands contribute, filling syringes to replenish bodies emptied out by effort. Though the rules governing prerace medications differ from state to state, all variety of drugs exist that can make a racehorse slower, faster, more supple, or fit. Some are considered therapeutic. Anabolic steroids build up muscles and help them rebound quickly from exertion. Clenbuterol, a bronchodilator often used to treat lung infections, expands the bronchial passages in animals troubled by labored breathing and allows them to swallow more air per stride.

Other substances, the sort more difficult to detect in blood or urine samples, are administered regardless of regulations meant to forbid them outright. These drugs are performance enhancers and nothing more. The most basic is something simple as bicarbonate of soda, which neutralizes the buildup of lactic acid in muscles and delays the onset of fatigue. On the opposite end of the scale, the slickest of trainers might dose their horses with Epogen, an expensive, human-engineered drug that increases the blood's capacity to carry oxygen. It's the same banned substance that earned the French Festina cycling team a disqualification from the 1998 Tour de France. Epogen is a genetically engineered human protein that stimulates bone marrow to produce extra red blood cells. It contains high doses of an endogenous protein already flowing through Thoroughbred blood, but, since it's derived from human ingredients, the horse's immune system often releases antibodies to kill the foreign invader, shutting down its own natural production of red blood cells as well. The side effects can range from lethargy and weight loss, to severe anemia requiring massive plasma transfusions, to death. On the flip side, horses high on extra oxygen run just a bit faster for just a bit longer than those whose blood still courses at sea level. In racing, victory is all about the bits, the necks and noses and hundredths of seconds that can deliver a horse first across the wire.

Perhaps the most dangerous drugs of all are the sort that had probably gone into my morning-sore gelding, simple painkillers delivered to block twinges of something clearly out of whack. Such cure-alls have therapeutic properties, but, overused, they allow an ailing horse to run full-out on body parts that threaten to crumble. In New York, medication rules allowed for administration of such anti-inflammatories (as well as hormones, steroids, diuretics, and adrenaline boosters like epinephrine) forty-eight hours before a race. Watching that unnaturally agile old fellow prance down the track, full and frisky and bucking lightly on his false legs, I imagined him just a bit puzzled at the wonders his body could achieve. As he approached the starting gate, I wanted to turn away. Whatever happened would happen whether I stood by or not.

I watched the race because I felt somebody should, and the only somebody at hand was me. Our tale came to an unexpectedly happy end. My ginger gelding not only ran cleanly but, most improbably, won at odds of 16–1. On paper, it was exactly what I came to see, Thoroughbreds once again defying probability, but I left the track that day feeling soured. There are physical impossibilities, even for racehorses, and such a transformation was one of them. An ingredient far more potent than plain moxie had entered that gelding's system, a tenuous Band-Aid wrapped around a runner who was worn out and shaking to pieces. No magic, just the chance he could earn somebody a bit more money and the absence of any higher concerns.

THE USE of artificial substances to jack up or wind down race-horses is far from a new phenomenon. News clippings from 1770s England reported horses fed arsenic and lead shot to keep them out of races or opium-laced treats to erase any lingering aches. In 1900, a shady American trainer who went by the name Wishard immigrated to England and inaugurated what came to be known as "the Epoch of the Yankee Alchemist." Wishard's horses flew down the racecourse, all wild eyes and foaming sweat, boosted up on an adrenaline enhancer commonly known as cocaine. His frequent misfires—horses going crazy, rearing over backward at the start, or collapsing dead as their hearts put a limit on unhindered effort—led to all race-day medications being ruled illegal. The law stands in England to this day.

Drug use on American racetracks flourished in the 1930s as stakes heightened with the influx of gangster cash. A pinch of heroin on the tongue regularly left both horse and human feeling no pain. By the end of the decade, drugging was so rampant that the Federal Narcotics Bureau demanded the industry do something clean up its trash. In 1932, saliva tests had been introduced, and they were followed shortly by blood and urine tests designed to spot residues of anything that might shoot a runner dangerously high. Tracks commonly ran such tests on the winner of every race, as well as the occasional randomly chosen entrant and any race favorites who didn't perform.

From its inception, equine drug testing garnered a stellar reputation for inaccuracy. In 1946, five Maryland trainers were accused of doping their horses based on the results of the Strob test. The test, originally developed to monitor human morphine addicts, entailed feeding a drop of equine blood to a mouse, then waiting to see whether the mouse's tail would curve into an S shape. If it did, both horse and trainer flunked. After much legal wrangling, the Maryland cases were eventually laughed out of court, but testing turned no more reliable. Artificial substances were difficult to pin-point. They could break down into ingredients that naturally occurred in a horse's bloodstream, leave behind the minutest levels of their original potency, or leave no clear traces at all. Chemists fell a neck behind alchemists, with fresh experimental drugs outpacing the ability to detect them. Horses kept running too unpredictably to pin down much of anything at all.

Such cutting-edge substances played a large part in Anthony Ciulla's arsenal in the mid-seventies, serving as backup when jock-eys couldn't be trusted to rig a race on their own. He tried every-thing from vials of cocaine to jack them up to a tranquilizer known as Acepromazine which, when injected shortly before post time, made a horse just dozy enough to lumber across the finish lengths behind the lead. One of Ciulla's Detroit-based crew, a man known as "Dr. Mule," specialized in finding chemists willing to bootleg the latest substances from high-tech drug laboratories. Half the time, Ciulla had only a sketchy knowledge of what he'd been handed. He would pay a groom a hundred bucks to deliver an injection before the race, then lean back to witness what occurred. Once or twice drugs guaranteed to "finesse" a horse's nervous system wound up killing them instead.

THE HAPPY ending to my old gelding's story wasn't especially happy. It wasn't even an ending. I guessed he would race again and again until eventually even science couldn't keep up with his degenerating body. Perhaps the wait would be shorter, perhaps the muffled pop of a bone breaking would intervene mid-stretch instead. Part of me just hoped I wouldn't be there when it hap-pened, the same part that had wanted to turn my head away the first time around. But ignoring seemed the same as condoning. I knew drugs existed, tapping away at the sport like a spoon against an eggshell, delivering hundreds of tiny cracks until the entire thing risked splintering. Surely, the only wrong choice would be to take no interest at all.

And so, ever so tentatively, I began to ask questions about just what went on with drugs on the racecourse. What I found were a boatload of secrets, people only willing to talk out of the sides of their mouths, suppositions, contradictions, and too many factors at work to isolate any single spot of blame. There are drugs that are undetectable and readily available, and there are vets willing to administer them for the proper fee. There's pressure from the owners for winners, and from the tracks for horses, gleaming or gutted, to fill ten and eleven races a day. There is real money, unreal hope, and human rather than Thoroughbred interest. There's a definition of responsibility that's gone seriously skewed.

The lines between which drugs are healers and which are performance enhancers is ever shifting, year to year, state to state. Horses all over the country are legally permitted to run on Lasix, a curative for "bleeders" who have thin-walled capillaries in their lungs that can burst and cause hemorrhaging in the effort of a race. Less than a decade ago, the question of whether to legalize Lasix generated heated debate. Now nearly every horse in the United States takes it, because Lasix also flushes out water weight and slows the buildup of lactic acid in muscles, and because not dosing up means lagging some indefinable step behind all those others who do. As a result, horses who bleed heavily are now indistinguishable from those who barely bleed at all. A bleeder can win the Kentucky Derby, turn valuable stallion, and produce a long string of second- and then third-generation bleeders, the equine version of the Russian royal family.

Depending on the state, other drugs—anti-inflammatories, steroids, hormones, or hormone suppressors—might be permitted days or hours before a race. They might be administered orally, via a rubber tube that snakes through the nasal passages down into the stomach, or perhaps by interarticular injection, a syringe full of painkillers jabbed straight into the swollen joint of an ankle or knee. When drug laws are broken, traces of forbidden chemicals found in blood or urine, the consequences are often unspectacular—trainers fined and suspended so that they have to stay physically off the track for a handful of days while their horses run in an assistant's name. Occasionally, racing officials figure the easiest way to stop cheating is the Lasix route: taking the banned substance everyone is using anyway and turning it legal. Meanwhile, the race-track's finer nature seems to be slowly trickling away.

I used to play a game when I was little, one reserved for particularly long and rainy Sunday afternoons. I would steal a ball of yarn from my mother's old knitting basket, something off-color and scratchy that no one wanted anymore. I'd shut myself in our upstairs den, clicking the latch on the old mortise lock, and tie the end of the skein to the glass doorknob. Then I would begin to unravel it. First there'd be a straight shot toward the far wall, looping the string through the window latch, then back over to the TV, up high around the closet-door hinges, down through the legs of the coffee table. I'd zigzag back and forth, up and down, until the full ball of yarn had unfurled behind me, the room woven into a massive burnt orange spider's web. When I reached the tail end, I would knot it around the heavy brass floor lamp opposite the door. Then I'd turn to crawl, back through the maze toward the door where it all began.

Navigating the drug issues at the racetrack is a bit like fording that mess of string. I can see the end goal—the welfare of the horses—just as I could see that crystal doorknob, but every step toward it presents another tangle. There are no simple answers, no line of red flags marching down the border between drugs that help a horse and hurt it, between professional athletes and creatures the way nature intended. Sometimes progress grows so convoluted that the only possible path seems to be to chuck everything and begin again from scratch. In this case, that would mean adhering to the British way of thinking. No race-day medications at all.

When I step back momentarily from stimulants and steroids, from blinkered ambition and a dangling fourth leg whose owner ran so hard he forgot it was even there, I can spot two things left in bas-relief.

The first is the fact that this thing I love is flawed. As am I. We are both, always, a work in progress. Sometimes our relationship will step along in perfect cadence, sometimes in clashing counter-beats. I can have my values and my sport, as long as I don't lose sight of either one.

The second thing is this: There are only so many races you can throw out before the record becomes permanently tarnished. We are the choices we make. It's a reality not even the magic of the Thoroughbred can transcend.

Part 4:

CROSSING THE WIRE

Chapter Nine

CONNECTIONS:

Chasing the Kentucky Derby

F or me, the Kentucky Derby will never cease to be a loaded proposition. It's inextricably linked to so much of what has gone right in my life—May-May and Real Quiet and Alydar—but also to so much that went wrong. I will never be able just to watch it as I might watch Wimbledon or the

Super Bowl, with an appreciation for fine athletic performance and a hand in the party unfolding all around. As I readied myself for Kentucky in May 2000, I knew I was going for Thoroughbreds and mint juleps and flurries of rose petals. I also realized that whenever this race and I met, something alive was bound to spring up. No matter how I tried to build it up or cut it down, my Derby trip would be a journey to the heart of my matter.

I gave myself extra time for acclimatization, first pulling into the blacktopped Churchill Downs parking lot a few mornings before the race. I took in the twin spires thrusting skyward above the grandstands, the seats below that come afternoon would spill over with people, and the horses walking, galloping, racing past on the track. All of it felt familiar, and the thought of tradition was reassuring. I was just a pilgrim headed back to her spiritual home.

The backstretch was surrounded by a decidedly nontraditional chain-link fence rimmed in barbed wire, the gate manned by a security guard sitting ramrod straight in an orange plastic chair. He let me through with a nod that left his aviator sunglasses crooked across the bridge of his nose. Once inside, I began to look for the ricketiest of barns, gnarled trees with decades worth of branches, anything that May-May might have seen eighty-five years before. Then, behind me, I heard a series of grunts accompanied by a long tinny clattering sound. A second later, two cameramen in sweat-stained baseball caps bumped past with electrical cords snaking out behind them like tails.

It seemed my pilgrimage would be going a bit differently than I'd planned.

The backside of a racetrack is meant to offer escape from the chaos of the races, serenity distilled to ease every raw equine nerve. Churchill Downs felt more like the South's biggest debutante ball taking place alongside a worldwide press conference. (In 1999, the track had issued credentials to 353 writers, 262 photographers, 669 television personnel, 177 radio employees, 106 ABC and NBC affiliates, and 69 "others.") Miss America strode past, trailed by a pack of still photographers. Impromptu interviews took place over feed barrels and hitching posts, and clumps of visitors, too chatty and well dressed for racing folk, migrated from barn to barn. What a moment earlier had been rosy nostalgia quickly reconfigured itself into the sense, rare at the racetrack, that I most definitely didn't belong. I retreated to the swathe of grass separating the stables from the road, searching out a switching tail or a long-lashed, liquid eye. Some reminder that I'd come to the right place after all.

The first horse I found was The Deputy, my gutsy little Irish-bred, grazing near more chain-link fencing accompanied by his groom. He looked too petite for a Derby contender, a slim rib of black flanked by a semicircle of casual observers. The noises floating back toward me—snap, jabber, flash, click—felt jarring, all human, no horse. I crouched down low beside a tree, so that The Deputy and I were at eye level. He'd done what Thoroughbreds do, donned something self-protective, a sheen of cool like a movie star presenting himself to the crowd. I knelt there for a long time, until most of the watchers had wandered away. Once or twice, he flicked a tolerant gaze in my direction, letting his eyes fan the entire human presence, then quickly dipped down again to his meal. When I finally stood and walked away, it seemed we'd shared something I didn't want for either of us. We both felt small and overwhelmed.

I swung around the front of his barn as I left, and almost smacked into another clutch of people, notebooks extracted, gathered around Jenine Sahadi, who wore dark glasses and fiddled with a can of Diet Coke. They tossed out the same question in endless formats: What did it mean, what did she think, what would it prove to be the first woman trainer to win the Kentucky Derby? The answers filtering back already sounded tired: I'm not a trailblazer, I'm not here to make any political statement, I'm just doing what I love to do. It began to sound as if she were apologizing for coming at all. I thought of May-May journeying to Churchill Downs in 1915 when trailblazing still had currency, women pushing for the vote and Margaret Sanger demanding access to birth control. Or 1937, when Mary Hirsch arrived, the first female trainer to be granted a license—in Illinois, after she was "politely" turned down in New York—and the first to run a horse in the

Derby, a colt called No Sir who finished thirteenth. Someone asked if it was true Sahadi had a thing for diamonds and she nodded.

"Diamonds and clothes, those are my weaknesses."

I waited for the question about her strengths, but when it didn't come, I slipped away again.

Bob Baffert's barn was easy to find, the doorway plastered with large placards in the Derby-winning colors of Silver Charm and Real Quiet. Baffert was busy working a gathering of reporters and well-wishers with much tempered ebullience, his goofiness and even a sliver of humility prevailing. I liked him best like this, simple, his usual spotlight eclipsed by the race favorite in another barn, a king-size bay colt named Fusaichi Pegasus, who looked like the Black Stallion and dumped his exercise riders as a matter of course. I leaned against a sawhorse, and pretty soon along came my Derby horse, hooves clacking against the concrete apron, ready for his bath.

Captain Steve's groom positioned him center stage, just yards from the audience, picked up a green rubber garden hose, and began spilling water back and forth across the chocolate brown back. Stray drops flew toward me and caught the sun like strands of a beaded curtain. Captain Steve kept ducking his head playfully, pulling left and right to dodge the sponge landing on his nose. For a moment, his attention lit on me, and I wondered if my blurred silhouette might look ever so slightly familiar. Then he noticed the full arc of people, the whine of microphones, and the shouldered cameras. In a moment, his bowed neck had flattened and strained upward, his gaze fixed over the line of heads. His eyes rolled white and even his hooves started to slide and scrape against the watered-down cement. When the groom finally switched off the hose, he had to jog to keep up with Captain Steve's line drive back to the barn. I was intensely relieved to see them go. It was strongest, surest emotion I'd felt all day.

I waited ten minutes or so before ducking down the shedrow to Captain Steve's stall. He stood still, braced against the webbing clipped across the doorway, his nose stretched forward to catch a ribbon of sunlight. As I approached, he relaxed his jaw and an expanse of long pink tongue emerged. I reached out tentatively, remembering our visit at Santa Anita when the tongue offering had been nefarious, a ruse to get his teeth latched onto my coat. Today, he just leaned into me like a dog rubbing up against my leg, and in the end I was the one who let go first. I rubbed my hands on the white stripe running down his nose, and he half closed his eyes and sighed into my chest. I was swamped by a protective, mama bear sort of feeling, none of it tinged with the awe he'd left behind earlier in the spring. As I left, the horse in the next stall curled back his lips and reached out to snap at my shoulder, depositing a trail of oat crumbs across my shirt.

I walked away jangled, and a bit depressed that even the backstretch had been invaded. What I'd hoped to find in Kentucky— my grandmother and my own live wires—seemed to have been tossed into a blender with those same things I'd come to shake loose. It was already late, after eleven, and the track had closed to training. Harrows bobbed along the surface, leaving furrows like fingernails dug into the dirt. Horses, bathed and blanketed, were invisible, tucked into stalls. The sun had pulled free of the few morning clouds, and the whole backstretch took on the baked, bleached feeling of the ground. Best of all, most of the people seemed to have disappeared.

I liked this downtime, this waiting. Instead of turning toward the front gate, I headed deep into the loosely stacked shedrows until I began passing the insignias of outfits that specialized in small-time races, barns doubled and tripled up with trainers who had only enough horses to fill a few stalls, into the area locals call "the ghetto." It was business as usual back there: peace and horses and rakes and bandages, grooms propped on their elbows in the grass waiting for the back half of the day to start. I sat down on the edge of a barrel planted with drooping pansies. Directly across from me, a gray horse stuck his head out of his stall, yawned, and licked his lips. That was all it took to carry me back. The rush of expectations I'd carted through the chain-link fence that morning

flexed into something else, into the comfort of an old, reliable relationship. Into knowing something—a horse, a sport, a passion—so
solidly it can anchor you to the ground.

YOU COULD travel as far back as the first Kentucky Derby, run
not on the first Saturday but on the seventeenth day of May 1875,
and find a history knotted with unreasonable expectations. That
inaugural Derby was run on a newly minted track built by the
Louisville Jockey Club, an association of Kentucky racing gentlemen headed by M. Lewis Clark, the grandson of explorer William
Clark of Lewis and Clark fame. New stands were erected for the
occasion, ambitious structures built to hold more than three thousand viewers. Some traveled from regions far to the north, arriving
via strips of newly constructed railway that joined the two halves of
a country still negotiating an uneasy post–Civil War détente. The
grassy infield between the two stretches of track was open to fans at
50¢ apiece, and the common folk—black and white, local and
imported—flooded in, driving horses of their own hitched to open
wagons.

Kentuckians and gambling had a serious past together, one that
covered everything from card games to chicken fights to horse
races run down the center streets of town. The Virginia settlers
who'd followed Daniel Boone across the Allegheny Mountains into
Kentucky's coal-rich valleys were mainly horsemen, and the first
governing bodies knew well what that entailed. The earliest local
constitution included a law titled "An Act to Suppress Excessive
Gaming." In August 1783, ten years before Kentucky split off to
become an independent state, a Harrodsburg settler named Hugo
McGary was tried and found guilty of illegally betting 12 pounds
on a horse race. He was condemned as an infamous gambler and
forbidden to hold any office of "trust or honor" within the state.

By 1874, McGary and his ilk had chipped away most of the
antigambling legislation. On that first Derby day, betting provided
its time-tested added heat. Imported pari-mutuel machines were
erected in one corner of the track, allowing fans a $5 bet on any
horse they chose. But the true action erupted amid the shoving and

sweating of the auction pools conducted along the rails. Auction-
eers lined up to sell off each horse in the race to the highest bidder,
and once the organizer had helped himself to a 3 percent cut, the
man who'd screamed out top price for the winning animal scooped
the rest of the pool. Heavy spenders monopolized such pools, with
one bettor often buying all the top horses in a race. Those of more
limited means struck side deals over champagne, silk hats, cigars,
and horseflesh. In 1874, ten thousand people showed up to take
part in the Derby's debut.

The race favorite that year was Chesapeake, a broad-chested colt
owned by flamboyant Irishman H. Price McGrath, another founding member of the track and a former partner in John Morrissey's
Saratoga Springs gambling dens. McGrath sauntered about the
new stands in his customary white hat and crimson tie, boasting
that Chesapeake couldn't be beaten. But he had little to say about
his second contender, a copper-colored speed horse called Aristides.
Aristides was only entered to run as "a rabbit" for his stablemate—
to zoom to the lead and set a breakneck pace that would tire the
other front-runners, allowing Chesapeake to sweep up from
behind and steal the race in the stretch. Aristides' jockey, Oliver
Lewis, one of thirteen black riders in the fifteen-horse race, had
instructions to pull up his horse after the far turn and allow Chesapeake room to streak through. Instead, despite Lewis's desperate
efforts to hold the colt back, Aristides delighted in playing prow to
the ship and kept it up all the way to the wire.

That initial Derby was a stakes race and nothing more, on a par
with similar contests run in Chicago, Maryland, and New York.
McGrath, Lewis, and Aristides' trainer, an ex-slave named Ansel
Williams, won a sterling silver punch bowl, and McGrath took
home a $2,850 purse. News of Aristides' victory traveled as far as
Europe via recently laid transatlantic telegraph cables, but it would
be several decades before the Derby made that crucial hard left
turn from mere horse race into international spectacle.

By the time May-May reached Churchill Downs forty years
later, the Kentucky Derby had transformed into a sports phenomenon. The hand guiding its conversion belonged to Colonel Matt

Winn, a business-savvy Kentucky hardboot, the son of a cart grocer
who'd quit school at age fourteen and made his racetrack reputation by betting two winning 100–1 long shots in a single day.
Colonel Winn was an obsessive cigar smoker with a flair for publicity that he threw full-throttle into promoting Churchill Downs.
He became general manager of the track in the early 1900s, just as
a fresh wave of antigambling laws were taking hold up north.
Winn took advantage of such Yankee distractions to promote his
Kentucky product. As his centerpiece, he decided to feature that
three-year-old race which for a quarter of a century had been
known simply as the Derby. Each year, Winn ratcheted up the
prize purse until by the time Regret nabbed it in 1915 the amount
had settled in at more than $11,000. He sweet-talked and manhan-
dled the national press, demanding that the race receive front-page
coverage. Spectator sports like boxing and baseball were gaining
ground as national pastimes, and Winn set about convincing the
country that his Derby offered the highest of those high stakes so
richly in demand.

Under Winn's reign, the Derby turned into a choice destination
not just for those seeking a rendezvous with the most divine Thoroughbreds imaginable, but for julep-sipping crowds made up of
the country's social, political, and financial elite. In 1925, the cream
of Chicago society reserved a specially outfitted Cuban Deluxe
train dubbed the "Edgewater Beach Hotel Special" to carry them
from downtown Chicago to Churchill Downs. The train was
advertised as "unsurpassed in distinctiveness, exclusiveness, comfort and completeness," and the four-day ride featured a layover in
French Lick, Indiana, renowned for its mineral spas and perfectly
manicured golf courses. Twenty thousand people journeyed south-
ward, including members of the Oriole dance band brought along
to entertain passengers on long carriage-bound nights and give a
track concert on Derby Day.

IN THE late 1930s, May-May began fleshing out the *Racing
Form*'s bare-bones Derby coverage with more of Robert's imported
literature, a *New Yorker* column written by a dry-witted scribe

named Audax Minor. Minor's weekly racing recaps brought news of the turf to the country's literati, and the Derby found him in prime, wry-humored form. His observations were littered with society doings and sardonic musings. Early on, he began periodically skipping the actual event for its radio and then television versions, complaining of the "excessive number of Colonels underfoot" and Fort Knox soldiers using rubber hoses to hold back the crowds. But his skeptical pose was only the thinnest of screens behind which rested a grand appreciation for the sport. He ended his Derby columns with observations collected under headings like "Notes on an old julep glass" or "Notes on a Derby ticket stub," in which he captured near sentimental bits—a policeman handing out sandwiches from a wooden basket slung over his arm, or a Derby colt who wiggled his legs like a coochie dancer whenever he walked.

Audax Minor's weekly *New Yorker* beat ended in the late seventies just as racing and I began. I used to read his Derby coverage by way of May-May's old clippings. His prose possessed a veneer of intellectual society and a tatty glamour that always seemed an implicit dividing line, the end of May-May's old world and the start of my buffed and shiny present. Then I reached Churchill Downs. Despite the million-dollar prize purse, the blimps and helicopters and skywriters, the crush of human superstars (not just Bob Baffert but Bo Derek, Miss America, and the George Bushes, junior and senior), another era continually rippled along beneath the modern buzz. Just as I'd start to feel fully coated in advertising banners and stadium views, I'd encounter a pinstriped summer suit or a building painted like a New England country club with whitewashed wood and flaking dark-green trim. After leaving the backside that first morning, I cut across the baked blacktop parking lots toward the main gate of the track. I wound up in front of a squat white building with a few small dark-tinted windows. A sign outside read "Kentucky Derby Museum."

Indoors, I roamed past tarnished punch bowls and silver pitchers and a gold-plated loving cup from 1922, past photos of clubhouse boxes containing Bob Hope, Babe Ruth, and the Duke and

Duchess of Windsor. Eventually, I came to a freestanding glass case alone in the center of the room. Inside, pinned up on an array of legless mannequins, were the racing silks of Derby runners spanning the race's full 125 years.

Silks first came to racing in 1862, introduced by the English Jockey Club in order to identify horses and riders as they whistled past. The caps and jackets began as simple designs sewn from bolts of brightly hued silk and velvet. Over time, more creative elements took hold, giving rise to stripes, checks, and diamonds, colored armbands, bow ties, and logos like smiley faces and tiger heads embossed on the back. Each design is drawn, constructed, and then registered with the Jockey Club, the property of the owner forever in exchange for $15 a year. The museum case ran the spectrum from frayed to immaculate, beach-ball brilliant to gauzy and faded with time. I saw Regret's silks up near the top, sea blue and a bit battered. The Calumet colors sat right below them in shades plucked from the baking-powder logo, the devil's red duller than I'd imagined, the twin midnight blue rings around the sleeves disappearing like grooves cut out of the cloth. I came around the case a second time and spotted Real Quiet's colors, the newest addition, an aerodynamic cherry-colored nylon with gold armbands and Mike Pegram's MP monogram stamped large across the back. The Lycra-based fabric reflected the light, making it shine like costume jewelry against the real silk of once upon a time.

The cloaked torsos weren't lined up chronologically but arrayed in random order, requiring me to keep circling to take it all in. The haphazardness was soothing. I felt my preconceptions shift once again. Coming to Kentucky seemed less about plunging than negotiating, finding a subtle and mobile balance, past and present, internal and external. Knowing when to let go of the past and when to tighten all ten fingers and hang on.

THERE'S A song played before every Kentucky Derby, usually by some local marching band, to accompany the horses from the paddock onto the track. It's the Kentucky state song, and like most state songs, it's a little bit seductive, a little bit hokey. The title is

"My Old Kentucky Home." It's played for the same reason almost everything is done at the Derby—out of tradition. It's also played because only part of this race is about saddlecloths and a dirt track. That's the Derby part. The other half is a place, a state, and a Thoroughbred source pool.

Racehorses blossom when they reach Kentucky. Whether they've come from California, New York, or Florida, shipped in via FedEx air cargo or overland trailer hitch, anxieties seem to unwind as soon as they set hooves against the bluegrass. On the surface, it's natural horse country—the temperate air, the proliferation of clover, and the give in the limestone soil filling all their most basic needs. But something also stretches deeper. Most Thoroughbreds hark back to Kentucky. If they weren't born there, one of their parents or grandparents probably was. I spotted such ease even along the cluttered Churchill Downs backstretch—necks loosened, haunches filled out, and coats allover rich and gleaming. I began to wonder if Thoroughbreds didn't keep themselves slightly held in everywhere else, intuitive protection from an alien environment. In some innate way, they knew the bluegrass was coming home.

The first Thoroughbreds, called "blood horses" because of their pure breeding, came to Kentucky in the early 1800s, arriving from England by way of Virginia and newly laid wagon paths through the Cumberland Gap. Their owners were mostly second or third sons from prominent Virginia families, those who aspired to the same Doric-columned mansions and rolling estates that had passed down to their older brothers. As soon as they arrived, they cast their blood horses loose in fields of local bluegrass, silvery-green blades that turned to periwinkle for a few weeks of late-spring bloom. The land was underlaid with a stratum of Ordovician limestone, rich in calcium and phosphorous from shells and skeletons deposited in the rock millenniums earlier when Kentucky had been an ocean bed. The supposedly fragile Thoroughbreds, traditionally confined to overheated stalls, thrived upon their new diet of ample space and organic nutrition. Kentucky horsemen, who until then had nursed their passion for racing by matching quarter horses down village thoroughfares, began voraciously breeding and running their newly imported stock. Laws had to be passed to forbid the coupling of stallions in public squares.

Early-nineteenth-century Kentucky was still considered frontier land, inhabited by log cabins and a meager population measured in free white males, of which there were relatively few. Easterners deemed the future of the territory too unpredictable, between Thomas Jefferson haggling with Napoléon over the nearby Louisiana territory and unknown Indian tribes lurking in the plains to the west. In their opinion, truly classic breeding required stability, and that meant the colonial South—Virginia, Maryland, and the Carolinas. Such stubborn beliefs held fast for the greater part of the century. Though a contract with the U.S. Cavalry and losses suffered by the other states in the financial panic of 1837 did something to help Kentucky's cause, it took a civil war to shake loose the old ways.

When North and South collided at Fort Sumter in April 1861, the futures of both the country and the racehorse were permanently altered. Within months, battles ripped across the once stable Southern states. Thoroughbreds, the pride of many a tidewater plantation, became as expendable as everything else. Horses of all breeds were donated to the cavalry, returning hobbled and wasted if they returned at all. Union forces razing the bottom half of the country left behind burned barns and slaughtered animals. Kentucky, that little backwater state closed inside the circlet of the Allegheny Mountains, remained safe and unharmed. Many Southerners shipped their prized stallions west to ensure the survival of bloodlines that rolled back centuries. Only in the bluegrass did horsemen keep right on breeding and running racehorses. When the ruin of war and Reconstruction finally settled decades later, Kentucky was undisputed home to the highest class of Thoroughbreds in the land.

The twenty-eight hundred square miles of central Kentucky concentrated around the city of Lexington are still knit together by racehorses. The town's entrance is marked by a pumpkin-shaped water tower painted with a mural of bays, blacks, and chestnuts,

standing, walking, and galloping against a pale-blue sky. An in-
scription printed underneath reads "Horse Capital of the World."
Old county roads fan out from Lexington like spokes on a wheel,
linked together by a honeycomb of rambling lanes. Every mile,
every switchback and dead end, is papered with horse farms. I
meant to see the countryside just as an adjunct to the Derby, a way
of passing part of a stray afternoon. Instead, I swung off the highway right outside Lexington, lured by an arrow-marked scenic
byway, and wound up driving for hours.

Kentucky horse country is the serenity of the backstretch poured
across an entire landscape, an atlas with its legend measured in
racehorses instead of miles. Everything was more of what I'd ever
seen before. The greens were greener, like limes and emeralds, and
the swags of the tree branches especially deep and swaggy. Tumble-
down tobacco barns sat lonely on hilltops, their roofs cut open for
drying. Walnut and buckeye and blue ash trees lined up like soldiers along each curve of road, backed by endless fences—planks,
rails, pickets, whitewashed, dark-stained, raw wood—cutting the
roll of the land into circles, squares, rectangles, ovals. There was
alfalfa and wild rye, grass close-clipped like a golf course or waving
long and loose like the strands of a girl's hair. Polka-dotted patterns
of light glancing through leaves dappled the roadways like feed
slung from a bucket.

Inhabiting it all, in every possible shape, tone, and definition,
were horses. Descending from a rise in the road, I could pick out
mamas who'd pulled their foals deep into pastures to let them wander a few tentative paces from their sides. Fields of older mares and
geldings gathered tail to nose, nose to tail, in shady corners, their
relaxed backs taking on the exaggerated sway of a hammock. Yearlings dashed along the fence lines, exploring the wonders of feet
and legs and hips in such marvelous construction, stretching and
striding smooth as water falling down a rock face. Old stallions,
long retired, just sank back into their haunches and blinked.

I felt as if I'd entered an alternate universe, one where time was
measured by the switch of tails and divisions meant nothing more
than the lines separating Bourbon County from Paris County, Old

Frankfurt from Versailles (pronounced Versayles with the accent
on the second syllable and a sharp southern twang). Every question
I'd had about how to take root seemed answered simply by knowing such country existed. Sometimes you just had to step back and
trust that a link was there, like the limestone in the soil. Like the
Kentucky in the horse.

OCCASIONALLY, AS I roped back toward the center of Lexington, the savannas would fall away, and I was reminded of civiliza-
tion in the form of a Texaco station or a freeway overpass bisecting
the horizon. Banked up against one such piece of highway was yet
another expanse of pasture, this one stitched together by miles of
whitewashed fencing. The acreage looked impressive even for the
bluegrass, barns roofed in devil's red mapping constellations over a
lime green sky. This was Calumet Farm. I stopped, but not to witness William Monroe Wright's faded legacy or the extravagances of
J. T. Lundy. I stopped for one reason only. To call on Alydar.

Calumet had changed hands and tempo since Alydar died, had
gone through bankruptcy and been sold at public auction to a Polish aircraft magnate named Henryk de Kwiatkowski. He kept the
farm's name and signature red-and-white décor, but the stables
were only half filled with racehorses of his own. Pastures were
inhabited by tiny bands of mares and foals nearly lost in the swells
of land. Most of J. T. Lundy's additions—the veterinary clinic, the
log cabin guest cabana, the equine swimming pool complex with
underwater treadmill and therapy tubs—had fallen into disuse. It
felt like a crumbling Victorian country house with half the rooms
sealed off, dust sheets draped over the furniture, and shutters
clapped up tight.

I asked the foreman, who was young and gung ho but a bit mud-
dled on the farm's history, to show me the stall where Alydar had
died. He led me through the rear door of the main offices into the
old stallion barn, another building gone cold, drafty, and empty.
The door to Alydar's stall, the one he'd supposedly sheared free
of its bracket, had been commissioned as evidence in the never-
ending fraud trials against Lundy. I examined its twin just opposite

the brick-red concrete floor. It was massive, heavy burnished oak, solid in that way they used to make things, because the world was expected to last. Tiny dents and pockmarks littered the bottom half of the eight-inch-thick wooden slab, near imperceptible damage inflicted by generations of lashing hooves. It seemed impossible that any horse, even Alydar, could have been mighty enough to kick the entire door free.

Less than a mile from Alydar's old stall sat Calumet's horse cemetery, an acre of land set just off one of the paved work roads crisscrossing the farm. The rectangle of clipped grass was planted with aged pin oaks, stone benches, and monuments to all of Calumet's greatest runners. Alydar's granite headstone wasn't the biggest but, as is custom with legendary horses, his whole body was buried there instead of just the usual head, heart, and hooves. He was slotted in among suitably grand company, Triple Crown winners and Calumet's other great sires and dams. His mother, Sweet Tooth, lay only a few yards away.

Despite all the rumors that had risen up around Alydar's death, the story that came to mind as I stood opposite his grave was a tiny one, its quirkiness the sole reason it had crossed the Atlantic into those London racing papers I'd read. The day after Alydar's funeral, four red roses had mysteriously appeared upon his grave. Despite the dawn-to-dusk buzz of farm life, his mystery mourner had come and gone from Calumet unseen. The flowers appeared again a few months later and then again a few months after that, always a quartet of perfect blossoms, always materializing against the granite marker without so much as a footprint left behind. The ghostly tributes continued for eighteen months. Then, just as inexplicably, they were gone for good.

Of all the newsprint I'd pored over after Alydar's demise, a paragraph-long article on those roses was the only thing I'd clipped out and held on to. It had provided a different sort of puzzle, a tiny, hopeful counterweight to even out the snarl of his undoing.

BY THE time Derby Day finally arrived, I was full on history, horse country, and Captain Steve, and primed for an experience unlike anything I'd ever known. I began the day determined to make each footstep fresh, no lapsing into tired old habits or expectations.

I ended the day watching the Kentucky Derby from the top of the stretch.

I hadn't intended it that way. For the biggest race in the country, I meant to select someplace grand and sweeping—the top level of the clubhouse or the pressbox, which balanced on the peaked roof like an aerie overlooking the track—someplace from which I could see every inch of the Derby's mile-and-a-quarter loop. The top of the stretch was for intimacy, and I'd come to Kentucky to create something bigger. I wanted one full afternoon's escape from everything confining about the ordinary world.

My dream day went wrong from the start. Churchill Downs was crowded and crazy and not about the Derby, or at least the Derby as I'd always imagined it—flowered hats and essence of racehorse—which perhaps wasn't really the Derby at all. I paid $30 to park my car on a patch of oil-soaked gravel, then spent the afternoon tugged and crushed by strangers in rumpled suit jackets with bourbon on their breath. I tried to think of simplicity, of May-May hanging over the paddock gazing at Regret without six cameramen and George Bush blocking her view, but spectacle kept getting in the way. I kicked aside beer glasses and popcorn buckets and half-eaten pork sandwiches and remembered one of Audax Minor's columns from the late thirties, one in which he pined for the days when Kentucky Derbies were just horse races. I wondered if I'd simply shown up a hundred years too late.

Eventually, I wandered over to the entry gate farthest from the track and sat down on an empty picnic table. For the first time, the day's hum went quiet. I knew I couldn't let the race pass by without my being fully in attendance. So I set about consciously reattaching myself to the Derby. I thought of Regret's silks and the pansy-planted barrel deep in the backstretch. I thought of the roses on Alydar's grave. I thought back to February and selecting Captain Steve as my Derby horse, pulling his tongue at Santa Anita and then prying his teeth off my coat, to The Deputy and Jenine Sahadi and the kiss she'd planted on his neck after they'd won the Santa Anita Derby. I went through the process again and again. Stop, gather, connect. Stop, gather, connect. Like joining up those long lines of hooks-and-eyes running down the backs of May-May's old party dresses. It was the best I could do at turning the Kentucky Derby back into a horse race.

By the time I stood up again, sweeping vistas had gone the way of the rest of my invented nostalgia. There seemed no question about which corner of the track I should head toward. While everyone else flooded the opposite direction, seeking out scraps of finish line viewed between ten-thick sets of straining shoulders, I aimed for the top of the stretch. I noticed details I'd missed earlier: a tray of real-glass julep glasses, each with a mint sprig trembling on its brim; the slow-flowing molasses of local voices. A man in a white suit strolled past humming a few bars of "My Old Kentucky Home."

When 150,000 people pack into one rickety old racetrack, there are few open spaces left. The top of the stretch was not one of them. Even more than an hour before post time, there was only the slimmest of person-sized openings available along the chain-link fence separating the cement apron from the track. I wedged myself in as tightly as I could until the honeycomb of metal dug into my hip. Then, as if to reward my change of faith, Churchill Downs provided an unexpected gift. The starting gate wheeled into place just yards from where I stood. I would get to double-down. First I'd see the horses pour out of the gate and onto the track. Then I'd watch them a second time, full-flower, coming around the far turn.

The grandstand chaos drifted toward me well filtered, the wind carrying only a faint purr of voices and a tinny marching band version of "My Old Kentucky Home." Horses and riders paraded formally in front of the crowds. By the time they reached me, all nineteen had shed their public faces and had begun coalescing into the race. Jockeys adjusted their equipment, fingers fiddling silks, straps, and goggles. Horses dipped their chins toward the track and experimented with the clank of the bit against their teeth. I could see the osmosis taking place as the base of each rider's back began to roll with the animal beneath. I tried my best to copy them, centering my thoughts in bones and muscles, tendons and ligaments, perfection each time they parted and met.

As they loaded, I could see the horses' individual faces through the doors of the starting gate. The Deputy flared his nostrils and tossed his head violently sideways, halting inches from the metal caging. It was as if he'd decided the whole pinwheeling Derby upheaval was too much for him, stretching him tauter than he was meant to stretch. A few stalls down Captain Steve ambled in looking his old steadfast, undaunted self. He was one of the last to load. There was a long still second in which they all stood packed like arrows in a giant quiver. Then the bell rang, and that intensity erupted onto the track.

They were gone in an instant, all force and energy. A muted crowd roar joined the clank of the starting gate being dragged to the side of the track. Then silence and that sense anything could be happening up around that first turn. Anything at all. I picked them up again along the far side, spread out along the rail. They gathered speed and distinction as they flowed into the turn, bending inward all at once as if someone were pulling them around the circle by yanking a giant string. They swept, some wide, some tight, around the hairpin.

My memory of what came next is like a snapshot, one horse in bold outline, the others a background blur. It wasn't The Deputy, sitting trapped somewhere in the muddy back of the pack, destined for a fourteenth-place finish. It wasn't Captain Steve, who through sheer grinding effort had cinched himself a spot just off the lead, only to be squeezed in the stretch and fade to eighth. The horse who hummed past, pulling me right out of myself and onto the track, was the race favorite, Fusaichi Pegasus. And he was awesome.

He kicked clear of the turn like some chimerical creature, all head and legs and massive chest leaving room for a massive heart. His muscles softened when everyone else's tensed, slipped clear of gravity and unfurled like a bolt of oiled silk. An internal cadence took over, the jockey atop a mere grace note, and that rhythm I'd searched out all afternoon swelled to the front of the pack. The racehorse, the racehorse, the racehorse.

In that moment, it no longer mattered whether I saw the finish or bet the winner or could distinguish anything at all from the back view of swaying rumps and flipping hooves. In that moment, I connected with a racehorse. And for all my searching in the days and hours leading up to the race, connection was exactly why I had come.

Chapter Ten

GROWTH:

The Future of the Track

S ometimes I look around at what I have at the racetrack—
the steam and speed and hard-candy colors—and wish I
knew how to preserve it, canned for future consumption.
But racing doesn't take well to confinement. As soon as I try to trap
a piece, it turns into one of those papery orange wildflowers I used
to pick in Montana, kicking my feet free of the stirrups and leaning
off Grey Lady's back to pluck a stem from the grass. By the time I'd
risen again, I was cupping nothing but a palm full of wilted petals.
All its seductive powers were tied to being alive.

In 1992, the year I graduated from college, the Longacres race-track shut down. The track had been built sixty years earlier, the baby of a local businessman named Joe Gottstein who made his fortune on the frontier, founding one of the first retail grocery chains in Alaska. Gottstein caught racing on the edge of popularity. Roosevelt's New Deal and a reviving economy had prompted numerous states to legalize betting and build splashy new tracks. Technology engendered nightly radio broadcasts to keep devotees in tune, and the end of Prohibition finally made enjoying the high life a legal endeavor. By the time Gottstein handed the track down to his son-in-law, Maury Alhadeff, several decades later, it was a prosperous business operation and a set piece in Seattle's social backbone.

Maury Alhadeff ran Longacres through the sixties and seventies, creating a haven for those career-type gamblers still shooting their cuffs. Then, in the late eighties, in the lull following America's boom economy, racing acquired a sheen of the passé that Longacres couldn't seem to overcome. Its charms were subtle; a rail that let you stand flush to the track, white fencing starting to peel around the edges as if waiting for a farmer to come along and lash it with another good coat of paint. The gift shop sold pencils and dark-blue lapel buttons emblazoned with the track's "Doo-dah" slogan adopted from the old "Camptown Races" song. Longacres was a neighborhood track, enough to please people like May-May and me who went purely for the horses, or gamblers whose field of vision didn't extend beyond the *Racing Form*. But Seattle—courtesy of a thriving international shipping port and the monopolistic rise of Boeing, the airplane manufacturer—was no longer a camp town. When Alhadeff died in 1990, ownership passed to his sons Mike and Ken, who looked into their laps and found a tarnished bit of history. The brothers sold the land to Boeing, which quickly drew up plans to erect a state-of-the-art flight simulator.

If racing had been my spirit home, Longacres formed the bricks and mortar. So many pleats and folds of my development could be traced there: that tingle of amazement provided by horses just off the highway; the anticipation, one long arc of tension building from September all the way into April, of opening day of the racing season; the way I'd squirmed to stay comfortable on the tottery box seats. Even the tint of seediness—the cigars and greased-back hair and shiny plaid pants that frightened my childhood friends away— had shaped me, made me feel dangerous and unique. My father clipped a column about the sale from the *Seattle Times* sports section and mailed it to me at college. Though I only professed the most casual link to racing at the time, that article felt as if it had ripped a hole right through me. The house I'd grown up in was being torn down.

The Alhadeff brothers gave Longacres a two-year grace period before the land would switch hands to Boeing. Two years in which to run races, two years for the sport to find a new Seattle home. An emergency team of thirty investors gathered, horse owners and enthusiasts with the means to help float the sport, and each anted up $100,000 to operate the track until its final bow. I went to Longacres only once in those two years, not so much to say good-bye as to seal shut my past. Longacres was about to go the way of May-May and those plastic horses still boxed and wrapped under the basement furnace, something abandoned because it could never be replaced. I wanted a fixed picture in my memory because, no matter what wonders rose up from the ashes, I knew I would never visit another Seattle track.

As they negotiated Longacres' final seasons, the impromptu board of directors commenced a search for land and investors to back a freshly minted track. Timing mattered. For each season Seattle went without local racing, more owners, trainers, horses, and fans would drift off towards rosier prospects. Even before Longacres officially shut its doors, there were rumblings of resurrection, a package of land purchased just south of the city. They tentatively called the projected entity Emerald Downs, after Seattle's nickname, "the Emerald City."

The thrust behind Emerald Downs was a local businessman named Ron Crockett. Crockett, like Longacres' founder Joe Gottstein, was an entrepreneur with King Midas leanings. In 1970, he'd started from scratch with a modest airline overhaul operation called Tramco; eighteen years later, he sold the business for a small fortune to the industrial conglomerate B. F. Goodrich. Racehorses formed a steady leitmotif in Crockett's success story. He'd grown up just minutes from Longacres, peering over his mother's shoulder as she handicapped the day's race card. As his wealth mounted, it seemed only natural that he float a bit of it into buying and running Thoroughbreds. He bought his first horse in 1974, and went on to amass one of Seattle's most profitable local stables. In 1990, as Longacres was scrabbling for financial footing, Crockett had just stepped off the corporate board at B. F. Goodrich and was looking for a worthwhile endeavor with which to occupy his time. Fate sent him to the track. He was named CEO of Seattle's informal racing preservation society, after which, being of a goal-oriented frame of mind, he set about overseeing the new land purchase. From there, it seemed a straight shot to revival.

Ron Crockett's smooth business plan lasted all of a month or two before things began to bob and swerve like a two-year-old first taking to the track. The land the committee had so carefully selected sat on a portion of native wetlands. As soon as Emerald Downs filed a request for permission to build, national environmental organizations swelled up in protest. They called in army engineers to evaluate the situation, generating lashings of negative press and freezing all forward momentum. Crockett had collected numbers and projected data for an Emerald Downs ready for operation exactly one year after Longacres shut down. Instead, months and then years passed, and the swamp only grew swampier. Some of Crockett's fellow board members began to waffle, wondering whether such a struggle was worth the now dubious outcome, each back-step adding to the suspicion that Emerald Downs was as thoroughly entrenched in fantasy as its *Wizard of Oz* namesake. Crockett didn't agree.

Ron Crockett is a lean, hawk-nosed man, outwardly warm but with hints of a whiplike intensity you wouldn't want to mess with over the negotiating table. He keeps his commitments, and he'd made one to the sport and the state. It would have been simple to wriggle free of a nightmare he'd entered into out of sheer generosity, but he saw more at stake than saving face. The racing industry doesn't generate highly versatile laborers. It breeds grooms with patchy English who've rubbed down steaming horses every morning since they were fourteen; jockeys who are gifted on a horse's back but just uneducated young men in miniature anyplace else; trainers who know the intricate architecture of a horse's legs but are lost in front of a keyboard. Blacksmiths, breeders, hay and alfalfa farmers—they all depended upon the racetrack. They made it difficult to walk away.

Instead, Ron Crockett poured $10 million of his self-made fortune into Emerald Downs. He brokered a long-term compromise with the environmental agencies, purchasing fifty-six acres of endangered wetlands across the highway from the track and designating it forever unspoiled. He battled the state legislature and special-interest lobbies and those trainers, owners, and fans who sat back on their heels and complained it would never be another Longacres. In the spring of 1996, Emerald Downs finally opened its doors.

The track's mere existence spins a classic tale of triumph over adversity, but, in the parlance of success, triumph is hardly enough. You need numbers. Emerald Downs debuted to only 60 percent of the old Longacres audience, the passage of time having lured all but the most blessedly loyal to the ready temptations of baseball games and Indian casinos or, like me, to the comforting cobwebs of the past. Again, Ron Crockett took advantage of disadvantage. Instead of trying to re-create Longacres and its shaky charms, he began to look around him for more forward-thinking options.

One of the first things Crockett spotted was Las Vegas, where he spends every New Year's Eve, an entertainment town busily revamping itself from mobsters' boudoir to neon-lit fantasy destination. Four years seemed ample lag time for Emerald Downs to undergo a similar metamorphosis. So Crockett set about engineering a perpetual holiday. He promoted family days and twilight racing, pony rides, rock concerts, and goggle tosses—an event in which jockeys pitched their racing goggles into the crowd like a bride ditching her bouquet. The numbers slowly began to climb. It was a quiet revolution, shaking up those married to the old, beckoning to those who didn't know they were even curious about the new. It was risky business, the sort of business at which racing truly excels.

EIGHT YEARS to the August after Longacres shut down, I finally decided I was ready to let go of how things used to be. It was time to pay a call on Emerald Downs. The changed terrain confronted me the second I spun through the gate, rose up in a passel of little girls in purple cowboy hats who strutted past licking Popsicles. Longacres had been my private domain. Most of the time, I was the only kid around. I paused to let newness and oldness wash through me, just a moment to acknowledge that the track that had raised me was gone. Then I stepped forward onto the paved apron of Emerald Downs.

I am lucky in the way of courtship. I begin anew all the time, a track in every port, and Emerald Downs did its job to charm. It wasn't a grandiose place. It was a regional racetrack, and like with any small town, that homespun quality—cleanly swept walkways, neon-colored signs, and beds of sweet william—provided most of the allure. Top tracks like Belmont and Churchill Downs operate on caste systems, laden with gateways labeled "Do Not Enter," permits, passes, and privilege required. At Emerald Downs, participation prevailed. Families lugged in coolers and spread picnics on white plastic tables. Jockeys had their own theme songs, played over the loudspeaker every time they reached the winner's circle— rock 'n' roll riffs like "Let's Get Jiggy," "Another One Bites the Dust," and "Louie, Louie" for Luis Jauregui, an angel-faced California rider who'd drifted north to join the family for the day. Even the bugler summoning the horses to the track jazzed up his traditional call with a few bars of John Denver or Billy Joel.

There were things I would never have found at Longacres, changes wrought by time and temperament. A mascot dressed in a fuzzy horse suit boogied down the track between races. A handful of women trainers cinched saddles around their charges, not impossible long shots but horses who went off as favorites and returned to the winner's circle. A female jockey, moon-faced, freckled, and taut and jaunty as her male counterparts, strode into the paddock for nearly every race. There were even a few comforting traces of the past: cows along the highway and narrow rails that allowed me to press up close to the finish line the same way I had when I was a child.

It was impossible to displace nostalgia altogether. Emerald Downs was allover shiny, bearing trace levels of Walt Disney, and I missed the hint of an underbelly always in residence at Longacres. I couldn't find anyplace to stand surrounded by cigarette smoke and square yards of people who held a martini and a hot tip fathoms above showering or square meals. Go-cart races and face painting seemed flimsy alongside the illicit thrill I used to get from men with jelly doughnut bodies who sported wads of cash and never said a word to me except maybe "Hey, kid." The suspense was diluted, Dorothy amid ruby slippers and polished gold brick, before she realized there was a wicked witch involved.

Some shrinkage had occurred, as it does when age and experience pull you taller. The starting gate—ten stalls long instead of the fourteen I'd grown used to at the larger tracks—looked flimsy, dwarfed by the horses when I was sure the mesh and bars and clanging metal doors had once made it the other way around. Even the horses themselves weren't as awesome as twenty years before. They were a few tiers down from elite, bred in Washington State or on obscure Kentucky farms, purchased for thousands instead of millions of dollars, too workmanlike or flighty to compete on the New York circuit that had become my home base. The Captain Steves had spoiled me, the same way chic Manhattan streets stripped downtown Seattle of any glamour, turning the Northwest runners thicker and shabbier than they'd ever been before. Too many of them showed signs of easy distraction, outfitted with blinkers or shadow rolls to curb wandering attention spans. I even spotted differences in the races themselves; times clocked a few fractions slower, gaits not as wondrously smooth, and a smattering of confoundedly stubborn creatures yanking against their riders all the way around the track.

Then I watched Luis Jauregui climb aboard a California import named Bold Words for the major race of the day, the Mount Rainier Breeders' Cup Stakes. Bold Words was classier than all his competition, straighter knees and a slim, elegant neck. If pedigree truly did win out, there would be no contest. A few minutes later, as the pack ripped down the homestretch, those Emerald Downs horses fought back as only underdogs can. It wasn't pretty. It was anarchy, all jagged paths, bumping gaits, and hearts that superseded anything less or more. Coming out of the far turn, Bold Words was still midpack, each runner in front of him unwilling to give in as he shouldered his way through. The leader, a Washington-bred bay called Edneator, stretched his neck long and toiled, waiting until his legs were bent and trembling before finally ceding to his worn-out speed a few yards from the wire. In the end, Bold Words had to pull out every ounce, and still nipped the race by only the tip of his nose. Galloping out after the finish, the also-rans hung their heads low and drew long heaving breaths, any hints of Thoroughbred pride lost in the fact that they'd spent everything they'd had. They were the same racehorses who'd once riveted me at Longacres, hell-bent and unencumbered by gloss.

I watched those horses pour past, and knew I would be back. They'd done their job. Longacres notwithstanding, I'd fallen for Emerald Downs.

WHEN I was a kid, my father and I used to go dawn fishing in the summers, trolling for trout along a protected offshoot of the Puget Sound. We'd always putter in close to shore where freshwater tributaries from mountain streams flowed into the salt. The fish congregated there, drawn to the cool influx of current and the delicacies of plant life that blossomed in the half-and-half watery medium. I liked to think they also came because day after day of a saltwater existence with the same old barnacles, sand dollars, and yellow-green strands of kelp grew dull after a while. Life gathers around indications of change.

In 1913, the most visible woman in the sport was a British suffragist who threw herself in front of the king's horse as he charged

down the stretch in the Epsom Derby. Now there are Jenine
Sahadi, Donna Barton, and Alice Chandler. In the 1930s, the Longacres vet May-May used for Dr. Rhythm and Countess Highland
traveled from barn to barn in a horse-drawn wagon, mixing herbed
poultices with the same straight alcohol that went into home-
brewed whiskey, his ingredients arrayed in drawers built into the
back of his open buggy like the shelves of an apothecary. The vet I
know now would've seemed an impossible fantasy figure seventy
years ago: a thirty-four-year-old woman manning a crack racehorse emergency clinic in Ocala, Florida, home to the finest Thoroughbreds outside the bluegrass.

Carol Clark came to horses as May-May and I did, a child
popped aboard a pony and launched into infatuation. There's a
hazy, girlish dream to somehow hang on to that drunkenness forever, but Carol tended toward more solid equations. If you wanted
horses, you became a large-animal vet. She started her career
with total immersion—animal medical school, a year-long equine
internship, a three-year residency at a university teaching hospital, case reports, publication in scientific journals, an original
research project on the effects of Lasix—all culminating in Veterinary Board certification. It was the sort of grinding marathon
meant to weed the waverers from the tough and impassioned.
Equine medicine, racehorse medicine, can appear especially
rigged against women, requiring physical strength and a certain
ballsy guile to match wits with a Thoroughbred. Carol fit all the
qualifications.

The Peterson & Smith Equine Hospital where she's worked
since 1996 would quickly push more timid temperaments over the
edge. It's the racehorse version of an ER, and Carol's job require-
ments are not negotiable. She must know everything, instantly,
life-hinging detective work conducted against the clink of scalpels,
saws, and surgical screws and the hum of diagnostic machinery.
She resides the other side of the globe from the typical veterinary
routine of toodling from farm to farm, checking on mares in foal,
delivering worm medicine and vaccinations.

"I didn't want something that would wind up boring me," she says about picking her area of specialization. "I don't think I'll need to worry."

Carol's average day might produce a broodmare in labor well past the half hour it should take to give birth, her foal stuck halfway down the birth canal as its blood and oxygen supplies dwindle, demanding an emergency cesarean section. It might require slicing open a pregnant mare's colic-swollen belly, then maneuvering around the full uterus to cut free a clump of knotted intestine. Mornings nearly always produce patients who arrive dull and washy with night-born fevers "of undetermined origin" that Carol must sort into viruses, hidden abscesses, or perhaps an undetected arrhythmia of the heart.

Surgery is common, often safer than drugs since horses' fragile digestive systems are hypersensitive to even the mildest doses of antibiotics. Treatment techniques advance daily, involving everything from high-tech X-ray bone scans to ice boots strapped around hooves literally crumbling from a blood-borne infection called laminitis. Carol learns via practical, often cutting-edge experimentation. The clinic is a repository for the most exceptional cases, an equine last resort, and she's treated illnesses so exotic that tenured veterinarians at national conferences gather around to hear her stories of diseases and defects they've never witnessed firsthand. It's a forum for constant stimulation, and occasional improvised genius. Mini-miracles make a regular appearance.

Come spring, birthing season, Carol's spectrum shifts from full-grown, half-ton animals to the most alarmingly fragile, neonatal foal work. Babies with untested organs and immune systems are susceptible to everything—pneumonia settling in the lungs, rampaging bacterial infections, or digestive tracts that spit back their mother's milk. In Ocala, foals begin to arrive by late January. Soon after, the first horse van will rumble through the clinic parking lot, its driver emerging clutching a twitching fuzzy bundle, a foal born healthy then gone punch-drunk with seizures a day later, unable to suck or stand. They're called dummy foals, babies deprived of oxygen at some point in the birth canal. Carol can treat the seizures with tiny doses of medication, drip food down their throats, and keep them in a stall monitored by cameras for twenty-four-hour observation. The pocket of brain damage usually passes after a day or two, the foal emerging as from a cocoon into full health and rampant curiosity. Such cases are the reward pinnacle, bridges perfectly constructed between helpless and whole.

"I probably shouldn't admit this," Carol laughs. "But when those foals come back, you start to feel a little bit like God."

The thorniest part of Carol's job isn't the schedule, though her days are long and unpredictable in the way doctors' days tend to be. She works fifty-hour weeks and one or two weekends on call each month, plus the inevitable midnight surgery summonses. During the February to June breeding season, her days often extend to unbroken twenty-four-hour stretches. She attempts to balance a husband, a small farm, and four pleasure horses of her own.

"I try to work smartly," she offers, "and to guard my personal time. But I can't say I'm all that successful." Wherever they appear, Thoroughbreds seem to reshape the environment, like some mythical creature growing bigger and bigger until it blocks out all the light. It's the exhausting, rewarding, manageable price Carol had expected for demanding that life never grow dull.

The toll she hadn't quite braced herself for was the psychological one. Thoroughbreds can't appreciate the need to factor financial cost into emotional choices. By default, this part of the equation falls to Carol, too. Emergency-room work involves extreme cases, expensive cures, and shaded questions of survival. She knows the owner of a racehorse will set out a scale, weigh the price of treatment against potential for recovery. If a colt's reset broken hip will leave it gimping into the future, if surgery on a clicking heart valve still forbids a wisp of stress or overstimulation, if the cost is prohibitive and the results chancy . . . Even though a mind weighted with veterinary knowledge yearns to try anything, the business backbeat often says otherwise. No Hippocratic oath exists to provide veterinarians with a code of moral obligation. Instead, a shot is prepared, a stall bedded, and the patient humanely and efficiently put down.

"For someone who grew up worshiping horses," she says, "those are the most difficult choices of all."

Carol was raised in a horse country far different from northern Florida's lush farmlands, the stripped prairies and barbed-wire fences of central Texas. When she'd finished her University of Florida veterinary residency and started searching for a place to settle, she thought first—as any good Texas girl might—about going home. Texas is rich in Thoroughbreds, breeding ranches ranging for thousands of sagebrush acres and races run spring to fall at Lone Star Park in the town of Grand Prairie. Back in 1929, a cattle baron named William T. Waggoner built his own $2 million racetrack halfway between Dallas and Fort Worth, staging a single eleven-day race meet in an effort to convince the state legislature to make racing legal. They did so in 1933. But sixty years later, the spurs and Stetsons still weren't quite ready for the likes of a girl vet talking high-risk surgeries, diagnostic imaging, and drug-treatment innovation. The few job offers Carol received included drought-level salaries and responsibility gauged at next to zero.

Ocala called more sweetly, with its palm trees, roadside Cuban restaurants, and the potential for partnership somewhere far down the line. But even after five years of documented proof, Florida isn't an open door for female practitioners. Owners are likely to second-guess, to summon their own vets to verify Carol's diagnosis of anything from a simple cornea infection to the nerve disorder equine protozoal myeloencephalitis. She spends long chunks of her over-extended days on the phone with consulting colleagues, explaining and justifying what she's done.

"I definitely get the feeling that if I had gray hair and balls people would listen more," she admits. "But I can't exactly wait around for that to happen."

Instead, she forges forward by way of education, attending veterinary conferences all over the country, reading medical journals, and tapping an evolving Internet database. She's chipped out a place as the youngster in the practice, the one schooled in scientific revisionism, aggressively networking and cultivating underexplored resources. She's learned that the surest way to alter convictions is by physical evidence, Thoroughbreds who limp into her care and gambol back out again. It's the nature of her career that loose ends will be left dangling—final outcomes evade finality, symptoms appear and vanish, patients recover seemingly by no actions of her own.

"I fight back by being as competent and well educated as I can. If that's not enough for people, I just have to move on."

CHANGE AT the track is unceasing, like water through the fingers. In the months after the Kentucky Derby, my unprepossessing goofball Captain Steve rebounded like a Superball. He finally managed that ruler-perfect line to victory in both the Swaps Stakes in California and the Iowa Derby, so that he and Bob Baffert boomeranged sky-high into the fall season. A year later they pulled off a three-length victory in the richest race on earth, the $6 million World Cup run over the Nad Al Sheba racetrack in Dubai. The Deputy, more delicate and easily rattled, took half the year off for a rest cure, lazing away his days in a shady green pasture someplace isolated and pristine. A few months after returning to the track, he strained a tendon during a workout and was retired to stud. Jenine Sahadi, having pulled up a few lengths short of her fairy-tale ending, went back to California and began nursing along the next generation, including one of the country's most promising two-year-old fillies, Golden Ballet. Their first big victory came in the Cinderella Stakes.

Alice Chandler accepted a seat as the only woman on the freshly formed Equine Drug Research Council, a committee designed to investigate and monitor medication use in racehorses. New drug controversies emerge from the industry almost daily as fresh ingredients loop through Thoroughbred bloodstreams and onto the track. Alice takes a sterner line than those toed by most of her colleagues. She's aiming toward stringent rules regulating substances and dosage, money funneled into sophisticated post-race drug-testing procedures, and stiffer penalties enforced against trainers caught using even trace levels of illegal goods. Her rigid stance will mean taking on the reigning chiefs of the sport, those officials prone to looking the other away when a buddy bends a rule or two or twelve. It's the sort of mission that will require serious political savvy, the maverick constitution instilled by her father, her horses, and Mill Ridge.

Down the road from Mill Ridge at Calumet Farm, after the ten-year impasse following Alydar's demise, J. T. Lundy's bankruptcy trial came to court in the spring of 2000. A jury found him guilty of bribery and deceit, defrauding the First National Bank of Houston out of $65 million in loans.

"Based on my review of the evidence," said the presiding judge, "Lundy is guilty as sin." He was sentenced to four and a half years at a medium-security prison in Pensacola, Florida, and ordered to pay $20.4 million in restitution.

Though the question of Alydar's death was never officially debated, the defense did bring in George Pratt, a biomechanical engineer from MIT, to study the physics of Alydar's injury. He concluded the twelve-hundred-pound stallion would have needed to jump twelve feet into the air to generate enough propulsion to kick his stall door free of its brackets. During Lundy's sentencing hearing, and in an accompanying letter to the FBI, Pratt outlined his belief that Alydar's leg was intentionally smashed and the scene later staged to look like an accident.

I didn't know whether to find such concrete information after so many years comforting or disturbing, until I remembered Frederico Tesio's guiding tenet. Racing isn't subject to the laws of science, only to the laws of chance. Then it was just Thoroughbred progress, precarious and fertile. One part moving forward, another part left behind.

IN 1945, Colonel Matt Winn, that honey-tongued granddaddy of the Kentucky Derby, set down his vision for racing's future in a book entitled *Down the Stretch*. He wrote:

> *As I look down the vista of the years ahead of us, I can envision an*
> *era of peace; I can see monster racetracks in operation; I can see*

crowds of 50,000 and 60,000 on normal days—100,000 crowds on
the Saturdays and holidays; I can see gigantic parking places for the
automobiles of the future; huge landing fields for the planes that will
carry race patrons almost to the gates of the track. The golden age
for Thoroughbred racing lies just beyond us now.

It was a grand dream, ambitious and romantic, spun sugar for an audience stripped bare by the Second World War. Fifty-five years later, it bears little resemblance to how things are. At Belmont Park's fall 2000 meet, the average daily attendance was 6,545 people. Winn hadn't counted upon competition from the likes of the NFL and college basketball, state-run lotteries and resort-casinos. Nor had he factored in the power exerted by those suspicious of any fresh vistas at all.

If Winn the visionary has a counterpart today, he would be a compact, white-haired Canadian automotive tycoon named Frank Stronach. Stronach is racing's wild card, querulous and quixotic, the sort of allover presence who makes traditionalists squirm in their Turf Club seats. His foray into the racetrack business began in the late 1980s when, despite owning a top-caliber racing stable, he couldn't wrangle his way into the cushy director's room at Santa Anita Park because it was filled with friends and acquaintances of racing's favored sons. He vowed to buy the track himself one day and to set about changing the sport's antiquated mode of operation. Ten years and $126 million later, Santa Anita was his. It was the first in a throng of independent tracks he would go on to purchase, and Stronach was neither reserved nor humble about his ambitions. He planned to construct a racetrack empire stretching from Florida to California. He was gunning toward a new version of master of the game.

Stronach possesses little if anything of Colonel Winn's southern country club aesthetic. He's a self-made multimillionaire, an Austrian-born manufacturer of car parts—mirrors, bumpers, speedometers, gearshifts—and the son of a Communist factory worker whose beliefs form slashes in the fabric of Stronach's capitalist leanings. Stronach's auto company, Magna International,

includes a formal corporate constitution designed to protect workers' rights. His grand plan for the racing industry is to bring the
headiness of the track eye-level with the common man. He owns
four thousand acres of breeding farms in Canada, Florida, and
Kentucky, and a stable full of champion racers. His unapologeti-
cally gluttonous aspirations include winning every high-profile
race mapped across the United States and Canada. Stronach may
be a businessman, but he also relishes—with hundred-proof adora-
tion—the bump and grind of the game.

Stronach aims to reinvigorate racing's old-fashioned pageantry
by injecting a dose of modern pizzazz. He wants to rebuild many
of the tracks he's purchased, adding hotels, rock concert pavilions,
and Wild West theme parks with restaurants and souvenir shops,
full-blown extravaganzas that feature live horse racing at the hub
of an ever-spinning entertainment wheel. In spring 2001, he set up
teams of racehorses, beginning with the Miami "Cruisers" and the
Los Angeles "Blaze," to face one another at "home" and "away"
confrontations. He plans to eventually generate team rivalries con-
tested by individual runners, a sort of four-legged version of
NASCAR. Traditionalists have squawked, and Stronach's aspirations do seem hazardous, in every way counter to the simple elegance of a Thoroughbred. Then you discover what most other
large tracks are concentrating on—pumping up offtrack betting,
pressing to legalize phone and Internet wagering, and facilitating a
future where gamblers can go to the races without ever leaving the
plush comfort of their La-Z-Boys. Held up against such an alterna-
tive, Frank Stronach begins to look something like a savior.

The ethics of change can be complex, and the racetrack proves no
exception. Many tiny regional tracks that have threatened again and
again to shut down are kept open because of roomfuls of slot
machines; hybrid racecourse-casinos that earn the tracks enough
money to boost prize purses and lure trainers and owners who
might otherwise have spirited their horses away. In 2000, at Prairie
Downs in Iowa, slots brought in around $295 million, enough light-
flashing, bell-ringing, quarter-clanging income for racing to survive. Even the larger, healthier tracks make much of their money

off simulcasting, the grandstands and clubhouses sprinkled with television screens offering betting opportunities from across the country, an endless gambling lollapalooza for any player who troubles to come to the track. I can see the intimacy seeping out of the sport, those moments reserved for just human and horses. But without changes, growth is impossible.

I've learned from May-May's ability to embrace imperfections, grown willing to ride through patchy places in the hopes that racing and I might pop out the other end richer and wiser than we were before. I can understand the slot machines and western theme parks, not as end goals but as a developmental stage. But there's something else I spot at the track, something that seems far more dangerous than all the questionable advances combined. It's that dusty, stale-air feel of nothing moving at all.

Racing has lost the glamour that buttressed it in the forties and fifties, and, for the most part, it's found no new catalyst to fill that empty space. It wants for fresh blood, the sort I found flowing into Emerald Downs. I can go to the track on a sunny Sunday afternoon and find myself one of a spotty crowd of potbellies and wash-and-wear suits, can eavesdrop on conversations about social security and sciatica as well as which horse looks good in the fifth. Things creak and move slowly—the clerks behind the grilled betting windows, the tired bands trotted out for Friday night concert series. The National Thoroughbred Racing Association (NTRA)—a newly formed, nationwide governing body designed to raise the sport in the public's eye—recently received an offer from IBM, the computer kingpin, pledging to revamp racing's entire antiquated technology sector from tote boards to online presence. Racing industry officials rejected the proposition as "too risky." Insiders voice vague worries about continually declining track attendance, but, aside from the NTRA—which has launched aggressive ad campaigns—few of them seem to mold such concerns into a plan. I hear all this and wonder how the business end of the sport can possibly hope to keep up with that glory whizzing past on the track. Racing seems caught behind an air of impoverished gentility, like someone in a

Chekhov play returning from a reverie, looking about lost and surprised, then asking, "Where has everybody gone?"

It's frustrating, this realization that the track can't always tap the sense of risk taking it's bestowed upon me, that my sport and I are not one and the same. I understand that part of my commitment is to weather what's difficult as well as what's magical. I just wish I knew the proper spell to cast what I've absorbed from racing back into the sport itself: to pass on the knowledge that you are never stuck, unless you choose to be.

AS ALWAYS when I'm troubled by the racing industry, when I need something solid to anchor me, I come back to the horses. Not long ago, I wound up on the Belmont backstretch in the middle of a lackluster racing day. It was mid-afternoon quiet, too early for the evening feed, too late for anything else. Most of the barns were deserted save a groom in a plastic chair, eyes closed, head back, mouth open, and an occasional horse's head peering out from the open top of its stall. A battered green pickup truck pulled up on the side of the road just ahead of me, a blacksmith with clippers and bent shoes rattling around loose on the metal floor of his flatbed. A trainer emerged from one of the barns leading a barrel-chested thug of a colt who already had his ears pinned flat to the crest of his head.

"How is the old bastard?" the blacksmith called out, fishing a fresh aluminum shoe from the mélange in the back.

"Dangerous," the trainer called back.

He had a bit of chain hooked to a length of rope dangling from his loose hand. At first I figured it for a second lead shank, that they were going to cross-tie the old bastard to keep him from jerking away in the middle of the shoeing. The colt was already straining, yanking his head hard left to avoid the rattle and clank of the approaching gear. Then the trainer reached up for the horse's nose, and I realized he was holding a twitch. A twitch is a bit of chain attached to a lead shank or stick that, when fastened to a horse's upper lip, gives humans a bit more control. It doesn't hurt as long

as the horse remains standing still, and its placement releases natural opiates into the horse's nervous system, creating a temporary—
usually about three to five minutes—valley of calm. The trainer
clipped the twitch onto the colt's lip and pulled down on the rope.
The drumming, the pulling, the panic, went still.

The blacksmith bent down, lifted the colt's left front hoof, and
balanced it on the flat of his thigh. He used the back end of a hammer to wrench off the old shoe and the front end to pound on the
new, lining up eight nails between his lips and pulling them out one
by one. It only took a minute or two, then the blacksmith was
upright again, shoving the worn shoe into his jacket pocket. The
trainer reached up to free the twitch, and the colt instantly began
jigging his feet, pushing his nose forward and back, claiming space
as his once again.

It was a plain, everyday backstretch occurrence, a feisty horse
getting a new shoe. I've seen a twitch, used plenty of times. It
requires that, some form of counterforce, to keep a racehorse standing still. Forward momentum is ingrained in his nature, inhabiting
every loose, leggy, wild, and untouchable inch.

Slot machines and empty grandstands will forever glide past,
twigs on a stream. The racehorses are the current. They are, always
have been, and always will be enough. Not because they're
anchored, but because they're moving all the time.

Epilogue

The Heartbeat

One of the first times I ever went to Longacres alone, the spring I was in sixth grade, a massive pileup on the highway made my father almost an hour late to pick me up. We'd planned to meet inside the gates at the corner where the paddock fence met the rail of the track. I waited there, watching as the entire place emptied out. First the fans drifted past, the last of them inching along with eyes pasted downward, hoping to cheat luck with a winning ticket someone had accidentally tossed away. Then came the maintenance staff, wielding plastic trash cans on rollers and push brooms taller than I was, erasing all signs of the day's play. Last, the jockeys emerged from their changing room, dressed for success in fancy-stitched cowboy shirts, creased blue jeans, and giant silver belt buckles, but their bodies disappointingly wingless when not coupled with that of a Thoroughbred.

A white-haired trainer, bent over a wooden walking stick, was schooling one of his young horses in the paddock. He stood in the center, like a Russian ballet master, brandishing his cane to direct the groom in and out of the saddling stalls, and around the parade circle. He halted them whenever the horse grew even faintly restless, letting her stand, shift, adjust, recover. I rested my hands on my chin, just high enough to reach the top railing, and watched the filly, an angular walnut-colored bay. Eventually, the trainer stopped the groom a few feet from me and limped over to where my chin sat balanced on the top board.

"You like horses, then?" he demanded, as if I were in for a lifetime of trouble if I answered either way.

I nodded.

"You ever touched one?"

"A horse?"

He snorted, dismissing the greater part of the species. "Any idiot can touch a horse. Did you ever touch a Thoroughbred?"

The answer was no, never. They were godlike, untouchable, Pegasus and Bucephalus and the Black Stallion. They were Thoroughbreds, and I was just me.

He lifted his cane toward the groom, and the younger man led the filly over to the railing, so close her nose was puffing warm air onto my knuckles. Still I kept my fingers clutched to the rail.

"Go on," the trainer said. "Won't bite you. Not this one, anyway."

I didn't even know how to do it, whether I should reach for her forehead or try stroking her ears, cupping them in my hand and stripping from base to tip the way I did to calm Sugar when she was itchy for anybody that wasn't me. Those ideas seemed too ordinary, already used up on something less worthy of the act. So finally I just reached up and laid my palm against the flat of her cheek. It was warm and soft and I could feel the tiny twitch of jaw muscles near the base of her head. She didn't move. Neither did I. Neither did the trainer or the groom. We stood there for what felt like minutes, until I felt something else. A slow pumping rhythm that seemed as if it rose up from deep in the center of the earth, pouring through the filly and straight into me. For a minute, I did think I was feeling something supernatural. Then I realized it was just her pulse, thumping along. That part of the track which kept on going when all else had been stripped away.

At age eleven, I had a theory about things like feeling the pulse of a Thoroughbred. I assumed that as you got older you collected more and more such items that mattered to you. By the time you reached May-May's age, you would possess a million sustaining passions, tiny and enormous, that you could pull out and enjoy whenever you pleased. I would wonder how, out of all the things she must have amassed over the years, May-May had known to hand over the racetrack.

That equation I pieced together so many years ago has proven upside down. Most of those fledgling passions I lit upon, Wonder Woman and Shetland ponies and rocky road ice cream, eventually became skins shed along the way. As a result, the things that mattered grew to matter even more. I see what May-May held on to across the near-century expanse of her lifetime—a few old stories, an overflowing sense of curiosity, and the racetrack—and I'm tempted to think she knew to couple me with racing because of what the sport had shown her. It's not about collecting, but about discovery, searching out a world that's authentic and rich and full.

I go to the races because I'm in love. It's that simple and that eternally complex. That deep, steady heartbeat has turned a part of me. I depend upon it.

It's the sound of being alive.

Photograph Credits

Introduction (also frontispiece). May-May on a pack trip in Alaska. *Courtesy of the author.*

Part 1: The Starting Gate. *Brandon Benson.*

Chapter One: Trust. *Brandon Benson.*

Chapter Two: Rewriting the Rules. May-May's favorite filly, Regret; trainer Jimmy Rowe; and owner H. P. Whitney. *Courtesy of the National Museum of Racing and Hall of Fame.*

Chapter Three: Leaps of Faith. Foals at Mill Ridge Farm. *Joy Brumagen Gilbert.*

Part 2: Early Speed. *Brandon Benson.*

Chapter Four: Courage. *Courtesy of the National Museum of Racing and Hall of Fame.*

Chapter Five: Generosity. *John Fort.*

Part 3: The Stretch Run. *Brandon Benson.*

Chapter Six: Risking It All. *Brandon Benson.*

Chapter Seven: Unconditional Love. *Courtesy of the author.*

Chapter Eight: Forming a Value System. *Brandon Benson.*

Part 4: Crossing the Wire. *Brandon Benson.*

Chapter Nine: Connections. A poster celebrating the 1941 Triple Crown winner, Whirlaway. *Courtesy of the National Museum of Racing and Hall of Fame.*

Chapter Ten: Growth. *Brandon Benson.*

Epilogue. *Brandon Benson.*